# Heitor Villa-Lobos

Heitor Villa-Lobos. Courtesy of the Brazilian Academy of Music (Academia Brasileira de Música).

# Heitor Villa-Lobos

## A Bio-Bibliography

**David P. Appleby**

**Bio-Bibliographies in Music, Number 9**

**Greenwood Press**
New York • Westport, Connecticut • London

**Library of Congress Cataloging-in-Publication Data**

Appleby, David P.
  Heitor Villa-Lobos : a bio-bibliography.

  (Bio-bibliographies in music, ISSN 0742-6968 ; no. 9)
  Discography: p.
  Bibliography: p.
  Includes index.
  1. Villa-Lobos, Heitor—Bibliography.
2. Villa-Lobos, Heitor—Discography.  3. Music—
Bio-bibliography.  I. Title.  II. Series.
ML134.V65A7  1988        016.78'092'4        87-28042
ISBN 0-313-25346-3 (lib. bdg. : alk. paper)

British Library Cataloguing in Publication Data is available.

Library of Congress Catalog Card Number: 87-28042
ISBN: 0-313-25346-3
ISSN: 0742-6968

First published in 1988

Greenwood Press, Inc.
88 Post Road West, Westport, Connecticut 06881

Printed in the United States of America

The paper used in this book complies with the
Permanent Paper Standard issued by the National
Information Standards Organization (Z39.48-1984).

10 9 8 7 6 5 4 3 2 1

To my wife, Martha, with love

# Contents

# Preface

Heitor Villa-Lobos was undoubtedly one of the most prolific composers of this century. His influence on the music of Latin America was enormous and during his lifetime his music was generally accepted as the embodiment of the spirit of his native Brazil. In 1987 centennial celebrations of his birth took place in all major nations. This is therefore an appropriate occasion on which to publish a bio-bibliography of his life and works.

This bio-bibliography is divided into four principal sections: the Biography, the Works and Performances section, the Discography and the Bibliography. In addition, there are two appendixes and one index.

The Biography gives a brief account of the composer's life. A discussion of major works written in each period of Villa-Lobos' life is included.

The Works and Performances section contains a chronological listing of 567 works, including dates of composition, commissions, dedications, information about first performances, and publishers. Since a chronological order within a given year could not be established, works within each year are listed in alphabetical order. Most standard reference sources state that the output of Villa-Lobos is more than a thousand compositions. One dictionary of contemporary music states that the works of Villa-Lobos number more than 3,000. The highly informative catalog of the Museu Villa-Lobos lists more than 650 items. The 567 entries listed in the Works and Performances section include only works for which it was possible to establish verifiable dates of composition. Any works for which this was not possible are listed in the chapter "Additional Works," and others written basically for pedagogical purposes are listed in the Collections chapter. The total of this prodigious output plus a large number of arrangements and original compositions that have been lost could well exceed 2,000 works. From 1899, the date of his first composition, Villa-Lobos composed in his words "by biological necessity" until very shortly before his death in 1959. Even on social occasions such as luncheon engagements, parties, and meetings with friends, Villa-Lobos frequently had manuscript paper and continued writing while  simultaneously engaged in animated conversation.

One of the most difficult tasks in compiling  this  catalog was avoiding any  duplications in listing the  various arrangements of works. It was not uncommon for Villa-Lobos to write a song for voice and orchestra, to write a voice and piano version the same year, and several years later to arrange the same material under a different title for chorus and string orchestra. Because  some versions of such a work could have been lost, in some cases it may not have been possible  to avoid duplication or erroneous listings. However, every effort was  made  to correct errors and provide scholars and musicians with a useful guide to the works of Brazil's most outstanding composer.

The Discography is a selected list of recordings either currently or recently available, or recordings of major importance. A complete discography would be of limited value, since the hundreds of early recordings made in Brazil or in Europe are generally unavailable. The Museu Villa-Lobos has more than five hundred  records, and a much larger selection on reel-to-reel tapes, which unfortunately have become brittle with  time. A series of recordings made at the Radiodiffusion Française remains one of the most valuable recorded legacies of the music of Villa-Lobos, since many of these recordings were conducted by the composer himself. A recently released  selection from this series is included  in the  discography.

The Bibliography contains a selected listing of books and articles by and about Villa-Lobos. During his lifetime Villa-Lobos had a fascinating relationship with the news media. His favorite game was testing the credibility of reporters. This was documented on numerous occasions.  Once, while in New York City, Villa-Lobos told a group of reporters  that his music contained Indian melodies of great antiquity. He then added that these melodies had been forgotten by the present generation of Indians in Brazil. A fast-thinking reporter immediately asked Villa-Lobos  how  the melodies had been obtained, if they were long  forgotten? Villa-Lobos replied that he had obtained them from the parrots. Brazilian parrots live a long time and heard the ancient melodies, learned them, and sang them to him. On another occasion in France, Villa-Lobos was asked how he had met his wife. He  told the reporters who were seeking sensational news that a beautiful young woman  was captured by a tribe of cannibal Indians. Wandering through the forest with his cello, he came upon the feast at which water was being heated in order to roast Lucilia, the beautiful young woman. At this point in the story, Villa-Lobos related that he played his cello so beautifully for the Indians that they agreed to release their prisoner, who promptly fell in love with him and married him.

As a result of Villa-Lobos' mischievous relationship with the press, the number of articles written about Villa-Lobos is enormous. A file of articles in the Villa-Lobos Museum contains eleven volumes of clippings collected by Arminda Villa-Lobos. A file in the *Jornal do Brasil* also contains a large number of articles. As a result of the enormous volume of articles and books of a popular nature that have been written about Villa-Lobos, the listing of articles and books in this bibliography is selective.

Because individual movements from some of Villa-Lobos' compositions are sometimes performed as separate pieces, the Index contains their titles as well as the titles of the main works. In order to facilitate the identification of the work from which a particular movement is taken, each movement is indexed to its corresponding main composition's entry.The index also contains titles of all short pieces arranged by Villa-Lobos in the collections. Names of individual performers, concert sites, and composition titles are also included. The titles that appear in the index are listed in Portuguese, whenever this was the langugage of the original title used by Villa-Lobos himself. Occasionally a work is better known by a title in a language different than the original title, in which case the work is listed in the index under both the original language title and the better known title in English or French.

A large selection of sources was used in the compilation of this book including materials in the Biblioteca Nacional in Rio de Janeiro; the Museu Villa-Lobos; and shelf lists from Indiana University; University of Illinois; University of Texas; New York Public Library; Boston Public Library; the British Library; and materials from the Bibliotèque Nationale in Paris. It is my purpose to provide scholars, musicians, and librarians with useful information for research and study of the life and works of Heitor Villa-Lobos.

# Acknowledgements

This book owes its existence to the help of a large number of persons with a common bond: an admiration for the life work of Heitor Villa-Lobos.

The untiring and unselfish help of Arminda Villa-Lobos, director of the Museu Villa-Lobos until her death in 1985, and Mercedes Reis Pequeno, director of the Music Section of the Biblioteca Nacional in Rio de Janeiro, were indispensable and a constant source of encouragement during the difficult months and years when completion of this monumental task appeared impossible. After the death of Dona Arminda, the new directors of the Museu Villa-Lobos, Sonia Vieira Strutt, and later Turibio Santos, and the staff of the Museu provided generous and unfailingly cheerful assistance.

The shelf lists and other information from libraries in the United States, England, and France were provided by the marvelous help of Ann Hartness-Kane, assistant director, Benson Latin American Collection, University of Texas at Austin; Kathy Talalay, Music Library, Indiana University; Pamela Bowden, graduate student, University of Illinois, Urbana, Illinois; Kathryn Appleby Ranger, Paris, France; and Dr. Wilson Luquire, Eastern Illinois University.

Grants for research were provided by the National Endowment for the Humanities; the Council for Faculty Research, Eastern Illinois University; the Eastern Illinois University Foundation; Heinz Endowment; and the College of Fine Arts, Eastern Illinois University.

The assistance with format suggestions by Dr. Don Krummel, bibliographer, University of Illinois, were invaluable. The work of manuscript preparation by my research assistant, Ron Roberts, was an essential element in the transfer of materials to computer discs, and the assistance of Professors John Gardner and Charles

Nivens in preparing the final copy was done with efficiency and cheerfulness. The final checking of Portuguese accents and spellings by Prof. Celso G.L. Chaves eliminated many errors which might otherwise have appeared in the final copy. Monsieur Pierre Vidal's discography research and his personal friendship with Villa-Lobos provided insight and information not otherwise available. The work of Roseane Yampolschi of the Museu Villa-Lobos  made available information concerning recordings in Brazil and the correction of many errors in the works and performance sections of the book. Dr. Janet Landreth was an ingenious and helpful friend who was able to locate a number of difficult- to- find Villa-Lobos memorabilia during her period of research in Rio de Janeiro. And  the eminent Brazilian musicologist, Dr. Luiz Heitor Correa de Azevedo, now living in Paris, France, provided both moral support and information from his personal file and from his recollections of many years of association with Villa-Lobos. My thanks to each of the persons named and to the many other contributors to this bio-bibliography of Heitor Villa-Lobos.

# Heitor Villa-Lobos

# Biography

In 1887 Dom Pedro II was emperor of Brazil. The nobility who frequented the brilliant social events in the imperial court lived mostly in a section of Rio de Janeiro called Catete, with a few in nearby Laranjeiras, (Orange Groves).

On 5 March 1887 in a section of Laranjeiras near an enormous rock quarry where rocks for the building of the homes for the nobility were carefully chosen, a boy was born in the home of Raul Villa-Lobos, a functionary in the National Library. The family named him Heitor, but during his boyhood they used the nickname "Tuhú."

The Villa-Lobos family lived in a "sobrado" type building in which a commercial type of establishment was located on the first floor and the family living quarters on the floor above. Dona Noêmia Umbelina Santos Monteiro Villa-Lobos, mother of eight children, attempted to provide from the meager salary of her husband, Raul, for the daily needs of the large family. Nevertheless, Heitor's recollections of the period of his early childhood were happy ones.

Raul Villa-Lobos was a man of conservative political views and great intellectual curiosity. He wrote several books on various subjects under the pseudonym Epaminondas Vilalba, had a keen eye for drawing portrait sketches, and was a fine amateur cellist. Soon aware that Tuhú had precocious musical talent, he personally undertook the boy's instruction in ear training and on the cello.

The city of Rio de Janeiro at the turn of the twentieth century had major sanitary problems and frequent epidemics had a devastating effect upon the population. The happiness of the Villa-Lobos household was shattered in July 1899 when Raul Villa-

Lobos died after a brief illness in a smallpox epidemic, leaving his family in dire financial circumstances. Dona Noêmia was forced to seek sources of income outside the home to support her family.

Shortly before the death of his father, Heitor had begun to study the guitar and clarinet, and had developed considerable skill on the cello. His first composition, a short song which he called "Os Sedutores" with a subtitle "Cançoneta" (Little Song) was written in 1899, the year of his father's death.

In the difficult period following the death of his father, Heitor sought the companionship of popular musicians who played an improvisatory kind of music called "choros." The term is related to the verb "chorar," to weep, and was used for the amorous melancholy type of music performed at "serestas" or serenades. The term was also used for groups performing this kind of music. Much to the distress of his mother, Heitor's growing interest in the activities of "choro" groups kept him away from home until late in the evenings and sometimes the entire night to the detriment of his schoolwork. Heitor finally decided to move to the home of an aunt more sympathetic to his friendships with the serenaders.

At the age of 18, Villa-Lobos became obsessed with the desire for travel. He wanted to see remote parts of Brazil, to travel beyond the frontiers of his country, to hear folk and indigenous music, and to see the world. Although travel during this period was dangerous, he sold several volumes from the rare book collection that he had inherited from his father, and traveled to northern Brazil. During the years 1905-1911 he was absent from his home, the capital city of Rio de Janeiro, except for brief periods of time such as the few months in 1907-1908 when he returned to Rio to enroll as a student at the National Institute of Music. After deciding that the formal classes at the institute were far less interesting than the folk and popular music he had heard during his travels, he resumed his journeys. The most fascinating music he heard was in northeastern Brazil where types of folk music almost totally unknown in the capital captivated his attention. Much of the music heard during these trips provided a basis for later musical works.

In spite of Heitor's frequent travelling in the period from 1905-1911, and refusal to accept formal musical training, the Villa-Lobos catalog includes forty-three compositions written during the years 1899 through 1911. Most of these compositions were short songs; pieces for the guitar, his favorite popular instrument; pieces for piano; a few chamber music works, and pieces for band or chorus. Two of the most significant compositions during this period were *Suite Populaire Brésilienne* (1908-1912) a five movement suite for solo guitar based on popular dance forms; and a Trio No. 1 for piano, violin and cello.

FIRST CONCERTS IN BRAZIL AND EUROPE

On 12 November 1913 Villa-Lobos married Lucilia Guimarães, a pianist and a graduate of the Instituto Nacional de Música. The marriage resulted in useful musical collaboration and Lucilia became an enthusiastic and able interpreter of the piano works of Villa-Lobos.

In 1915 he felt a need to establish a reputation as a composer through public performances of his works. The first three concerts were scheduled in Friburgo, in the state of Rio de Janeiro, and the first major performance of his works in the capital was scheduled in Rio de Janeiro on 13 November 1915. The program included a sonata for violin and piano, songs, pieces for cello and piano, and the Trio No. 1 for piano, violin, and cello. Reviews for the first performances of works by Villa-Lobos in Rio de Janeiro were generally favorable. Critics recognized his talent while commenting on his inexperience and relative merits of his first works. At this point in his career, Villa-Lobos was twenty eight years old and had written more than one hundred works, but was relatively unknown outside of a small circle of friends and admirers in Rio de Janeiro.

The friendship of pianist Arthur Rubinstein was an important factor in the establishing the professional reputation of Villa-Lobos. The first meeting took place in 1918, when Rubinstein went to hear Villa-Lobos play at the Cinema Odeon in Rio de Janeiro. At this time Villa-Lobos was thirty one years old, and still had no regular source of income, except the salary and music lesson fees of his wife and the occasional fees earned by performing in restaurants and cinemas. A strong friendship developed and Rubinstein was able to persuade wealthy patrons in Brazil that Villa-Lobos was a composer of major talents and that funds should be provided for him to go to Europe.

Villa-Lobos' first trip to Europe was in 1923. The Brazilian government had provided a limited subsidy for him to present concerts of the music of Brazilian composers, and several friends provided the remainder of the funds necessary for him to remain in Europe a few months. On 30 May 1924, a concert of his works was held in the Salle des Agriculteurs in Paris, consisting of several new compositions, including *Nonetto,* one of the most important chamber music works written by Villa Lobos, and *A prole do bebé No. 1,* a suite of piano pieces performed by Arthur Rubinstein. In the concert reviews, critics noted the use of native Brazilian instruments such as "reco-reco," a notched stick, and "xucalho," a gourd filled with beans, highly unusual instruments for a chamber music work.

In 1927, after concerts in Brazil and Argentina, Villa-Lobos was able to return to Paris with his wife, having received additional financial help from his Brazilian friends Arnaldo and Carlos Guinle, who provided the use of an apartment on the Place St. Michel. The apartment soon became a popular meeting place for many of

Place St. Michel. The apartment soon became a popular meeting place for many of the artists and musicians in Paris at the time. On 24 October and 5 December 1927 two major concerts of works by Villa-Lobos were held in the Salle Gaveau, in Paris. Performers at the concerts included pianists Arthur Rubinstein, Aline Van Berentzen, and Thomas Teran; singers Vera Janacopulos and Elsie Houston; an orchestra and a chorus of 260 voices. The programs included *Choros* 2, 4, 7, 8, and 10, *Nonetto, Trois Poèmes Indiens* for voice and orchestra and other recent works by Villa-Lobos, which were enthusiastically received by critics and the public. The startlingly innovative qualities of the *Choros* and the outstanding performances contributed to the enormous success of these concerts. In a brief period of time, he received invitations for concerts in London, Amsterdam, Vienna, Berlin, Brussels, Madrid, Liège, Lyons, Amiens, Poitiers, Barcelona and Lisbon.

## VILLA-LOBOS AND THE VARGAS REGIME

In 1930 Villa-Lobos returned to Brazil for a brief vacation. Distressed because of the low level of public school music instruction, he sent a sweeping proposal for total reorganization of public music instruction in the state of São Paulo. The time for such a proposal appeared highly unfavorable because of the instability of the political climate. Nevertheless, the proposal was accepted by the state government in São Paulo, and Villa-Lobos spent much of the 1930s and early 1940s in an attempt totally to reorganize musical instruction, first in the state of São Paulo, and after 1932, in Rio de Janeiro on a nationwide basis.

Villa-Lobos attempted to arouse the Brazilian public from its apathy regarding educational value of the arts by means of gigantic "canto orfeônico" concerts, in which thirty thousand, and at one time forty thousand performers presented demonstrations at the Vasco da Gama stadium in Rio de Janeiro. These demonstrations were first held in São Paulo, and after his appointment as director of the Superintendencia de Educação Musical e Artistica (S.E.M.A.) in 1932, in Rio de Janeiro. During a period in political history in which the Brazilian president Getúlio Vargas, who had been a minority candidate in the 1930 elections was seeking to consolidate his power, Villa-Lobos persuaded the government that the patriotism they sought to instill in Brazilian youth by political means could more readily be achieved through musical education. Since, for the first time, Brazil had an authoritarian rather than a democratic government, the organizational aspects of mass choral performances were made possible by a close working of the government and S.E.M.A.

The public demonstrations in the 1930s by enormous choral groups were feats never before or since duplicated in Brazil or elsewhere. The sheer size of groups was unprecedented, and the organizational aspects were carefully planned and carried out with the help of musical assistants and the government, which had passed a law requiring "canto orfeônico" instruction of every Brazilian schoolchild. In 1932 a school for the preparation of teachers was established with Villa-Lobos as the director, Curso de Pedagogia de Música e Canto Orfeônico, and Orfeão de Professores, founded by Teixeira Bastos. Music was carefully chosen for civic and patriotic purposes and arranged for performances with massed choruses. Villa-Lobos used an individualized system of solmization hand signals in working with choral groups that had been carefully prepared and taught by teachers and choral assistants. A demonstration with thirty thousand participants and one thousand instrumentalists performing music with body gestures portraying the wind rushing through the trees in an Amazon forest, or the waves pounding a magnificent Brazilian beach was not an experience easily forgotten by any performer or listener.

The period during which Villa-Lobos worked as director of S.E.M.A. was a time of incredible activity that did not provide the creative circumstances necessary for a composer to produce his best work. The challenge, however, of having readily available groups to perform choral compositions led to an increase in his productivity of choral works during these years, and he was able also to complete additional works such as the *Ciclo brasileiro* for piano (1936), one of his best piano works; the four suites for orchestra *Descobrimento do Brasil* (1937); and several of the *Bachianas brasileiras*.

## CONCERTS IN THE UNITED STATES AND THE LAST YEARS

Villa-Lobos made his first trip to the United States in 1944, at the age of 57. He had had invitations to visit the United States for many years, but arrangements for the trip in the difficult days of World War II were not completed until late in 1944, and he arrived in Los Angeles a few days prior to a scheduled appearance on 26 November to conduct the Jenssen Symphony of Los Angeles in a program of his works. During his first trip to the United States, Villa-Lobos' works were presented in concerts in New York, Boston, and Chicago with enormous success. Thereafter, until his death in 1959, Villa-Lobos returned to the United States every year, and fulfilled an impressive number of commissions for prestigious individuals and organizations.

In 1948 Villa-Lobos was admitted to Sloan-Kettering Memorial Hospital where his illness was diagnosed as cancer of the bladder. The bladder was removed and he was able to lead an active life as composer and conductor for the last eleven years of his life. The incredibly demanding schedule of composing and conducting, however, would have taxed the physical resources of even a man in perfect health, and during his last years Villa-Lobos was able to survive only by means of a carefully supervised program of medical treatment. The creative accomplishments of his last years are therefore all the more amazing.

Prior to his first concerts in the United States, Villa-Lobos frequently chose compositional forms that  by title and content expressed Brazilian elements. The enthusiastic reception given his works in the United States encouraged him to think of himself as a international composer whose music unavoidably expressed his origins, background, and individual style of writing. From the years 1944-1945 until his death, the output of works in traditional forms multiplied, and the series of distinctively Brazilian works,  such as the *Choros*  and *Bachianas brasileiras*, were completed. The universality of inspiration of the last years produced some of Villa-Lobos' finest writing in traditional forms such as the Symphony No. 10 for solo, mixed choir, and orchestra, the last string quartets, several fine symphonic poems, the choral composition *Bendita sabedoria*, the opera *Yerma*, and an enormous number of commissioned and non-commissioned works. During this period of prodigious productivity, he traveled incessantly to the United States, Europe, and South America conducting concerts of his works.

In 1959, the last year of his life, he traveled in Europe and continued his schedule of composing, arranging, and conducting until July, when his physical condition required hospitalization at the Hospital dos Estrangeiros in Rio de Janeiro. He died in his apartment on Rua Araújo Porto Alegre in downtown Rio on 17 November 1959.

# Works and Performances

Works are listed by year of composition. Works within a given year are listed alphabetically, since it is not always possible to establish an exact date of composition. Definite and indefinite articles are disregarded in the alphabetization in all languages.

## Key to Abbreviations

MUSICAL INSTRUMENTS AND TERMS

Whenever possible, abbreviations are used in listing musical instruments in the Works and Performances section. Instruments will usually be listed in English. In a few cases, Villa-Lobos has requested the use of instruments used in the music-making of popular Brazilian musicians, and no ready English equivalent is available. In such cases the instrument is listed in Portuguese in the Works and Performances section. A key to abbreviations and a brief explanation of typical Brazilian instruments is provided in the section which follows.

| | |
|---|---|
| a | alto (instrument) |
| A | Alto (voice) |
| assobio | whistle |
| b | bass (instrument) |
| B | Bass (voice) |
| b cl | bass clarinet |
| baguette de pau | wooden drum stick |
| bar | baritone (instrument) |
| Bar | Baritone (voice) |
| bn | bassoon |

| | |
|---|---|
| bomb | bombo (bass drum) |
| bombardino | euphonium |
| bug | bugle |
| ca | caixa (side drum) |
| caixa de madeira | (wooden drum) |
| camisão | (large or small) a Brazilian type of bass drum |
| caracaxá | a bamboo cylinder filled with small stones |
| castanholas | castanets |
| cax | caxambu, tom-tom played by hand |
| cbn | contrabassoon |
| cel | celesta |
| cho | chocalho (metal or wood) a metal container or bamboo cylinder filled with beans or small stones (also spelled in scores as "chucalho", "xocalho"or "xucalho" |
| cho inf | chocalho infantil, small rattle |
| cl | clarinet |
| coco | coconut (dry coconut hulls) |
| cond | conductor |
| cont | contrabass (E-flat and B-flat) trombones |
| cor | cornet |
| cuica | cuíca or puíta (lion's roar) sound produced by friction, native Brazilian percussion instrument |
| cymb | cymbals |
| db | double bass |
| eng hn | English horn |
| eup | euphonium (baritone) |
| ferrinho | triangle |
| fl | flute |
| folha de Flandres | tin plate sheet |
| ganza | cow bell |
| garrafa | bottle |
| gongo | gong |
| guizos | sleigh bells |
| hn | (French) horn |
| maceta | mallet: Maceta de metal (metal); maceta de madeira (wood) |
| madeiras | wood block |
| mat | matraca |
| novachordion | novachord |
| ob | oboe |
| org | organ |
| pan | pandeiro (tambourin with jingles) |
| pf | piano(forte) |
| pic | piccolo |

| | |
|---|---|
| pic fl | piccolo flute |
| pio | a type of baton with a harmonic box at the end which sounds when the baton is rubbed with a piece of resined leather |
| prato | Portuguese for "plate" |
| | prato de louça- dinner plate |
| | prato de metal- cymbals |
| | prato com maceta de madeira- cymbals played with a wooden mallet |
| | prato com maceta de metal-cymbals played with a metal mallet |
| puita | (see cuica) |
| reco | reco-reco, guïro, a notched gourd scraped with a stick |
| req | requinta, a small clarinet in E Flat |
| saxhn | saxhorn |
| s | soprano (instrument) |
| S | Soprano (voice) |
| sin | sinos, bells or chimes |
| som agudo | high pitch |
| som medio | medium pitch |
| som grave | low pitch |
| str | strings |
| surdo (copo) | mute cup; (de papelão) large straight mute |
| t | tenor (instrument) |
| T | Tenor (voice) |
| t-t | tam-tam (tom-tom) |
| tambi | replaced by xylophone |
| tamb | tambor, generic name in Portuguese for drum |
| | tambor africano- large tambourine without bells |
| | tambor de Basque- tambourine |
| | tambor indiano -Indian drum |
| | tambor militar- Military drum |
| | tambor de Provence- tom-tom |
| | tambor surdo-big drum (no snares) |
| tamborim de samba | tom-tom |
| tambu | replaced by xylophone |
| tarol | snare drum |
| tartaruga | literally "turtle", Indian drum of medium pitch |
| timp | timpani |
| tri | triangle |
| trbn | trombone |
| trocano | Indian drum made out of a hollow log |
| tpt | trumpet |
| v | voice |

| | |
|---|---|
| va | viola (English) |
| vassourinha | brushes |
| vc | (violon)cello |
| vibrafone | vibraphone |
| violão | guitar |
| vn | violin |
| xyl | xylophone |

## PUBLISHERS

The publisher of each work by Villa-Lobos is listed in the Works and Performances list. If the information about publication is not listed, the work was not published. The original publisher is listed regardless of whether the work is still available, or out of print. In works originally published by a French or Brazilian editor and subsequently published by an American company, both the original and American publishing companies are  listed. The names and available addresses of publishers of Villa Lobos music are:

Associated

Associated Music Publishers Inc.

Music sales:
Hal Leonard
8112 W. Blue Mound
Milwaukee, Wisconsin 53213
Phone (414-774-3630)

Music rentals:
5 Bellvale Road
P.O. Box 572
Chester, NY 10918

Belwin

Belwin Mills Publishing Corp.
Theodore Presser Co.
Presser Place
Bryn Mawr, PA 19010

CMP

Consolidated Music Publishers
Music Sales Corporation
24 E. 22nd Street
New York, NY 10010

| | |
|---|---|
| Eschig | Editions Max Eschig,<br>48, Rue de Rome<br>75008 Paris<br>France |
| Carl Fischer | Carl Fischer, Inc.<br>62 Cooper Square,<br>New York, NY 10003 |
| Israeli | Israeli Music Publications<br>Theodore Presser Co.<br>Presser Place<br>Bryn Mawr, PA 19010 |
| Leduc | Alphonse Leduc SA<br><br>(U.S.)<br>Theodore Presser Co.<br>Presser Place<br>Bryn Mawr, PA 19010<br><br>(France)<br>175, Rue Saint Honoré<br>Paris Ier, France |
| Mercury | Mercury Music Co.<br>Theodore Presser Co.<br>Bryn Mawr, PA 19010 |
| Napoleão | Editora Arthur Napoleão Ltda.<br>FERMATA do Brasil<br>Av. Ipiranga, 1123<br>01039 São Paulo, SP, Brazil |
| Peer | Peer Southern Concert Music Division,<br>Theodore Presser Co.<br>Presser Place<br>Bryn Mawr, PA 19010 |
| Peters | C.F. Peters Corporation<br>373 Park Avenue South<br>New York, NY 10016 |

G. Ricordi

Ricordi and Co.

Music sales:
Hal Leonard Publishing Co.
8112 W. Blue Mound
Milwaukee, Wisconsin 53213
Phone (414-774-3630)

Music rentals:
5 Bellvale Road
P.O. Box 572
Chester, NY 10918

P. Robbins

Robbins Music Corporation
Columbia Pictures Publications
15800 Northwest 48th Ave.
Miami, FL 33014

G. Schirmer

G. Schirmer, Inc.

Music sales:
Hal Leonard
811 W. Blue Mound
 Milwaukee, Wisconsin 53213

Music rentals:
5 Bellvale Road
P.O. Box 572
Chester, NY 10918

Southern

See: Peer Southern  Concert Music Division

Villa-Lobos
Music Corp.

Villa-Lobos Music Corporation
1585 Broadway
New York, NY 10019

I. Vitale

Irmãos Vitale S.A.
Rua França Pinto 42
04016 São Paulo, S.P.,Brazil

V. Vitale

Vicente Vitale
Avenida Almirante Barroso 2, Segundo Andar
20.000 Rio de Janeiro, R.J., Brazil

## OTHER ABBREVIATIONS

Names of persons and performance halls have frequently been cited in abbreviated form. Salão Nobre da Associação dos Empregados do Comercio, in Rio de Janeiro, where many first performances of Villa Lobos works were performed, appears simply as Salão Nobre in the Works and Performances list. Rio de Janeiro appears simply as Rio. The most frequent dedicatee of Villa-Lobos works was Arminda Villa-Lobos, his beloved companion of the last 23 years of his life. Dedications to Arminda are cited as her name appears in manuscripts. Most frequently her name appears as Mindinha (little Arminda), sometimes as Arminda Neves de Almeida, sometimes as Arminda Neves d'Almeida. Rather than rigid consistency, the writer has sought to retain the dedications as they appear in the original scores.

## *The Catalog*

**1899**

**Os sedutores** (Cançoneta)
    Voice and piano; 2 min.                                W001

**1900**

**Panqueca**
    Guitar; 2 min.                                        W002

**1901**

**Dime perché**
    Voice and piano; 2 min.
    Poetry by P. de Tasso                            W003

**Mazurka em ré maior**
    Guitar; 2 min.                                        W004

**1904**

**Celestial** (Waltz)
    Piano; 2 min.                                        W005

**História de Pierrot**
    Piano; 2 min                                        W006

**Nuvens**
    Piano; 2 min.                                        W007

**Paraguai** (Dobrado)
Band                                                          W008

**Valsa brilhante**
Guitar; 3 min.
Originally entitled Valsa Concerto  no. 2                     W009

*1905*

**Brasil** (Dobrado)
Band                                                          W010

**Imploro**
Piano or harmonium; 2 min.
Dedicated to Father Escaligero Maravalho                      W011

**O Salutaris**
Chorus and piano or harmonium; 2 min.                         W012

*1907*

**Cânticos sertanejos** (Fantasia característica)
String quintet and piano; 3 min.
Also for 2 flutes, clarinet and strings (*See*: W014)        W013

**Cânticos sertanejos** (Fantasia característica)
Two flutes, clarinet and strings; 3 min.
Also for string quintet and piano (*See*: W013)              W014

**Japonesa**
Voice and piano; 2 min.
Poetry by Luiz Guimarães Filho
Premiere: Manaus, Teatro Amazonas; Santos Moreira, v;
   Joaquim França, pf; 1911                                   W015

**Valsa romântica**
Piano; 3 min.                                                 W016

*1908*

**Confidência** (canção)
Voice and piano; 2 min.

Poetry by Honório Bastos de Carvalho
Premiere: Rio, Salão Nobre; Alberto Guimarães, v; Lucilia
   Villa-Lobos, pf; 11/13/1915
Napoleão                                                                    W017

**As crianças**
   Four part chorus, a cappella, 2 min.
   Poetry by Lauro Sales
   Napoleão                                                                 W018

**Recouli**
   Orchestra; 3 min.
   Flute, clarinet and strings
   Written especially for the students of the city of
      Paranaguá, Brazil
   Premiere: Paranaguá, Paraná, Brazil, Teatro Santa
      Isabel; Villa-Lobos, conductor; 1/26/1908              W019

*1908-1912*

**Suite populaire brésilienne**
   Guitar; 12 min.
      *Mazurka-choro*
      *Schottisch-choro*
      *Valsa-choro*
      *Gavota-choro*
      *Chorinho*
   *Mazurka-choro* dedicated to Maria Tereza Teran
   Eschig                                                                    W020

*1909*

**Aglaia**
   Opera in two acts
   Later incorporated in Izaht (*See*: W055)                 W021

**Ave Maria**
   Voice, cello and organ; 2 min.                               W022

**Fantasia**
   Guitar; 3 min.                                                         W023

**Memorare**
   Two part chorus and organ; 2 min.
   Premiere: Rio, Teatro Municipal; Chorus of the Schola

Cantorum, Alpheo Lopes de Souza, org;  Villa-Lobos,
cond; 11/11/1922                                                          W024

**Um beijo**
Piano; 2 min.
Dedicated to Eduardo Gomes                                      W025

**1909-1912**

**Dobrados** (eight)
Guitar; 12 min.
  *Paraguaio*
  *Brasil*
  *Chorão*
  *Saudade*
  *Paranaguá*
  *Cabeçudo*
  *Rio de Janeiro*
  *Padre Pedro*                                                         W026

**1910**

**Canção brasileira**
Guitar; 2 min.                                                          W027

**Dobrado pitoresco**
Guitar; 2 min.                                                          W028

**Elisa**
Opera in one act
Later incorporated in Izaht (*See*: W055)                       W029

**Fuga** (arrangement)
Cello and piano; 2 min.
Transcribed from *The Well-Tempered Clavier* of J.S. Bach     W030

**Prelúdio em fá sustenido menor**
Cello and piano; 3 min.
Transcription of a prelude by Chopin                             W031

**Quadrilha**
Guitar; 2 min.                                                          W032

**Tarantela**
Guitar; 3 min.                                                      W033

**Tristorosa** (valsa)
Piano; 2 min.
Premiere: Rio; Arnaldo Estrella, pf; 11/20/1968
Written under the pseudonym Epaminondas Villalba Filho      W034

*1911*

**Bailado infantil**
Piano; 2 min.                                                      W035

**Canto oriental**
Voice and piano; 2 min.
Poetry by Honório de Carvalho                                      W036

**Comédia lírica em 3 atos**
Opera in 3 acts
Transcription for piano (incomplete)
Libretto by Octávio F. Machado                                     W037

**Mazurlesca**
Piano; 2 min.                                                      W038

**Num berço de fadas**
Piano; 2 min.                                                      W039

**Simples** (Mazurka)
Guitar; 2 min.
Written for Eduardo Luiz Gomes, guitar student of Villa-
   Lobos                                                          W040

**Tarantela**
Piano; 3 min.
Excerpted from *Suite for piano and orchestra* (*See*: W068,
   À Itália - Tarantella)
Premiere: (Programmed as op. 30) Rio, Salão Nobre; Ernãni
   Braga, pf; 11/17/1917                                          W041

**Trio no. 1**
Piano, violin, and cello; 20 min.
Premiere: (Programmed as op.25) Rio, Salão Nobre;
   Lucilia Villa-Lobos, pf; Humberto Milano, vn and

Oswaldo Allionni, vc; 11/13/1915
Eschig                                                                    W042

**Valsa lenta**
Piano; 2 min.                                                             W043

*1912*

**Ave Maria**
Voice and organ; 2 min.                                                  W044

**Brinquedo de roda**
Piano; 10 min.
   *Tira o seu pezinho*
   *A moda da carranquinha*
   *Uma, duas angolinhas*
   *Os três cavalheiros*
   *Garibaldi foi à missa*
   *Vamos todos cirandar*
Peer                                                                     W045

**Mal secreto**
Voice and piano; 2 min.
Poetry by Raimundo Correa
Premiere: Rio, Salão Nobre; Frederico Nascimento Filho,
   Bar; Ernani Braga, pf; 11/13/1915
Consolidated Music Publishers                                            W046

**Noite de luar**
Voice and piano; 3 min.
Poetry by Batista Junior
Premiere: Rio, Salão Nobre; Lydia Albuquerque Salgado, S;
   Lucilia Villa-Lobos, pf; 2/3/1917                                     W047

**Petizada**
Piano; 15 min.
   *A mão direita tem uma roseira*
   *Assim ninava mamãe*
   *A pobrezinha sertaneja*
   *Vestidinho branco*
   *Saci*
   *História da caipirinha*

História da caipirinha, dedicated "to my adopted daughter
Izaht"
Peer, V. Vitale                                                                                                W048

**Pro-pax** (Marcha Solene)
Band; 10 min.
Pic, fl, ob, cl, sax, B-flat cor, bug, hn, saxhn,
trbn, bar, bass drum, tuba (E-flat and B-flat), drum,
ca, cymb, timp, and tri
Published by the Conservatório de Canto Orfeônico as
*Partituras de banda*                                                                                 W049

**Quinteto duplo de cordas**
Double string quintet; 20 min.
Violins, violas, celli, and double basses
Premiere: Rio, Instituto Nacional de Música, 9/17/1925           W050

**Sonata fantasia no.1** (Première Sonate-Fantaisie)
(Désespérance)
Violin and piano; 10 min.
Also called *Sonata fantasia e capricciosa no.1*, op.35
Premiere: Rio, Salão Nobre; Judith Barcelos, vn; Lucilia
Villa-Lobos, pf; 2/3/1917
Eschig                                                                                                           W051

**Suíte brasileira**
Orchestra; 8 min.                                                                                        W052

**Suíte infantil no.1**
Piano; 12 min.
*Bailando* (minueto piu animato)
*Nenê vai dormir* (andante melancolico)
*Artimanhas* (allegretto quasi allegro)
*Reflexão* (allegro)
*No balanço* (allegro non troppo)
Napoleão                                                                                                     W053

**Suíte para quinteto duplo de cordas**
Double string quintet or string orchestra; 10 min.
*Tímida*
*Misteriosa*
*Inquieta*
Inquieta later used in *Evolução dos aeroplanos* (*See*:
W271)

Premiere: (programmed as Suíte característica para
instrumentos de cordas) Rio, Teatro Municipal;
Orchestra of the Sociedade de Concertos Sinfônicos;
Francisco Braga, cond; 7/31/1915                    W054

### 1912-1914

**Izaht**
Opera in four acts; 90 min.
Soloists, Chorus and Orchestra
Pic, 2 fl, 2 ob, eng hn, 2 cl in B-flat, 2 cl in A, b cl,
  2 bn, cbn, 4 hn in F, 2 hn in D, 2 hn in E, 2 tpt in F,
  2 tpt in B-flat, tpt in D, 4 trbn, tuba, tim, t-t,
  cymb, ca, chimes, tri, bomb, xyl, cel, harps and str
Libretto by Azevedo Júnior and Villa-Lobos under the
  pseudonym Epaminondas Villalba Filho
Adapted from the operas Agalia (*See*: W21) and Elisa
  (*See*: W29)
Premiere:
  (3rd act) Rio, Teatro Municipal; 11/16/1921
  (4th act) 8/15/1918
  (complete) 11/13/1958                    W055

### 1912-1917

**Miniaturas**
Voice and piano; 12 min.
  *Cromo no.2*
  *A viola*
  *Cromo no.3*
  *Sonho*
  *Japonesa*
  *Sino da Aldeia*
Poetry by Abílio Barreto Sylvio Romero, B. Lopes, A.
  Guimarães, Luiz Guimarães Filho,and Antônio Maria C. de
  Oliveira
*Japonesa* composed in Bahia; March 5, 1912
Arranged for voice and orchestra (*See*: W057)
Premiere:
  (*Cromo no.2*, *Sonho*, *Japonesa*, and *Sino da aldeia*) Rio,
    Salão Nobre; Alberto Guimarães, v; Lucilia Villa-Lobos,
    pf; 11/17/1917
  (*Cromo no.3* and *A viola*) Rio, Teatro Municipal;
  Frederico Nascimento Filho, Bar; Lucilia Villa-Lobos,

pf; 11/12/1919
Napoleão, Eschig                                                W056

**Miniaturas**
Voice and orchestra; 8 min.
*Cromo no.2*
*A viola*
*Cromo no.3*
*Japonesa*
*Sino da aldeia*
Two fl, 2 ob, eng hn, 2 cl in A, 2 cl in B-flat, 2 bn,
   2 hn, timp, cymb, cel, harp and strings
Poetry by Abílio Barreto Sylvio Romero, B. Lopes, A.
   Guimarães, Luiz Guimarães Filho, and Antônio Maria C.
   de Oliveira
*Japonesa* composed in Bahia; March 5, 1912
Arranged for voice and piano (*See*: W056)
Premiere:
   (A viola) Rio, Teatro Municipal; Frederico Nascimento
   Filho, bar; Villa-Lobos, cond; 12/1/1922                     W057

*1913*

**Ave Maria**
Voice and strings; 2 min.
Premiere: Rio, Teatro Municipal; Asdrubal Lima, v; Villa-
   Lobos cond; 11/11/1922                                       W058

**Fleur fanée**
Voice and piano; 2 min.
Poetry by A. Gallay
Premiere: Rio, Salão Nobre; Frederico Nascimento Filho,
   Bar; Ernâni Braga, pf; 11/13/1915
Napoleão                                                        W059

**Louco**
Voice and piano; 3 min.
Poetry by J. Cadilhe
Premiere: Rio, Salão Nobre; Frederico Nascimento Filho,
   Bar, Lucilia Villa-Lobos, pf; 11/17/1917
Napoleão                                                        W060

**Marcha solene no.3**
Orchestra; 3 min.                                               W061

## L'oiseau blessé d'une flèche
Voice and piano; 3 min.
Based on a fable of La Fontaine
Premiere: Rio; Frederico Nascimento Filho, Bar; Lucilia
   Villa-Lobos, pf; 2/3/1917
Napoleão                                                              W062

## Pequena sonata
Cello and piano; 12 min.
Premiere: (Programmed as op.20) Friburgo, state of Rio
   de Janeiro, Teatro Dona Eugênia; Villa-Lobos, vc;
   Lucilia Villa-Lobos, pf; 1/29/1915                                W063

## Pequena suíte
Cello and piano; 15 min.
   *Romancette*
   *Legendária*
   *Harmonias soltas*
   *Fugato* (All'antica)
   *Melodia*
   *Gavotte-scherzo*
Premiere: (*Romancette*, *Legendária*, and *Gavotte-Scherzo*)
   Rio, Salão Nobre; Villa-Lobos, vc; Robert Soriano, pf;
   9/5/1919
Napoleão                                                              W064

## Prelúdio no.2
Cello and piano; 3 min.
Premiere: Rio, Salão Nobre; Alfredo Gomes, vc; Lucilia
   Villa-Lobos, pf; 2/3/1917
Napoleão                                                              W065

## Suíte da terra
Chamber orchestra; 10 min.                                           W066

## Suíte infantil no.2
Piano; 10 min.
Napoleão                                                              W067

## Suíte para piano e orquestra
Piano and orchestra; 25 min.
   *À Espanha e Portugal*
   *Ao Brasil*
   *À Itália* (Tarantela)

Pic, 2 fl, 2 ob, 2 cl, 2 b cl, 2 bn, 2 hn, 2 tpt, 2 tpt
  in B-flat, 2 trbn, tuba, timp, and str
  Reduction for two pianos
  *Tarantela* arranged for piano (*See*: W041)
  Premiere: São Paulo; Orchestra of the Sociedade de
    Concertos Sinfônicos, Lucilia Villa-Lobos, pf; Villa-
    Lobos, cond; 4/21/1923
  Eschig                                                    W068

**Trio**
  Flute, cello and piano; 12 min.
  Also called Trio op.25
  Premiere: Friburgo, state of Rio de Janeiro, Teatro Dona
    Eugênia; Agenor Bens, fl; Heitor Villa-Lobos, vc;
    Lucilia Villa-Lobos, pf; 1/29/1915                      W069

**Valsa-scherzo**
  Piano; 3 min.
  Premiere: (Programmed as op.17) Rio, Salão Nobre; Sylvia
    Figueiredo, pf; 11/13/1915
  Napoleão                                                  W070

**A Virgem**
  Voice and piano; 2 min.
  Sonnet by Anthero de Quental
  Premiere: Rio, Salão Nobre; Alberto Guimarães, v; Lucilia
    Villa-Lobos, pf; 11/13/1915
  Napoleão                                                  W071

*1914*

**Ave Maria no.6**
  Voice and piano; 2 min.
  Text in Latin
  Originally for string quartet
  Napoleão                                                  W072

**Canção árabe**
  Voice and piano; 2 min.
  Poem by Honório de Carvalho
  Premiere: Marieta W. Campelo, soloist; 11/17/1919
  Napoleão                                                  W073

## Canção ibérica
Piano; 2 min.
Premiere: (Programmed as op.40) Friburgo, state of Rio de
   Janeiro, Teatro Dona Eugênia; Lucilia Villa-Lobos, pf;
   1/29/1915                                              W074

## Danças aéreas (ballet)
Chamber orchestra; 5 min.
Commissioned by the School of Music of the University of
   Brazil                                                W075

## Fábulas características
Piano; 8 min.
   *O cuco e o gato*
   *A araponga e o irerê*
   *O gato e o rato*
Premiere: (Programmed as op.60) Rio, Salão Nobre; Rubens
   Figueiredo, pf; 2/3/1917
The first two movements are lost
Napoleão (*O gato e o rato*)                              W076

## Ibericarabé (Poema sinfônico)
Orchestra; 10 min.
Transcribed for piano (*See*: W078)                      W077

## Ibericarabé (Poema sinfônico)
Piano
Original for orchestra (*See*: W077)
Napoleão                                                 W078

## Louco
Voice and orchestra; 3 min.
Pic, 2 fl, 2 ob, eng hn, 2 cl in A, b cl,2 bn, cbn, 4 hn,
   4 tpt, 3 trbn, tuba, timp, cymb, bomb, cel, harp and
   str
Poetry by J. Cadelhe
Premiere: São Paulo, Teatro Municipal; Orchestra of the
   Sociedade de Concertos Sinfônicos de São Paulo;
   Frederico Nascimento Filho, Bar; Villa-Lobos, cond;
   2/8/1925                                               W079

## Les mères
Voice and piano; 2 min.
Poetry by Victor Hugo (Les enfants)

Premiere: Rio, Salão Nobre; Frederico Nascimento Filho,
    Bar; Lucilia Villa-Lobos, pf; 2/3/1917
Napoleão                                                          W080

**Octeto** (Dança negra)
Flute, clarinet, bassoon, two violins, cello, and piano;
3 min.                                                           W081

**Ondulando** (estudo)
Piano; 3 min.
Napoleão                                                          W082

**Sonata fantasia no.2** (Deuxième Sonate-Fantaisie)
Violin and piano; 22 min.
Also called *Sonata-fantasia* no. *2* (op.29)
Premiere: Rio, Salão Nobre; Humberto Milano, vn; Lucilia
    Villa-Lobos, pf; 11/3/1915
Eschig                                                           W083

**Sonhar**
Violin and piano; 2 min.                                         W084

**1914-1915**

**Danças características africanas**
Piano; 12 min.
    *Farrapós op.47* (Dança dos moços - Dança indígena no.1)
    *Kankukus op.57* (Dança dos velhos - Dança indígena no.2)
    *Kankikis op.65* (Dança dos meninos - Dança indígena no.3)
    Based on themes of the Caripunas Indians (from Mato
        Grosso)
    Dedicated to Ernáni Braga (*Kankukus*) and Nininha Veloso
        Guerra (Kankikis)
    Transcribed for *Octet* (*See*: W087) and orchestra
    (*See*: W107)
    Premiere:
    (*Farrapós*) Friburgo, state of Rio de Janeiro, Teatro
        Dona Eugênia; Lucilia Villa-Lobos
    (*Kankukus*) R. Figueiredo - Ernáni Braga
    (*Kankikis*) Rio, Salão Nobre; Nininha Veloso Guerra;
        11/17/1917
Napoleão                                                          W085

**Sonhar** (melodia)
  Cello and piano; 2 min.
  Premiere: (Programmed as op.14) Friburgo, state of Rio de
  Janeiro, Teatro Dona Eugênia; Heitor Villa-Lobos, vc;
  Lucilia Villa-Lobos, pf; 11/29/1915
  Napoleão                                                    W086

*1914-1916*

**Danças africanas**
  Octet; 14 min.
  *Farrapós* (Dança dos moços)
  *Kankukus* (Dança dos velhos)
  *Kankikis* (Dança dos meninos)
  Two violins, viola, cello, continuo, flute, clarinet and
  piano
  Original for piano (*See*: W085); transcribed for
  orchestra (*See*: W107)
  Premiere: (First program of the Semana de Arte Moderna)
  São Paulo, Teatro Municipal; Paulina d'Ambrozio, vn;
  George Marinuzzi, Orlando Frederico, va; Alfredo Gomes,
  vc; Alfredo Corazza, Pedro Vieira, Antão Soares and
  Fructuoso Viana, pf; 12/13/1922                             W087

*1915*

**Berceuse**
  Cello and piano; 2 min.
  Also for violin and piano (*See*: W089)
  Dedicated to the composer's mother, Noêmia Villa-Lobos
  Premiere: (programmed as op. 50) Rio, Salão Nobre;
  Oswaldo Allioni vc; Lucilia Villa-Lobos, pf; 11/13/1950
  Napoleão                                                    W088

**Berceuse**
  Violin and piano; 2 min.
  Also for cello and piano. (*See*: W088)
  Dedicated to the composer's mother, Noêmia Villa-Lobos
  Premiere: 11/13/1915
  Napoleão                                                    W089

**Il bove** (The Bull)
  Voice and piano (cello ad libitum); 3 min.
  A setting of a poem by Carducci on the monotony of work

in the fields
Premiere: Rio, Salão Nobre; Lydia Albuquerque Salgado, S;
 Lucilia Villa-Lobos, pf; Alfredo Gomes, vc; 2/3/1917
Napoleão                                                                    W090

**Capriccio**
 Cello and piano; 2 min.
 Also for violin and piano (*See*: W092)
 Originally programmed as op.49
 Napoleão                                                                   W091

**Capriccio**
 Violin and piano; 3 min.
 Also for cello and piano (*See*: W091)
 Premiere: Rio, Salão Nobre; 11/13/1915
 Napoleão                                                                   W092

**Cegonha, A** (The Stork)
 Voice and piano; 3 min.
 Poetry by Anivel Teôfilo
 Premiere: Rio, Salão Nobre; Frederico Nascimento Filho,
  Bar; Ernâni Braga, pf; 11/13/1915
 Napoleão                                                                   W093

**Élégie**
 Orchestra; 4 min.
 Two fl, 2 ob, 2 cl, 2 bn, 2 hn, 2 tpt, 2 trbn, tuba,
  timp, cel, harp and str
 Premiere: Rio, Teatro Municipal; Roberto Soriano, cond;
  11/10/1917                                                                W094

**Grande concerto para violoncelo no.1**
 Cello and orchestra; 22 min.
 Pic, 2 fl, 2 ob, 2 cl, 2 bn, 4 hn, 3 tpt, tuba, timp,
  harp and str
 Premiere: Rio, Teatro Municipal; Newton Pádua, vc; Villa-
  Lobos, cond; 5/10/1918
 Eschig                                                                     W095

**Improviso no.7** (Melodia)
 Violin and piano; 2 min.
 Premiere: Rio, Salão Nobre; Mário Caminha, vn; Lucilia

Villa-Lobos, pf; 11/17/1917
Napoleão                                                          W096

**Marcha religiosa no.1**
Orchestra; 6 min.
Premiere: São Paulo; Symphonic Orchestra of São Paulo;
   Villa-Lobos, cond; 6/12/1915                                  W097

**Il nome di Maria**
Voice and piano; 2 min.
Poetry by Lorenzo Stechetti
Premiere: Rio, Salão Nobre; Lydia Albuquerque Salgado, S;
   Lucilia Villa-Lobos, pf; 2/3/1917
Napoleão                                                          W098

**Quarteto de cordas no.1**
Two violins, viola and cello; 18 min.
   *Cantilena* (Andante)
   *Brincadeira* (Allegretto scherzando)
   *Canto lírico* (Moderato)
   *Cançoneta* (Andantino quasi allegretto)
   *Melancolia* (Lento)
   *Saltando como um Saci* (Allegro)
Premiere: Nova Friburgo, state of Rio de Janeiro, in the
   home of Brazilian composer Homero Barreto; 2/3/1915
Peer                                                             W099

**Quarteto de cordas no.2**
Two violins, viola and cello; 20 min.
Premiere: Rio; Judith Barcelos, vn; Dagmar Gitahy, vn;
   Orlando Frederico, va; Alfredo Gomes, vc; 2/3/1917
Eschig                                                           W100

**Salutaris hostia** (motet)
Four part mixed a cappella chorus; 3 min.
Premiere: Rio, Teatro Municipal,; Schola Cantorum of
   Santa Cecilia School, Canon Alpheo Lopes de Araújo,
   cond; 11/11/1922                                              W101

**Sonata no.1**
Cello and piano; 12 min.
Eschig                                                           W102

## Sonata no.2 (Deuxième Sonate)
Cello and piano; 20 min.
Premiere: (Programmed as op.46) Rio, Salão Nobre; Gustavo
  Hess de Melo, vc; Lucilia Villa-Lobos, pf;
  11/17/1917
  Also performed: (First program, Semana de Arte Moderna)
  São Paulo, Teatro Municipal; Alfredo Gomes, vc; Lucilia
  Villa-Lobos, pf; 2/13/1922
  Eschig                                                    W103

## Tantum ergo
Chorus and orchestra; 4 min.
Flute, oboe, clarinet, bassoon and strings                 W104

## Trio no.2
Piano, violin, and cello; 25 min.
Premiere: Rio, Teatro Municipal; Mario Ronchini, vn;
  Newton Pádua, vc; Lucilia Villa-Lobos, pf; 11/12/1919
  Also performed: (First program, Semana de Arte Moderna)
  São Paulo, Teatro Municipal; Paulina d'Ambrosio, vn;
  Alfredo Gomes, vc; Fructuoso Vianna, pf; 2/13/1922
  Eschig                                                    W105

## *1916*

## Centauro de ouro
  Orchestra; 18 min.
  Symphonic poem based on a text by Ruy Pinheiro Guimarães   W106

## Danses africaines (Danses des indiens métis du Brésil)
  Orchestra; 14 min.
  *Farrapós* (Dança dos moços)
  *Kankukus* (Dança dos velhos)
  *Kankikis* (Dança dos meninos)
  Pic, 2 fl, 2 ob, eng hn, 2 cl, b cl, 2 bn, cbn, 4 hn, 4
  tpt, 3 trbn, tuba, timp, t-t, cax, tri, pan, cymb,
  African drum, large and small tambourines, reco,
  bells (large and small), bomb, xyl, cel, 2 harps, pf
  and str
  Original score for piano (*See*: W085)
  Transcribed for chamber orchestra (octet) (*See*: W087)

Premiere: (Under the title Danças características
   africanas) Rio, Teatro Municipal; Villa-Lobos, cond;
   12/9/1922
Eschig                                                                W107

**Élégie**
   Cello and piano; 3 min.
   Also for violin and piano (*See*: W109)
   Premiere: (Programmed as op.87) Rio, Salão Nobre; Alfredo
   Gomes, vc; Lucilia Villa-Lobos, pf; 2/3/1917
   Napoleão                                                          W108

**Élégie**
   Violin and piano; 2 min.
   Also for cello and piano (*See*: W108)
   Napoleão                                                          W109

**Myremis** (Symphonic poem)
   Orchestra; 18 min.
   Pic, 2 fl, 2 ob, eng hn, cl, b cl, 2 bn, cbn, 4 hn, 4
      tpt, timp, cymb, bomb, mat, drum, pan, viola d'amore,
      bowed kithara, cel, hp and str
   Based on mythology and a poem by his father, Raul Villa-
      Lobos
   Premiere: Rio, Teatro Municipal; Francisco Braga, cond;
      8/15/1918                                                      W110

**Naufragio de Kleônicos** (Symphonic poem and ballet)
   Orchestra; 12 min.
   Pic, 2 fl, 2 ob, eng hn, 2 cl, b cl, 2 bn, cbn, 4 hn, 3
      tpt, 4 trbn, tuba, timp, t-t, cymb, tri, bomb,
      ca, hp and str
   Adaptation by Teixeira Leite
   Ballet version danced by dancer Ruskaia
   Used as musical source material for *O canto do cisne
      negro* (*See*: W122 and W123)
   Premiere: Rio, Teatro Municipal; A. Soriano, cond;
      7/27/1920
   Also performed: Rio; Orchestra of the Sociedade de
      Concertos Sinfônicos, Felix Weingartner, cond; 11/27/1920
   Eschig                                                            W111

**Quarteto de cordas no.3** (Quarteto das pipocas, Pop-corn
   Quartet)

Two violins, viola and cello; 20 min.
Premiere: Rio, Teatro Municipal; Pery Machado,vn; Mário
Ronchini, vn; Orlando Frederico, va; Newton Pádua, vc;
11/12/1919
Eschig                                                          W112

**Quinteto**
Two violins, viola, cello, and piano; 12 min.                   W113

**Sinfonia no.1** (O Imprevisto)
Orchestra; 22 min.
Two pic, 3 fl, 2 ob, eng hn, 2 cl, 2 cl in A, b cl, 2 bn,
  cbn, 4 hn, 4 tpt, 3 trbn, tuba, timp, tam-tam, bass
  drum, cymb, tri, side drum, glock, cel, 2 hp and str
Written under the pseudonym Epaminondas Villalba Filho
Premiere: (Originally programmed as op. 112)
  (1st and 4 movements) Rio; Grande Companhia Italiana;
    Marinuzzi, cond; 9/29/1919
  (complete) Rio, Teatro Municipal; Orchestra of the
    Sociedade de Concertos Sinfônicos do Rio; Villa-Lobos,
    cond; 8/30/1920
Eschig                                                          W114

**Sinfonieta no.1** (Em memória de Mozart)
Orchestra; 15 min.
Two fl, 2 ob, 2 cl, 2 bn, 2 hn, 2 trbn, timp, str
Peer                                                            W115

**Tédio de alvorada**
Orchestra; 15 min.
Three fl, 2 ob, eng hn, 2 cl in A, b cl, 2 bn, 2 hn in
  F, 2 hn in E, 2 trpt in B-flat, 3 trpt in C, bg, 3
  trbn, timp, cymb, bones, xyl, cel, hp and str.
Premiere: Rio, Teatro Municipal; Villa-Lobos, cond;
  8/15/1918                                                     W116

*1916-1918*

**Suíte floral**
Piano; 6 min.
  *Idílio na rede*
  *Uma camponesa cantadeira*
  *Alegria na horta*
Premiere: (Idílio na rede) Rio, Salão Nobre; Ernâni

Braga, pf; 11/17/1917
(Uma camponesa) Nininha Veloso; 11/19/1919
(Cantadeira) Arthur Rubinstein; 10/21/1921
Napoleão
Villa-Lobos Music Corp.                                    W117

*1917*

**Amazonas** (ballet and symphonic poem based on an Indian story
    told by his father, Raul Villa-Lobos; music based on
    the symphonic poem *Myremis*)
Orchestra; 14 min.
    *Contemplação do Amazonas*
    *Ciúme do Deus dos ventos*
    *O espelho da jovem índia*
    *Traição do Deus dos ventos*
    *A prece da jovem índia*
    *Dança ao encantamento das florestas*
    *A dança sensual da jovem índia*
    *Região dos monstros*
    *A marcha dos monstros*
    *A alegria da índia*
    *Um monstro se destaca*
    *A ânsia do monstro*
    *O espelho enganador*
    *A descoberta*
    *O abismo*
    *O precipício*
Two pic, 2 fl, 2 ob, eng hn, pic cl in E-flat, 2 cl in A,
    b cl, 2 bn, cbn, sarrusophone, 4 or 8 hn, 2 tpt in F, 2
    tpt in B-flat, 3 trbn, tuba, timp, t-t, tri,
    tambourine, cymb, pan, bomb, cho, mat, Citara de arco
    (Violinofone), viola d'amore, cel, hp, pf and str
Transcribed for piano (*See*: W119)
Premiere: Paris, Maison Gaveau; Orchestre des Concerts
    Poulet (with added musicians, a total of 120
    performers), Gaston Poulet, cond; 5/30/1929
Eschig                                                     W118

**Amazonas** (Bailado indígena brasileiro)
Piano; 12 min.
Original for orchestra. (*See*: W118)
Eschig                                                     W119

**Ave Maria no.18**
   Four part mixed a cappella chorus
   Also for voice and piano or harmonium (*See*: W121)
   This musical setting appears in *Música Sacra* (*See*:
   Collections M.S. #3) for four part female chorus      W120

**Ave Maria no.18**
   Voice and piano or harmonium
   Also for four part mixed a cappella chorus (*See*: W120)
   This musical setting appears in *Música Sacra* (*See*:
   Collections M.S. #3) for four part female chorus      W121

**O canto do cisne negro** (Poema ballomístico)
   Cello and piano; 3 min.
   Source of musical material is *Naufrágio de Keônicos*
   (*See*: W111)
   Transcribed for violin and piano (*See* W123)
   Napoleão      W122

**O canto do cisne negro**
   Violin and piano; 3 min.
   Source of musical material is *Naufrágio de Kleônicos*
   (*See*: W111)
   Original for cello and piano (*See*: W122)
   Napoleão
   S. Araujo      W123

**Canto oriental**
   Violin and piano      W124

**Cascavel**
   Voice and piano; 2 min.
   Poetry by Costa Rego Júnior
   Premiere: Rio, Teatro Municipal; Frederico Nascimento,
    Bar; Lucilia Villa-Lobos, pf; 11/12/1919
   Napoleão      W125

**Iara** (Symphonic poem)
   Orchestra; 10 min.      W126

**Lobisomem** (Werewolf)
   Orchestra; 10 min.      W127

**Memorare**
Two part chorus and orchestra; 3 min.
Two flutes, 2 ob, 2 cl, 2 bn, 2 hn, 2 trumpets, 2 trbn,
  timp, harmonium and str                                      W128

**Quarteto de cordas no.4**
Two violins, viola and cello; 20 min.
Dedicated to Frederico Nascimento
Premiere: Rio de Janeiro; Borgerth String Quartet;
  10/8/1949
Associated Music Publishers                                    W129

**Saci pererê** (Symphonic Poem)
Orchestra; 15 min.                                             W130

**Sexteto místico** (Sextuor Mystique)
Sextet; 12 min.
Flute, oboe, E-flat alto sax, harp, celeste and guitar
Premiere: Rio; Moacyr Liserra, José Cocarelli, Sebastião
  de Barros, Romeu Fassate, Maria Célia Machado and
  Turíbio Santos; 11/16/1962
Eschig                                                         W131

**Sinfonia no.2** (Ascensão)
Orchestra; 35 min.
Two pic, 2 fl, 2 ob, eng hn, 2 B-flat cl, 2 cl in A, 2
  bn, cbn, 4 hn, 4 tpt in B-flat, 4 tpt in A, 4 trbn,
  tuba, timp, tam-tam, bomb, cymb, ca, tambor de basque,
  cel, 2 harps and str
Premiere: (Originally programmed as op.160) Rio;
  Orquestra Sinfônica de Rádio Nacional; Villa-Lobos,
  cond; 5/6/1944
G. Ricordi                                                     W132

**Uirapuru** (The Enchanted Bird) (Symphonic poem and ballet)
Orchestra; 14 min.
Pic, 2 fl, 2 ob, eng hn, 2  cl, b cl, sop sax, 2 bn, cbn,
  4 hn, 3 tpt, 3 trbn, tuba, timp, t-t, bells, reco,
  coconut, bass drum, tambourine, cymb, bomb, glock  xyl,
  violinophone, cel, 2 harps, pf and str
Based on the legend of the enchanted bird
Dedicated to Serge Lifar
Also available in piano reduction
Premiere: (On the occasion of the visit of Brazilian

President Getúlio Vargas to Argentina) Buenos Aires,
Teatro Colón; Orchestra and ballet of the Teatro Colón;
Nemanoff, choreographer; Villa-Lobos, cond; 5/25/1935
Associated Music Publishers                              W133

## 1917-1919

### Simples coletânea
Piano; 6 min.
*Valsa mística*
*Um berço encantado*
*Rodante*
*Valsa mística* later used in *Evolução dos aeroplanos* (*See*:
W271)
Premiere: (*Valsa mística*) Rio, Teatro Municipal; Nininha
Veloso Guerra, pf; 11/12/1919
Also performed: (First program, Semana de Arte
Moderna) São Paulo, Teatro Municipal; Ernâni Braga,
pf; 2/13/1922
(Rodante) Ernâni Braga, pf; 10/21/1921
(Complete) Rio, Antonieta Rudge Muller, pf
Napoleão                                                W134

## 1918

### Amor y perfidia
Voice and piano; 2 min.
Dedicated to Roberto Soriano
Napoleão                                                W135

### Jesus
Opera in 3 acts; 90 min.
Soloists, chorus and orchestra
Libretto by Goulart de Andrade                          W136

### Marcha religiosa
Orchestra; 10 min.
Premiere: Rio, Teatro Municipal; Orchestra of the
Sociedade de Concertos Sinfônicos, Francisco Nunes,
cond; 12/5/1918                                         W137

**Marcha religiosa no.3**
Orchestra; 10 min.
Two fl, 2 ob, cl, 2 bn, 3 hn, 3 tpt, 3 trbn, timp
and str                                                    W138

**Marcha religiosa no.7**
Orchestra; 8 min.
Premiere Rio, Teatro Municipal; Villa-Lobos, cond;
11/11/1922                                                 W139

**A prole do bebê no.1** (A família do bebê)
Piano; 24 min.
*Branquinha* (A boneca de louça)
*Moreninha* (A boneca de massa)
*Caboclinha* (A boneca de barro)
*Mulatinha* (A boneca de borracha)
*Negrinha* (Boneca de pau)
*A pobrezinha* (A boneca de trapo)
*O polichinelo*
*A bruxa* (A boneca de pano)
Dedicated to Lucilia Villa-Lobos
Premiere: (Complete) Rio, Teatro Municipal; Arthur
   Rubinstein, pf; 7/5/1922
Napoleão, Belwin                                           W140

**Tantum ergo**
Four part mixed a cappella chorus
Transcription of a 1910 *Tantum ergo* transposed to key of
F major (*See*: Collections, M.S. v.1 #13, for four part
mixed a cappella chorus)
Premiere: Rio, Teatro Municipal; Schola Cantorum Santa
Cecilia; Canon Alpheo Lopes de Araújo, cond;
11/11/1922                                                 W141

**Trio no.3**
Violin, cello and piano; 25 min.
Premiere: Rio, Salão Nobre; Paulina d'Ambrozio, vn;
Alfredo Gomes, vc; and Lucilia Villa-Lobos, pf;
10/21/1921
Eschig                                                     W142

**Valsa brasileira**
Band; 8 min.                                               W143

**1919**

**Dança frenética**
Orchestra; 8 min.
Pic, 2 fl, 2 ob, eng hn, 2 cl, b cl, 2 bn, cbn, 4 hn,
   4 tpt, 3 trbn, tuba, timp, t-t, cymb, bomb, tri, xyl,
   cel, harp and str
Premiere: Rio, Teatro Municipal; Villa-Lobos, cond;
   3/7/1922
Eschig                                                           W144

**Festim pagão**
Voice and piano; 2 min.
Poetry by Ronald de Carvalho
Premiere: Rio, Teatro Municipal; Frederico Nascimento
   Filho, Bar; Lucilia Villa-Lobos, pf; 11/12/1919
Napoleão                                                         W145

**Folia de um bloco infantil**
Piano and orchestra; 3 min.
Two fl, ob, cl, sax, bn, 3 hn, trbn, timp, bomb, tamb,
   cho, reco, drum and str
Based on *Carnaval das crianças* (*See*: W157)
Premiere: São Paulo; Lucilia Villa-Lobos, pf; Villa-Lobos
   cond; 9/22/1925                                               W146

**Hino dos artistas**
Voice and piano; 3 min.
Text by Raul Pederneiras
Dedicated to Casa dos artistas
Also called *Canção dos artistas* (*See*: Collections, C.O.
   v1, #41)
V. Vitale                                                        W147

**Histórias da carochinha**
Piano; 10 min.
   *No palacio encantado*
   *A cortesia do principezinho*
   *E o pastorzinho cantava*
   *E a princezinha dançava*
Dedicated to Nylzota Ahygarita, Russenha and Kilzota
Napoleão                                                         W148

**Meu país**
  Chorus and orchestra; 2 min.
  Text by Villa-Lobos under pseudonym Zé Povo
  Also for chorus and band (*See*: W258); and five part
  chorus (*See*: Collections, C.O. v1, #24)
  Premiere: Rio, Teatro Municipal; 11/15/1926                    W149

**Sertão no estio** (Cântico brasileiro)
  Voice and piano; 2 min.
  Text by Arthur Iberê Lemos
  Also for voice and orchestra (*See*: W151)
  Napoleão                                                       W150

**Sertão no estio** (Cântico brasileiro)
  Voice and orchestra; 2 min.
  Flute, clarinet, piano and strings
  Poetry by Arthur Iberê Lemos
  Also for voice and piano (*See*: W150)
  Premiere: Rio, Teatro Municipal; Vicente Celestino, v;
    Robert Soriano, cond; 6/11/1921                              W151

**Sinfonia no.3** (A Guerra)
  Orchestra and fanfare brass section (mixed chorus ad
    libitum); 25 min.
  *Allegro quasi giusto* (A vida e o labor)
  *Como scherzo* (Intrigas e cochichos)
  *Lento e marcial* (Sofrimento)
  *Allegro impetuoso* (A batalha)
  Pic, 2 fl, 2 ob, eng hn, 2 cl, b cl, 2 bn, cbn, 4 hn, 4
    tpt, 4 trbn, tuba, timp, t-t, xyl, cymb, mat, bomb,
    fanfarra, cel, harp and str
  Premiere: (Concert in homage to the King of Belgium) Rio,
    Teatro Municipal; Villa-Lobos, cond; Sept. 1920
  G. Ricordi                                                     W152

**Sinfonia no.4** (A Vitória)
  Orchestra and fanfare section; 25 min.
  Orchestra: 2 pic, 3 fl, 2 ob, eng hn, 2 cl, b cl, s sax,
    a sax, t sax, bar sax, 3 bn, cbn, 4 hn, 4 tpt, 4 trbn,
    tuba, timp, cymb, bonb, tambor, ca, t-t, sin, pan, cho,
    guizos, tri, xyl, cel 2 harps, pf and str
  Fanfare: E-flat cl, s sax, a sax, eup, cor(s), bug(s),
    hn, saxhn(s), b trbn, E-flat contrabass trbn, B-flat

contrabass trbn, bomb
Internal ensemble: E-flat cl, s sax, a sax, t sax, eup,
  pan, tri, cymb and bomb
Significant performance: Paris, Theatre Champs Elysées;
  Orchestre Nationale et Fanfare de la Radiodiffusion
  Française; Villa-Lobos, cond; 6/6/1955
G. Ricordi                                          W153


**Vidapura** (Oratorio Mass)
  Four part mixed chorus, soloists and organ; 22 min.
  *Kyrie*
  *Gloria*
  *Credo*
  *Sanctus*
  *Benedictus*
  *Agnus Dei*
  Reduction from orchestral version (*See*: W155)
  Eschig                                            W154


**Vidapura** (Oratorio Mass)
  Orchestra, mixed chorus and soloists; 22 min.
  *Kyrie*
  *Gloria*
  *Credo*
  *Sanctus*
  *Benedictus*
  *Agnus Dei*
  Two fl, 2 ob, 2 cl, 2 bn, 2 hn, tpt, 2 trbn, tuba, timp,
    t-t, bomb, org and str
  Inscribed on the score: "This mass was comissioned by
    Father Romualdo da Silva. I began in November and
    ended in December of 1919. May God forgive this sin."
  Also for four part mixed chorus, soloist and organ
    (*See*: W154)
  Premiere: (Performed under the title of *Second Mass*) Rio,
    Teatro Municipal; Escola Coral do Teatro Municipal
    (Sylvio Piergili, cond); Arnaud Gouvêa, org; Margarida
    Simões, Mariana Leal, Doloris Belchior, Antonieta de
    Souza, Armando Ciuffi, Asdrubal Lima and João Athos
    soloists; Villa-Lobos, cond; 11/11/1922
  Eschig                                            W155

**Zoé** (Bailado Infernal)
Opera in three acts
Excerpts arranged for piano (*See*: W160 and W163)          W156

*1919-1920*

**Carnaval das crianças**
Piano; 22 min.
*O ginete do Pierrozinho*
*O chicote do diabinho*
*A manhã de Pierrete*
*Os guizos do dominozinho*
*As peripécias do trapeirozinho*
*As traquinices do mascarado Mignon*
*A gaita de um precoce fantasiado*
*A folia de um bloco infantil* (four hands)
Dedicated to his nephews
*Folia de um bloco infantil* arranged for piano and
  for orchestra (*See*: W144)
Later arranged for piano and orchestra with the title
  *Momoprecoce* (*See*: W240 and W259)
Premiere: (Complete) Rio, Salão do Instituto Nacional de
  Música; Antonieta Rudge Muller, pf; 9/17/1925
Napoleão                                                    W157
*1919-1935*

**Canções típicas brasileiras** (Chansons typiques brésiliennes)
Voice and orchestra; 14 min.
*Mokocê-cê-maká*: fl, ob, eng hn, cl in A, bn and str
*Nozani-ná*: eng hn (ad libitum), cl, 2 hn, and str
*Xangô*: 2 bn, 2 hn, timp, bomb, tambor surdo, t-t, harp,
  pf and str
*Estrela é lua nova*: 2 fl, ob, 2 B-flat cl, 2 bn, 3 hn,
  harp and str
*Itabaiana*: harp and str
*Onde o nosso amor nasceu*: fl, ob, eng hn, cl, b cl, bn,
  a sax, b sax, bass sax, 2 hn and str
*Xangô*: eng hn, bn, 2 hn, tpt, trbn, timp, bomb, pf (or
  harp) and str
*Estrela é lua nova*: cl in A, bn, 2 hn and str
Also for voice and piano (*See*: W159)
*Estrela é lua nova* also arranged for voice, clarinet in
  A, bassoon 2 horns and strings (See W331)
Premiere: (*Mokocê-cê-maká, Nozani-ná* and *Xangô*) Paris,

Salle Chopin; Orchestre de Chambre; Croiza, soloist;
Villa-Lobos, cond; 3/14/1930
Eschig                                                          W158

**Canções típicas brasileiras** (Chansons typiques brésiliennes)
Voice and piano; 25 min.
*Mokocê-cê-maká* (Dorme na rede)
*Nozani-ná* (Ameríndio)
*Papai curumiassú* (Berceuse de caboclo)
*Xangô* (Canto de macumba)
*Estrela é lua nova* (Fetichista)
*Viola quebrada* (Toada caipira)
*Adeus Ema* (Desafio)
*Pálida Madona* (Modinha antiga)
*Tu passaste por este jardim* (Modinha carioca)
*Cabocla de caxangá* (Embolada do norte)
*Pássaro fugitivo* (Guriatar do coqueiro pernambuco)
*Itabaiana* (da Paraíba do Norte)
*Onde o nosso amor nasceu* (Modinha antiga)
Songs with texts and melodies collected from various
  sources including Mário de Andrade and Catulo da Paixão
  Cearense
Also for voice and orchestra (*See*: W158)
*Estrela é lua nova* also arranged for voice, clarinet in
  A, bassoon 2 horns and strings (See W331)
Premiere: (*Itabaiana*) Buenos Aires; Stefana Macedo, v;
  Villa-Lobos, pf; 5/28/1935
Eschig                                                          W159

*1920*

**Bailado infernal**
Piano; 3 min.
Excerpt from the second act of the opera *Zoé* (*See*: W156)     W160

**Choros no.1**
Guitar; 3 min.
Dedicated to Ernesto Nazareth
Eschig, Napoleão                                               W161

**Dança diabólica**
Orchestra; 8 min.                                              W162

**Dança infernal**
Piano; 3 min.
From the third act of the opera *Zoé*. (*See*: W156)
Associated Music Publishers                                    W163

**Historiettes** (Historietas)
Voice and orchestra; 16 min.
  *Solitude*
  *Le petit peloton de fil*
  *Hermione et les bergers*
  *Car vite  s'écoule la vie*
  *Le marché*
Pic, 2 fl, 2 ob, eng hn, 2 cl, b cl, 2 bn,
cbn, 4 hn, 2 tpt in F, 3 trbn, tuba, timp, t-t, cymb,
cel, harp, pf and str
Poetry in Portuguese by Ribeiro Couto and Manuel
  Bandeira, and in French by Ronald de Carvalho and
  Albert Samain
Dedicated to Vera Janacopulos
Also for voice and piano (*See*: W165)
Casa Mozart                                                   W164

**Historiettes** (Historietas)
Voice and piano; 12 min.
  *Solitude*
  *Lune d'Octobre*
  *Le petit peloton de fil*
  *Hermione et les bergers*
  *Car vite s'écoule la vie*
  *Le marché*
Poetry in Portuguese by Ribeiro Couto and Manuel
  Bandeira, and in French by Ronald de Carvalho and
  Albert Samain
Dedicated to Vera Janacopulos
Premiere: (*Le petit peloton*) Vera Janacopulos, pf;
  8/11/1921
  (Complete) Rio, Salão Nobre; Maria Emma, v; Lucilia
  Villa-Lobos, pf; 10/21/1921
Also for voice and orchestra (*See*: W164)
Casa Mozart                                                   W165

**A lenda do caboclo**
Piano; 5 min.
Dedicated to Arthur Iberê Lemos

Premiere: Rio, Arthur Iberê Lemos, pf; 6/11/1921
Also for orchestra (*See*: W188)
Napoleão                                                                W166

**Marcha solene no.6**
Orchestra; 6 min.
Two fl, 2 ob, 2 cl, 2 bn, 4 hn, 3 tpt, 3 trbn and str
Premiere: Rio, Teatro Municipal; Villa-Lobos, cond;
11/11/1922                                                        W167

**Marcha triunfal**
Orchestra; 6 min.                                                W168

**Poema do menestrel**
Piano; 6 min.
*Pobre ceguinho*
*Canção de esmola*
*Abandono*                                                          W169

**Sinfonia no.5** (A Paz)
Orchestra, chorus and fanfare brass section; 25 min.
Eschig                                                              W170

**Sonata no.3**
Violin and piano; 15 min.
Eschig                                                              W171

*1921*

**Cantiga boêmia**
Voice and orchestra; 2 min.
Arrangement by Villa-Lobos of a song by Henrique Oswald,
text by Olegario Mariano
Premiere: Rio, Teatro João Caetano; Orquestra do Teatro
Municipal; Julieta Teles de Menezes, v; Villa-Lobos,
cond; 6/18/1934                                                W172

**Epigramas irônicos e sentimentais**
Voice and orchestra; 20 min.
Two fl, ob, eng hn, 2 cl, a sax, bn, 2 hn, 2 trbn,
timp, t-t, bomb, cymb, cel, harp or pf and str
Poetry by Ronald de Carvalho
Dedicated to Maria Emma

Premiere: Rio, Teatro Municipal; Concertos Viggiani;
   Elsie Houston, v; Villa-Lobos, cond; 8/26/1929            W173

**Fantasia de movimentos mistos**
   Violin and orchestra; 25 min.
   *Alma convulsa*
   *Serenidade*
   *Contentamento*
   Pic, 2 fl, 2 ob, eng hn, 2 cl in A, 2 cl in B flat, 2 bn,
   cbn, 4 hn, 2 tpt in A, 2 tpt in B-flat, 2 trbn, tuba,
   timp, t-t, cymb, cel, harp, pf and str
   Dedicated to Paulina d'Ambrozio
   Arranged for violin and piano (*See*: W175)
   Premiere: (Second movement) Rio, Teatro Municipal;
      Paulina d'Ambrozio, vn; Villa-Lobos, cond; 12/9/1922
   (Complete) Rio, Orquestra do Teatro Municipal; Oscar
      Borgerth, vn; Albert Wolff, cond; 4/23/1941
   Peer                                                     W174

**Fantasia de movimentos mistos**
   Violin and piano; 25 min.
   *Serenidade*
   *Alma convulsa*
   *Contentamento*
   Dedicated to Paulina d'Ambrozio
   Original for violin and orchestra (*See*: W174)
   Premiere: (*Alma convulsa* and *Serenidade*) Paulina
      d'Ambrozio, vn; Lucilia Villa-Lobos, pf
   (*Serenidade*) Napoleão
   (Complete) Peer                                          W175

**Fiandeira, A** (La Fileuse)
   Piano; 3 min.
   Dedicated to Ernani Braga
   Premiere: Rio, Salão Nobre; Ernani Braga, pf; 10/21/1921
      Also performed: (First program, Semana de Arte Moderna)
      São Paulo, Teatro Municipal; Ernani Braga, pf;
      Feb. 1922
   Napoleão                                                 W176

**Malazarte**
   Opera in three acts
   Voices and orchestra; 120 min.
   Libretto by Graça Aranha                                 W177

**Pierrot**
 Voice and orchestra; 2 min.
 Arrangement by Villa-Lobos of a song by Henrique Oswald
 Text by Olegario Mariano                                             W178

**Poema úmido**
 Piano; 6 min.
 *Pingos d'água*
 *Gotas de lágrimas*
 *Brilhantes de orvalho*                                              W179

**prole do bebê no.2** (Os bichinhos)
 Piano; 30 min.
 *A baratinha de papel*
 *A gatinha de papelão*
 *O camundongo de massa*
 *O cachorrinho de borracha*
 *O cavalinho de pau*
 *O boizinho de chumbo*
 *O passarinho de pano*
 *O ursinho de algodão*
 *O lobozinho de vidro*
 Dedicated to Aline Van Barentzen
 Premiere: Paris; Aline Van Barentzen, pf; 12/5/1927
 Eschig                                                               W180

**Quatour**
 Flute, E-flat alto saxophone, harp, celeste and female
 voices; 20 min.
 Dedicated to Mme. Santos Lobo, patroness
 Premiere: (Under the title of *Quarteto simbólico*) Rio,
 Salão Nobre; Pedro de Assis, Antão Soares, Rosa
 Farraiola and female chorus; Villa-Lobos, cond;
 10/21/1921
 Eschig                                                               W181

**Trio**
 Oboe, clarinet and bassoon; 18 min.
 Premiere: Paris, Salle des Agriculteurs; L. Gaudard,
 Hamelin and G. Dherin; 4/9/1924
 Eschig                                                               W182

*1921-1923*

**Epigramas irônicos e sentimentais**
Voice and piano; 20 min.
*Eis a vida*
*Inútil epigrama*
*Sonho de uma noite de verão*
*Epigrama*
*Perversidade*
*Pudor*
*Imagem*
*Verdade* (como ópera lírica)
Poetry by Ronald de Carvalho
Dedicated to Maria Emma
Premiere: Rio, Salão Nobre; Maria Emma, v; Lucilia Villa-
Lobos, pf;
Napoleão                                                                    W183

*1921-1926*

**Rudepoema**
Piano; 24 min.
Dedicated to Arthur Rubinstein
Transcribed for orchestra (*See*: W312)
Premiere: Paris, Maison Gaveau; Arthur Rubinstein, pf;
10/24/1927
Eschig                                                                      W184

**1922**

**Brasil novo**
Chorus and orchestra; 3 min.
Poetry by Villa-Lobos under the pseudonym Zé Povo
Also for band (*See*: W186); and for soloist and four part
mixed chorus with piano and percussion accompaniment
(*See*: Collections, C.O. v1, #18)                                        W185

**Brasil novo**
Band; 5 min.
Pic, fl, cl, tpt, bug, sax, bar, trbn, eup, cont (E-flat
& B-flat), cymb, drum and bomb
Also for chorus and orchestra (*See*: W185); and for
soloist and four part mixed chorus with piano and
percussion accompaniment (*See*: Collections, C.O. v1,

#18)
Published by the Conservatório Nacional de Canto
Orfeônico as *Partituras de banda*                              W186

**Dança dos mosquitos**
Orchestra; 4 min.
Pic, 2 fl, 2 ob, eng hn, 2 cl, b cl, 2 bn, cbn, 4 hn, 4
   tpt, 4 trbn, tuba, timp, t-t, cymb, cho (metal),
   pan, mat, cel, vibraphone, harp, pf and str
Dedicated to Mindinha in 1936
Premiere: Rio, Teatro Municipal,; Orquestra Sinfônica
   Nacional da Rádio MEC; Mário Tavares, cond; 11/23/1974
Eschig                                                          W187

**A lenda do caboclo**
Orchestra; 5 min.
Two fl, 2 ob, 2 cl, 2 bn, 2 hn, timp, tri, harp and str
Dedicated to Arthur Iberê Lemos
Original  for piano (*See*: W166)
Also orchestrated by Adalberto de Carvalho
Premiere: Rio; Orquestra do Teatro Municipal; Alberto
   Soriano, cond; 6/13/1921                                     W188

**Verde velhice** (Divertimento)
Orchestra; 8 min.
Two fl, 2 ob, 2 cl, b cl, 2 bn, 4 hn, 2 tpt, 3 trbn,
   tuba, timp, t-t, harp, pf, and str
Dedicated to Counsellor Antônio Prado
Premiere: São Paulo; Villa-Lobos, cond; 1926                    W189

*1923*

**Coleção brasileira**
Voice and orchestra; 3 min.
   *Tempos atrás*
   *Tristeza*
Fl, ob, cl, a sax, bn, tamb, and str
Poetry by Godofredo da Silva Telles
Dedicated to Olivia Guedes Penteado and Carolina da Silva
   Telles
Arranged for voice and piano (*See*: W211)
Premiere: São Paulo, Teatro Sant'Ana; Frederico
   Nascimento Filho, Bar; Villa-Lobos, cond; 2/18/1925          W190

**Noneto** (Impressão rápida de todo o Brasil)
Orchestra and mixed chorus; 18 min.
Flute, oboe, clarinet, alto and baritone sax, celeste,
    harp, piano, mixed chorus and percussion: (timp, xyl,
    t-t, tamb, bomb, ca, cymb (bronze and pottery dinner
    plate), cho (metal and wood), tri, reco, coco large and
    small, puita, pand grande and caxambu)
Dedicated to Dona Olivia Guedes Penteado, patroness
Premiere: Paris; Choeur Mixte de Paris; L. Fleury, L.
    Gaudard, H. Declacoix, R. Briard, G. Dherin, G. Truc,
    J. Souza Lima, Inghelbrecht, Caillette, and L. Perret;
    Villa-Lobos, cond; 5/30/1924
Eschig                                                          W191

**Poème de l'enfant et de sa mère**
Voice, flute, clarinet and cello; 6 min.
Text by Villa-Lobos under the pseudonym Epaminondas
    Villalba Filho
Also for voice and piano (*See*: W193)
Premiere: Paris, Salle Chopin; Croiza, v; Grunelle,
    Cahuzac and Aniceto Palmia; 3/14/1930
Eschig                                                          W192

**Poème de l'Enfant et de sa Mère**
Voice and piano; 4 min.
Text by Villa-Lobos under the pseudonym Epaminondas
    Villalba Filho
Also for voice and instruments (*See*: W192)
Eschig                                                          W193

**Sonata no.4**
Violin and piano; 20 min.
Eschig                                                          W194

**Suíte para canto e violino**
Voice and violin; 12 min.
    *A menina e a canção*
    *Quero ser alegre*
    *Sertaneja*
Poetry by Mário de Andrade
Dedicated to A. Stall, Vera Janacopulos, and Yvonne
    Astruc
One movement (*Sertaneja*) arranged for voice, violins and
    violas (*See*: W196)

Premiere: Rio, Instituto Nacional de Música; Julieta
  Teles de Menezes, v; Paulina d'Ambrozio, vn; 9/17/1925
Eschig                                                    W195

**Suíte para canto e violino**
  Voice, violins and violas; 2 min.
  *Sertaneja*
  Poetry by Mário de Andrade
  Also for voice and violin (*See*: W195)
  Premiere: Rio, Teatro João Caetano; Julieta Teles de
    Menezes, v; Villa-Lobos, cond; 6/18/1934
  Eschig                                                  W196

*1924*

**Choros no.2**
  Flute and clarinet; 3 min.
  Dedicated to Mário de Andrade
  Transcribed for piano (*See*: W198)
  Premiere: Spartaco Rossi, Antenor Driussi; 2/18/1925
  Eschig                                                  W197

**Choros no.2**
  Piano (transcription); 3 min.
  Dedicated to Mário de Andrade
  Original for flute and clarinet (*See*: W197)
  Napoleão and Eschig                                     W198

**Choros no.7** (Setemino)
  Instrumental ensemble; 10 min.
  Fl, ob, B-flat cl, E-flat a sax, bn, vn, vc, and
    t-t (off-stage)
  In this work, the clarinet is played without a reed and
    is blown as a French horn
  Dedicated to Arnaldo Guinle
  Premiere: Rio, Instituto Nacional de Música; Ary
    Ferreira, fl; Antão Soares; Rodolfo Atanásio; Felipe
    Dechamps; Assis Republicano; Cardoso Menezes; Newton
    Pádua, vc; 9/17/1925
  Eschig                                                  W199

*1925*

**Canção da terra**
  Female chorus and orchestra; 3 min.
  Poetry by Ronald de Carvalho
  Dedicated to Francisco Albuquerque da Costa for his
    students at Colégio Bennet
  Also for female chorus and piano (*See*: W201); and for
    voice and piano (*See*: W202)
  Napoleão                                                      W200

**Canção da terra**
  Female chorus and piano; 3 min.
  Poetry by Ronald de Carvalho
  Dedicated to Francisco Albuquerque da Costa for his
    students at Colégio Bennet
  Also for female chorus and orchestra (*See*: W200); and
    for voice and piano (*See*: W202)
  Napoleão                                                      W201

**Canção da terra**
  Voice and piano; 3 min.
  Poetry by Ronald de Carvalho
  Arranged for female chorus and orchestra (*See*: W200); and
    for female chorus and piano (*See*: W201)
  Napoleão                                                      W202

**Canção do parachoque** (Bumper Song)
  Three part a cappella chorus; 1 minute
  Written under the pseudonym Epaminondas Villalba Filho     W203

**Cantiga de roda**
  Three part female chorus and piano; 3 min.
  Dedicated to Italiano Tabarin
  Napoleão                                                      W204

**Cantiga de roda**
  Female chorus and orchestra; 3 min.
  Premiere: Rio; Orchestra of the Orfeão de Professores;
    Villa-Lobos, cond; 5/8/1933
  Napoleão                                                      W205

**Choros no.3** (Picapau)
Instruments; 4 min.
Cl, a sax, bn, 3 hn, trbn, and male chorus
Dedicated to Tarsila and Oswaldo de Andrade
Based on the theme "Nozani-ná" collected by E. Roquette
    Pinto from the Pareci Indians (from Mato Grosso)
Premiere: Paris; Cahuzac, Poimbeuf, G. Dherin, Entraigue,
    Penable, Marquette and Dervaux; Ribert Siohan, cond;
    12/5/1927
Eschig                                                          W206

**Choros no.5** (Alma brasileira)
Piano; 5 min.
Dedicated to Arnaldo Guinle
Eschig and Consolidated                                          W207

**Choros no.8**
Orchestra and two pianos; 20 min.
Pic, 2 fl, 2 ob, eng hn, 2 cl, b cl, a sax, 2 bn, cbn, 4
    hn, 3 tpt, 3 trbn, tuba, timp, t-t, tri, cymb, tambor
    de campanha, ca, cho, reco, caracaxá, caraxa, puita,
    mat, bomb, xyl, cel, 2 harps and str
Dedicated to Tomas Teran
The percussion section requires 8 performers
The performance of one section of this work requires a
    sheet of paper to be placed over the strings of the
    piano
Premiere: Paris, Salle Gaveau; Orquestra "Concerts
    Colonne"; Aline Van Barentzen and Tomas Teran, pf;
    Villa-Lobos, cond; 10/24/1927
Eschig                                                          W208

**Choros no.10**
Orchestra and mixed chorus; 16 min.
Pic, 2 fl, 2 ob, 2 cl in A, a sax, 2 bn, cbn, 3 hn, 2 tpt
    in A, 2 trbn, timp, t-t, gong, tamb, ca, tambor, cax,
    caixa de madeira, 2 puitas, 2 bomb, reco (large and
    small) cho (metal and wood), pf, harp and str
Poetry by Catulo da Paixão Cearense, "Rasga o coração"
Dedicated to Paulo Prado
Ballet version of same work is called Jurapary; danced in
    Rio and Paris
Premiere: Rio, Teatro Lírico; Grande Orquestra da Empresa
    Viggiani; chorus of Brazilian singers and the Deutscher

Männerchor; Villa-Lobos cond; 11/11/1926
Eschig                                                                     W209

## Cirandinhas
Piano; 26 min.
*Zangou-se o cravo com a rosa*
*Adeus bela morena*
*Vamos maninha*
*Olha aquela menina*
*Senhora pastora*
*Cai, cai, balão*
*Todo mundo passa*
*Vamos ver a mulatinha*
*Carneirinho, carneirão*
*A canoa virou*
*Nésta rua tem um bosque*
*Lindos olhos que ela tem*
Napoleão                                                                   W210

## Coleção brasileira
Voice and piano; 3 min.
Text by Godofredo da Silva Telles
Dedicated to Olivia Guedes Penteado and Carolina da Silva
   Telles
Original for voice and orchestra (*See*: W190)
Napoleão                                                                   W211

## Marcha solene no.8 (Entrada) (A caminho da reza)
Orchestra; 6 min.
Premiere: Rio, Teatro Municipal; Villa-Lobos, cond;
   11/11/1922                                                              W212

## Martírio dos insetos
Violin and orchestra; 15 min.
*A cigarra no inverno*
*O vagalume na claridade*
*Mariposa na luz* (1916)
Pic, 2 fl, 2 ob, eng hn, 2 cl, 2 bn, cbn, 2 hn, 2 tpt,
   2 trbn, tuba, timp, cymb, harp, cel, and str
Dedicated to Oscar Borgerth, Mariuccia Iacovino and Mário
   Caminha
Arranged for violin and piano (*See*: W214)
Mariposa na luz later used in *Evolução dos aeroplanos*
   (*See*: W271)

Premiere: (*Mariposa na luz*) Rio, Teatro Municipal;
  Paulina d'Ambrozio, vn; Villa-Lobos, cond; 12/9/1922
  (Complete) Rio; Orquestra Sinfônica de Rádio Nacional;
  Oscar Borgerth, vn, Leo Perachi, cond; 12/9/1922
Eschig                                                                W213

**Martírio dos insetos**
  Violin and piano; 18 min.
  *A cigarra no inverno*
  *O vagalume na claridade*
  *Mariposa na luz* (1916)
  Dedicated to Oscar Borgerth, Mariuccia Iacovino and Mário
  Caminha
  Original for violin and orchestra (*See*: W213)
  *Mariposa na luz* later used in *Evolução dos aeroplanos*
  (*See*: W271)
  Premiere: Rio, Salão Nobre; Mário Caminha, vn; Lucilia
  Villa-Lobos, pf; 11/17/1917
  Napoleão (*Mariposa na luz*)                                         W214

**Serestas**
  Voice and orchestra; 25 min.
  *Pobre cega*
  *Canção da folha morta*
  *Saudades da minha vida*
  *Modinha*
  *Na paz do outono*
  *Cantiga do viúvo*
  *Canção do carreiro*
  *Abril*
  *Desejo*
  *Redondilha*
  Pic, 2 fl, 2 ob, eng hn, 2 cl, 2 b cl, a sax, 2 bn, cbn,
  4 hn, tpt, 2 trbn, tuba, timp, t-t, cho, reco, harp,
  cel and str
  *Canção da folha morta* is for mixed chorus and orchestra
  Also for voice and piano (*See*: W216)
  Premiere: (*Cantiga do Viúvo*) Rio; Orquestra do Teatro
  Municipal; Alicinha Ricardo Mayerhofer, v, Villa-Lobos,
  cond; 11/6/1936                                                      W215

**Serestas**
  Voice and piano; 35 min.
  *Pobre cega*

*Anjo da guarda*
  *Canção da folha morta*
  *Saudades da minha vida*
  *Modinha*
  *Na paz do outono*
  *Cantiga do viúvo*
  *Canção do carreiro*
  *Abril*
  *Desejo*
  *Redondilha*
  *Realejo*
  *Vôo*
  *Serenata*
  Also for voice and orchestra (*See*: W215)
  Premiere: (*Serenata*) Alma Cunha Miranda, v; 8/27/1940
  (*Vôo*) Maria Sylvia Pinto, v; Francisco Mignone, pf;
  8/15/1944
  Napoleão (songs 1-12)
  Eschig (songs 13 and 14)                                           W216

**Sul América**
  Piano; 4 min.
  Commissioned by the Argentine newspaper *La Prensa*
  Impressions of various South American countries
  Napoleão                                                          W217

*1926*

**Choros no.4**
  Three French horns and 1 trombone; 4 min.
  Dedicated to Carlos Guinle
  Premiere: Paris; Entraigue, Penable, Marquette,and
  Dervaux; 10/24/1927
  Eschig                                                            W218

## Choros no.6
Orchestra; 24 min.
Two pic, 2 fl, 2 ob, eng hn, 2 cl, b cl, 2 bn, cbn, 4 hn,
4 tpt, 4 trbn, tuba, timp, t-t, sax, xyl, glock, cymb,
bomb, cuíca, reco, tambu and tambi, tambores, roncador,
tamborim de samba, tambor surdo, cel, 2 harps and str
Dedicated to Arminda Neves d'Almeida in 1936
Premiere: Rio; Orquestra do Teatro Municipal; Villa-
Lobos, cond; 7/18/1942
Eschig                                              W219

## Cirandas
Piano; 48 min.
*Teresinha de Jesus*
*A condessa*
*Senhora Dona Sancha*
*O cravo brigou com a rosa*
*Pobre cega (Toada de rede)*
*Passa, passa, gavião*
*Xô, xô, passarinho*
*Vamos atrás da serra, Calunga*
*Fui no itororó*
*O pintor de Canahy*
*Nesta rua, nesta rua*
*Olha o passarinho domine*
*A procura de uma agulha*
*A canoa virou*
*Que lindos olhos*
*Có-có-có*
*Terezinha de Jesus* arranged for guitar (*See*: W559)
Dedicated to Alfredo Oswald
Premiere: Rio, Teatro Lírico; Tomas Teran, pf; 8/13/1929
Napoleão                                            W220

## Filhas de Maria
Voice and piano; 3 min.
Impressions of the interior of the Candelária church in
Rio
Poetry by Dante Milano
Peer                                                W221

## A prole do bebê no.3 (Esportes)
Piano; 30 min.

*Gude*
*Diabolô*
*Bilboquê*
*Peteca*
*Pião*
*Futebol*
*Jôgo de bolas*
*Soldado de chumbo*
*Capoeiragem*                                                    W222


**Três poemas indígenas**
   Voice and piano; 12 min.
   *Canidé-Ioune-Sabath* (Ave amarela, canção elegíaca)
   *Teiru* (Canto fúnebre pela morte de um cacique)
   *Iara* (Poem by Mário de Andrade)
   Melody of Canide-Ioune-Sabath collected by Jean de Léry
      (16th century)
   Dedicated to Roquette Pinto
   Also for voice, mixed chorus and orchestra (*See*: W224)
   Eschig                                                       W223

**Três poemas indigenas**
   Voice, mixed chorus and orchestra; 12 min.
   *Canidé-Ioune-Sabath* (Ave amarela, canção elegíaca)
   *Teiru* (Canto funebre pela morte de um cacique)
   *Iara* (Poem by Mário de Andrade)
   Pic, 2 fl, 2 ob, eng hn, 2 cl in B-flat, cl in A, b cl,
      a sax, 2 bn, cbn, 3 hn, 2 tpt, 4 trbn, timp, t-t,
      tamborim de provence, matraca selvagem, bomb, cel,
      harp, pf and str
   Melody of *Canide-Ioune-Sabath* collected by Jean de Léry
      (16th century)
   Dedicated to Roquette Pinto
   Also for voice and piano (*See*: W223)
   Premiere: Paris, Maison Gaveau; Orchestra of the Concerts
      Colonne e L'Art Choral; Vera Janacopulos, v; Villa-
      Lobos, cond; 12/5/1927
   Eschig                                                       W224

**Vira**
   Voice and piano; 2 min.
   Portuguese melody

Premiere: Rio; Alma Cunha Miranda, v; 7/31/1944
Eschig                                                                    W225

*1927*

**Saudades das selvas brasileiras**
Piano; 10 min.
Dedicated to Mademoiselles Lile and Beatriz Lucas
Premiere: Paris, Salle Chopin; Janine Cools, pf;
  3/14/1930
Eschig                                                                    W226

*1928*

**Choros bis** (Deux Choros)
Violin and cello; 10 min.
Premiere: Paris, Salle Chopin; Tony Close and André
  Asselin; 3/14/1930
Eschig                                                                    W227

**Choros no.11**
Piano and orchestra; 65 min.
Two pic, 3 fl, 2 ob, eng hn, 2 cl, b cl, E-flat cl,
  s sax, a sax, 2 bn, cbn, 4 hn, 4 tpt, 4 trbn, tuba,
  timp, t-t, bomb, cymb, reco, cho, ca, tamb, tambor,
  côco, cabacinhas, cax, cuica, xyl, cel, 2 harps and str
Dedicated to Arthur Rubinstein
Premiere: Rio; Orchestra of the Teatro Municipal; José
  Vieira Brandão, pf; Villa-Lobos, cond; 7/18/1942
Eschig                                                                    W228

**Choros no.14**
Orchestra, band, and choirs                                               W229

**Quatuor** (Quarteto para instrumentos de sopro)
Flute, oboe, clarinet, and bassoon; 20 min.
Eschig                                                                    W230

**Quinteto em forma de choros**
Quintet; 12 min.
Flute, oboe, clarinet, English or French horn, and
  bassoon
Premiere: Paris, Salle Chopin; Crunelle, Mercier, Brun,

Cahuzac and Lenon; 3/14/1930
Eschig                                                      W231

*1929*

## Choros no.9
Orchestra; 25 min.
Pic, 2 fl, 2 ob, eng hn, 2 cl, b cl, 2 bn, cbn, 4 hns,
  4 tpt, 4 trbn, tuba, timp, t-t, bomb, tamb, tambor
  surdo, camisão (large and small), pio, tri, reco,
  tartaruga, cax, cho (metal and wood), xyl, vibraphone,
  cel, 2 harps and str
Dedicated to Arminda Neves d'Almeida in 1936
Premiere: Rio; Orchestra of the Teatro Municipal; Villa-
  Lobos, cond; 7/15/1942
Eschig                                                      W232

## Choros no.12
Orchestra; 40 min.
Two pic, 3 fl, 3 ob, eng hn, 3 cl, b cl, 2 a sax, 3 bn,
  cbn, 8 hn, 4 tpt, 4 trbn, tuba, timp, t-t, cymb, cuíca,
  bomb, tambor, camisão grande, cho, reco, pan, xyl,
  vibraphone, cel, pf, 2 harps and str
Dedicated to José Cândido de Andrade Muricy in 1942, at
  the suggestion of Mindinha
Premiere: Boston Symphony Orchestra; Villa-Lobos, cond;
  2/21/1945
Eschig                                                      W233

## Choros no.13
Two orchestras and band                                     W234

## 12 Études (12 Estudos)
Guitar; 45 min.
Dedicated to Andres Segovia
Segovia was invited by Villa-Lobos to provide a fingering
  for the guitar *Etudes*. Segovia's reply was as follows:
  I did not wish to change any of the fingerings which
  Villa-Lobos wrote in the score.  He knows the guitar
  perfectly.  If a certain fingering was chosen for
  specific phrases, his instructions should be strictly
  observed, even if greater technical efforts must be
  made.
Eschig                                                      W235

**Fado**
Voice and piano; 2 min.
Popular Portuguese melody                                      W236

**Francette et Pià**
Piano; 30 min.
*Piá veio a França* (Pià est venu en France)
*Piá viu Francette* (Pià a vu Francette)
*Piá falou a Francette* (Pià a parle à Francette)
*Piá e Francette brincam* (Pià et Francette jouent
  ensemble)
*Francette ficou zangada* (Francette est fachée)
*Piá foi para a guerra* (Pià est parti pour la guerre)
*Francette ficou triste* (Francette est triste)
*Piá voltou da guerra* (Pià revint de la guerre)
*Francette ficou contente* (Francette est contente)
*Francette e Piá brincam para sempre* (Francette
  et Pià jouent pour toujours) (Piano four hands)
Commissioned by Max Eschig for the precocious Paris
  Conservatory students of Marguerite Long. The music is
  based on the story of a Brazilian boy, Piá, son of
  Indian parents, who goes to France and meets a French
  girl, Francette.
Transcribed for orchestra (*See*: W552)
Eschig                                                         W237

**Funil** (Ballet)
Orchestra                                                     W238

**Introdução aos choros**
Orchestra and guitar; 10 min.
Pic, 2 fl, 2 ob, eng hn, 2 cl, b cl, sax, 2 bn, cbn,
  4 hn, 4 tpt, 4 trbn, tuba, timp, tam-tam, xyl, cel, 2
  harps, pf and str
Dedicated to Mindinha
Premiere: Rio; Orchestra of the Rádio Nacional; Menezes,
  guitar; Leo Perachi, cond
Eschig                                                        W239

**Momoprecoce** (Fantasia)
Piano and orchestra; 18 min.
Pic, fl, ob, eng hn, cl, a sax, bn, 3 hn, tpt in C, trbn,
  timp, tambor, tambor de Basque, tamborim de Campagne,
  ca, tambor infantil, bomb, cho infantil, choc (metal

and wood), bomb, reco and str
Based on *Carnaval das Crianças* (*See*: W157)
Dedicated to Magda Tagliaferro
Reduction for 2 pianos
Transcribed for piano and band, performed in 1931 in the
   Teatro Municipal of São Paulo (*See*: 259)
Premiere: Amsterdam; Magda Tagliaferro, pf; Pierre
   Monteaux, cond; 1929
Eschig                                                                                 W240

**Possessão** (Ballet)
Orchestra
Premiere: Oslo, Norway; Adolfo Bolm, dancer; 1929              W241


**Suíte sugestiva** (Cinema)
Chamber orchestra, Soprano and Baritone; 14 min.
   *Ouverture de l'homme tel*
   *Prelude, choral et funèbre* (ciné journal)
   *Cloche pied au flic* (comédie)
   *Le recit du peureux* (drame)
   *Charlot aviateur* (comique)
   *l'Enfant et le iouroupari* (tragédie)
   *La marche finale*
Pic, fl, ob, cl in A, bn, tpt in B-flat, tpt in C,
   tpt in A, trbn, timp, t-t, bomb, tri, cymb,
   caixa clara, 3 metronomes, xyl, cel, pf, vn, va, vc and
   db with 5 strings
Poetry by Oswaldo de Andrade, René Chalupt and Manuel
   Bandeira
Dedicated to Mme. Frederic Moreau
Also for voice and piano (*See*: W243); *Ouverture de
   l'homme tel* arranged for orchestra (*See*: W508)
Premiere: Paris, residence of Mme. Frederic Moreau;
   Anthony Bernard, cond; 4/3/1930
Eschig                                                                                 W242


**Suíte sugestiva**
Voice and piano; 14 min.
   *Ouverture de l'homme tel*
   *Prelude, choral et funèbre* (ciné journal)
   *Cloche pied au flic* (comédie)
   *Le recit du peureux* (drame)

*Charlot aviateur* (comique)
*L'Enfant et le iouroupari* (tragédie)
*La marche finale*
Poetry by Oswaldo de Andrade, René Chalupt and Manuel
Bandeira
Dedicated to Mme. Frederic Moreau
Also for Chamber orchestra, Soprano and Baritone
(*See*: W242); *Ouverture de l'homme tel* arranged for
orchestra (See: W508)
Premiere: Rio, Teatro Lírico; Elsie Houston, Adalto
Filho, Lucilia Villa-Lobos and Brutus Pereira;
8/26/1929
Eschig                                                                    W243

**Veículo** (Ballet)
Orchestra; 18 min.
Le Roll (Paris)                                                           W244

**Vocalises-Estudos**
Voice and piano; 2 min.
Commissioned and edited under the direction of A.L.
Hettich
Leduc                                                                     W245

*1930*

**Bachianas brasileiras no.1**
Orchestra of celli; 18 min.
*Introdução* (Embolada)
*Prelúdio* (Modinha)
*Fuga* (Conversa)
Dedicated to Pablo Casals
Premiere: Rio, Casa d'Italia; Ensemble of 8 cellists;
Villa-Lobos, cond; 11/13/1938
Associated Music Publishers                                               W246

**Bachianas brasileiras no.2**
Orchestra; 20 min.
*Prelúdio* (O canto do capadócio)
*Ária* (O canto da nossa terra)
*Dansa* (Lembrança do sertão)
*Toccata* (O trenzinho do caipira)
Pic, fl, ob, cl, t sax, bar sax, bn, cbn, 2 hn, trbn,

timp, ganzá, cho, pan, reco, mat, ca, tri, cymb, t-t,
  bomb, cel, pf and str
Dedicated to Mindinha
*Prelúdio* (O canto do capadócio) transcribed for cello and
  piano (*See*: W251)
*Ária* (O canto da nossa terra) transcribed for cello and
  piano (*See*: W250)
*Dansa* (Lembrança do sertão) transcribed for piano (*See*:
  W252)
*Toccata* (O trenzinho do caipira) transcribed for cello
  and piano (*See*: W254)
Premiere: Venice; Festival Internacional de Veneza;
  Dimitri Mitropulos, cond; 9/3/1934
G. Ricordi                                                                    W247

**Canções indígenas**
Voice and orchestra; 2 min.
  *Ualalocê*
Pic, fl, ob, eng hn, cl in A, bn, 2 hn, tpt, trbn, timp,
  t-t, tambor, coco and str
Premiere: Paris, Salle Chopin; Orchestra de Camara de
  Paris; Croiza, v; Villa-Lobos, cond; 3/14/1930            W248

**Canções indígenas**
Voice and piano; 5 min.
  *Pai do Mato* (Poema Ameríndio)
  *Ualalocê* (Lenda dos índios Parecis para comemorar a
  caça)
  *Kamalalô*
*Pai do Mato* text by Mário de Andrade
*Ualalocê* and *Kamalalô* based on themes of the Pareci
  Indians (from Mato Grosso)
Southern Music Publishers, Inc.                             W249

**Canto da nossa terra, O**
Cello and piano; 3 min.
Transcribed from *Bachianas brasileiras no.2* (*See*: W247)   W250

**Canto do capadócio, O**
Cello and piano; 3 min.
Transcribed from *Bachianas brasileiras no.2* (*See*: W247)
Premiere: Friburgo, state of Rio de Janeiro, Teatro Dona
  Eugênia; Heitor Villa-Lobos, vc; Lucilia Villa-Lobos,
  pf; 1/29/1915                                             W251

**Lembrança do sertão**
Piano; 3 min.
Dedicated to Georgette Baptista
Transcribed from *Bachianas brasileiras no.2* (*See*: W247)          W252

**Pai do mato**
Voice and piano
Poetry by Mário de Andrade
Peer          W253

**O trenzinho do caipira**
Cello and piano; 2 min.
Transcribed from *Bachianas brasileiras no.2* (*See*: W247)
Premiere: São Paulo, Pirajuí; Villa-Lobos, vc; Souza
Lima, pf; 1930          W254

*1931*

**O brasileiro** (Gritos da rua)
Voice          W255

**Caixinha de música quebrada**
Piano; 3 min.
Original version entitled *Realejo quebrado*
Premiere: São Paulo; João de Souza Lima, pf; 1931
Consolidated Music Publishers          W256

**Fuga no.10** (Arrangement)
Cello and piano; 3 min.
Transcribed from *The Well-Tempered Clavier* of J.S. Bach          W257

**Meu país**
Chorus and band; 2 min.
Poetry by Villa-Lobos under pseudonym Zé Povo
Original version for soloist and five part chorus (*See*:
Collections, C.O. v.1 #24); also for chorus and
orchestra (*See*: W149)          W258

**Momoprecoce** (Fantasia)
Piano and band; 18 min.
Based on *Carnaval das crianças* (*See*: W157)
Original for piano and orchestra (*See*: W240)
Premiere: São Paulo, Teatro Municipal; 1931          W259

**Noturno op.9, no.2** (Arrangement)
Cello and piano; 3 min.
Original by Chopin                                                        W260

**Prelúdio no.8** (Arrangement)
Cello and piano; 3 min.
Transcribed from *The Well-Tempered Clavier* of J.S. Bach
Arranged for orchestra of cellos (*See*: W431)                            W261

**Prelúdio no.14** (Arrangement)
Cello and piano; 3 min.
Transcribed from *The Well-Tempered Clavier* of J.S. Bach
Arranged for orchestra of cellos (*See*: W431)
Premiere: São Paulo, Pirajuí, concert tour; Villa-Lobos,
   vc; Souza Lima, pf; 1930                                               W262

**Quarteto de cordas no.5**
Two violins, viola and cello; 18 min.
Dedicated to João Alberto Lins de Barros
Originally titled *Quarteto Popular no.1*
Associated Music Publishers                                               W263

*1930-1941*

**Bachianas brasileiras no.4**
Piano; 24 min.
   *Prelúdio* (Introdução) 1941
   *Coral* (Canto do sertão) 1941
   *Ária* (Cantiga) 1935
   *Dansa* (Miudinho) 1930
Dedicated to: Tomas Teran (*Prelúdio*), José Vieira Brandão
   (*Coral*), Silvio Salema (*Ária*), and Antonietta Rudge
   Muller (*Dansa*)
Transcribed for piano and orchestra (*See*: W424)
Premiere: Rio; José Vieira Brandão, pf; 11/27/1939
CMP & Vitale                                                             W264

*1932*

**Caixinha de boas festas** (Vitrine encantada - Symphonic poem
   and ballet)
Orchestra; 22 min.
Pic, 2 fl, 2 ob, eng hn, 2 cl, b cl, 2 bn, cbn, 4 hn,
   3 tpt, 2 trbn, tuba, timp, drums (various), t-t, reco,

small bells, cymb, mat, cho, bomb, xyl, cel, harp, pf
and str
Dedicated to Burle Marx
Symphonic poem and childrens ballet written at the
request of Walter Burle Marx for the Concertos da
Juventude (Youth Concerts)
Premiere: Rio, Teatro Municipal; Childrens group of the
dance school of the Teatro Municipal; Maria Oleneva,
dir; Orquestra Filarmônica, Walter Burle Marx, cond;
11/23/1932;
G. Ricordi                                                           W265

## A canoa virou
Band; 4 min.
Pic, fl, E-flat cl, cl, tpt, sax, bug, trbn, bar, bomb,
Eb and Bb contrabass trbn, cymb, tambor, and bomb          W266

## Consolação
Four part mixed a cappella chorus; 3 min.
Theme by Mendelssohn
Text by Pedro Mello
Premiere: Rio; Orfeão de Professores; Villa-Lobos, cond;
April 1933                                                           W267

## Constância
Band; 1 min.
Pic, fl, ob, E-flat cl, cl, hn, bug, sax, tpt, bar, bomb,
trbn, E-flat and B-flat contrabass trbn, ca, cymb and
bomb
Also for voice with piano, instrumental ensemble or piano
solo (*See*: Collections, G.P. #41)
Published by the Conservatório de Canto Orfeônico as
*Partituras de banda*                                           W268

## Élégie
Mixed a cappella chorus with tenor and soprano soloists;
2 min.
Theme by Massenet
Premiere: Rio; Orfeão de Professores; Pery Machado, v;
Villa-Lobos, cond; 9/14/1932                                   W269

## Entrei na roda
Band; 1 min.
Pic, fl, E-flat cl, cl, sax, hn, saxhn, B-flat cor, bug

Also for two part chorus (*See*: Collections, G.P. #49)
Published by the Conservatório de Canto Orfeônico as
*Partituras de banda*                                                                     W270

**Evolução dos aeroplanos**
Orchestra; 6 min.
Adapted from *Inquieta* (*See*: W054), *Valsa mística* (*See*:
W134), and *Mariposa na Luz* (*See*: W213 and W214)          W271

**Fuga no.1**
Four voice mixed a cappella chorus; 5 min.
Transcribed from *The Well-Tempered Clavier* of J.S. Bach
Premiere: Rio; Orfeão de Professores do Distrito Federal;
Villa-Lobos, cond; April 1933                                                    W272

**Fuga no.5**
Four voice mixed a cappella chorus; 3 min.
Transcribed from *The Well-Tempered Clavier* of J.S. Bach
Premiere: Rio; Orfeão de Professores do Distrito Federal;
Villa-Lobos, cond; April 1933                                                    W273

**Fuga no.8**
Four voice mixed a cappella chorus; 4 min.
Transcribed from *The Well-Tempered Clavier* of J.S. Bach
Premiere: Rio; Orfeão de Professores do Distrito Federal;
Villa-Lobos, cond; April 1933                                                    W274

**Fuga no.21**
Four voice mixed a cappella chorus; 4 min.
Transcribed from *The Well-Tempered Clavier* of J.S. Bach
Premiere: Rio; Orfeão de Professores do Distrito Federal;
Villa-Lobos, cond; 9/7/1933                                                      W275

**Guia prático**
A practical guide to musical and artistic education
Music for various choral ensembles (*See*: Collections,
G.P.)
V. Vitale                                                                                    W276

**Guia prático** Album 1
Piano; 10 min.
*Acordei de madrugada*
*A maré encheu*
*A roseira* (2nd version)

*Manquinha*
  *Na corda da viola*
Dedicated to José Vieira Brandão
Premiere: (Nos. 1, 2, 3, and 5) Rio:11/11/1939
(*Manquinha*) Rio: José Vieira Brandão, pf; 11/13/1941
V. Vitale and CMP                                         W277

**Guia prático** Album 2
Piano; 8 min.
  *Brinquedo*
  *Machadinha*
  *Espanha*
  *Samba-le-le*
  *Senhora Dona Viúva* (1st. version)
Dedicated to Julieta d'Almeida Strutt
Premiere: (Nos. 1, 2, 4, and 5) Rio; José Vieira
  Brandão; pf 11/27/1939
Eschig                                                    W278

**Guia prático** Album 3
Piano; 6 min.
  *O pastorzinho*
  *João Cambuête*
  *A freira*
  *Garibaldi foi à missa*
  *O pião*
Dedicated to Arnaldo Estrela
Premiere: (Nos. 2, 4, and 5) Rio; José Vieira
  Brandão, pf; 11/27/1939
Eschig                                                    W279

**Guia prático** Album 4
Piano; 8 min.
  *O pobre e o rico*
  *Rosa amarela* (2nd version)
  *Olha o passarinho, domine*
  *O gato*
  *O sim*
Dedicated to Magdalena Tagliaferro
Eschig                                                    W280

**Guia prático** Album 5
Piano; 10 min.
  *Os pombinhos*

*Você diz que sabe tudo*
*Có-có-có*
*O bastião*  or Mia gato
*A condessa*
Dedicated to Anna Stella Schic
Premiere: (Nos. 1 and 2) Rio; 11/13/1941
   (No. 3) Rio; José Vieira Brandão, pf; 11/27/1939
Eschig                                                          W281

**Guia prático** Album 6
Piano; 10 min.
   *Sonho de uma criança*
   *O corcunda*
   *O carangueijo* (1st version)
   *A pombinha voou*
   *Vamos atrás da serra, Oh! Calunga!*
Dedicated to William Kapell
Mercury                                                        W282

**Guia prático** Album 7
Piano; 10 min.
   *No fundo do meu quintal*
   *Vai, abóbora*
   *Vamos Maruca*
   *Os pombinhos*
   *Anda `a roda*
Premiere: (nos. 1 and 3) Rio; 11/13/1941
   (no.2) Rio; José Vieira Brandão, pf; 11/27/1939
Mercury                                                        W283

**Guia prático** Album 10
Piano; 12 min.
   *De flor em flor*
   *Atché*
   *Nésta rua*
   *Fui no itororó* (1st. version)
   *Mariquita muchaca*
   *No jardim celestial*
Dedicated to Sônia Maria Strutt
Premiere: (nos. 2 and 6) Rio; José Vieira Brandão, pf;
   11/13/1941
   (no. 3) Noemi Bittencourt, pf; 10/12/1949
Eschig                                                         W284

## Hino às árvores
Two part a cappella chorus; 2 min.
Melody and text by C. Júnior and Arlindo Leal
V.Vitale                                                                    W285

## Hino da independência do Brasil
Three part a cappella chorus; 2 min.
Melody and text by D. Pedro I and Evaristo da Veiga          W286

## Hino nacional brasileiro
Two part a cappella chorus; 2 min.
Music by Francisco Manuel da Silva and text by Osorio
    Duque Estrada
Arranged by Villa-Lobos                                              W287

## Iphigénie en aulide
Four part mixed a cappella chorus; 2 min.
Melody by Gluck, text by Rollet
Premiere: Rio; Orfeão de Professores; Villa-Lobos, cond;
    April 1933                                                           W288

## Juventude
Three part a cappella chorus; 2 min.
Theme by J. Tebaldine
Premiere: Rio; 18,000 students; Villa-Lobos, cond;
    10/24/1932                                                           W289

## Lá na ponte da vinhaça (Passa, passa gavião)
Band; 1 min.
Pic, fl, E-flat cl, cl, sax, B-flat cor, bar, trbn, eup,
    Eb and Bb contrabass trbn, ca, cymb and bomb
Also for two part chorus (*See*: Collections, G.P. #104)
Published by the Conservatório de Canto Orfeônico as
    *Partituras de banda*                                            W290

## Lamento
Six part mixed a cappella chorus; 3 min.
Melody by Homero Barreto                                         W291

## Marselhesa, A
Two part a cappella chorus; 2 min.
Original French song by Rouget de Lisle                        W292

## Meu benzinho
Vocal sextet; 1 min.
Based on a popular theme
Premiere: Rio, Auditório do Instituto de Educação; Odila
  Macedo Lima, Francisca Nóbrega de Vasconcelos, Maria da
  Conceição da Cruz Rangel, Canuto Roque Regis, Sylvio
  Salema and Asdrubal Lima; Villa-Lobos, cond          W293

## Minha mãe (Andante)
Four part mixed a cappella chorus; 2 min.
Theme by Beethoven
Poetry by F. Haroldo                                    W294

## Os moinhos (Minueto)
Four part mixed a cappella chorus; 2 min.
Theme by Beethoven
Poetry by F. Geraldy                                    W295

## Moteto
Three part mixed a cappella chorus; 3 min.
Adapted from a motet by Palestrina
Premiere: Rio; Orfeão de Professores; Villa-Lobos, cond;
  9/14/1932                                            W296

## Na Bahia tem
Band; 3 min.
Pic, fl, E-flat cl, cl, B-flat cor, sax, bug, trbn, bar,
  bomb, cont Bb and Eb contrabass trbn, cymb, tambor and
  bomb
Also for four part male chorus (*See*: W576); chorus and
  band (*See*: W577); and voice with piano or
  instrumental accompaniment (*See*: Collections, G.P. #12)
Published by the Conservatório de Canto Orfeônico as
  *Partituras de banda*                                W297

## Na risonha madrugada
Four voice female a cappella chorus; 2 min.
Melody  by Haydn and poetry by F. Haroldo
Also for four part mixed a cappella chorus (*See*:
  Collections, C.O. v.2 #41)                          W298

## Na roça
Two part a cappella chorus; 1 min.

Melody by J. Gomes Júnior
Poetry by Aristeo Seixas                                        W299

**Nesta rua**
Band; 1 min.
Pic, fl, E-flat cl, bug, sax, trbn, bar, bomb, Eb and Bb
   contrabass trbn, ca, cymb and bomb
Also for two part chorus (*See*: Collections, G.P. #82)
Published by the Conservatório de Canto Orfeônico as
   *Partituras de Banda*                                       W300

**O´ciranda, o´cirandinha**
Band; 1 min.
Pic, fl, ob, E-flat cl, cl, sax, hn, bn, tpt, B-flat cor,
   bug, saxhn, trbn, bomb, Eb Bb and F contrabass trbn,
   tambor de Campanha, tarol, cymb and bomb
Also for voice and piano, instrumental ensemble or piano
   solo (*See*: Collections, G.P. #35)
Published by the Conservatório de Canto Orfeônico as
   *Partituras de Banda*                                       W301

**Papagaio do moleque** (Le cerf volant du gamin) (Episódio
   sinfônico)
Orchestra; 14 min.
Pic, 2 fl, 2 ob, eng hn, 2 cl, bass cl, 2 bn, cbn, 4 hn,
   4 tpt, 4 trbn, tuba, timp, t-t, cymb, cho, pan, xyl,
   cel, 2 harps, pf and str
Dedicated to Serge Lifar
Premiere: Paris, Maison Gaveau; Orchestra Pasdeloup;
   Villa-Lobos, cond; 3/21/1948
Eschig                                                         W302

**Pátria**
Two part male chorus and military drums; 4 min.
Dedicated to the Orfeão de Professores do Distrito
   Federal
Also for six part mixed a cappella chorus, and for four
   part female a cappella chorus (*See*: Collections, C.O.
   v.2 #34 & #35)                                              W303

**Prelúdio no.8**
Six part mixed a cappella chorus; 4 min.
Transcribed from *The Well-Tempered Clavier* of J.S. Bach

Premiere: Rio; Orfeão de Professores; Villa-Lobos, cond;
   April 1933                                                W304

**Prelúdio no.14**
   Four part mixed a cappella chorus; 3 min.
   Transcribed from *The Well-Tempered Clavier* of J.S. Bach     W305

**Prelúdio no.22**
   Six part mixed a cappella chorus; 5 min.
   Transcribed from *The Well-Tempered Clavier* of J.S. Bach
   Premiere: Rio; Orfeão de Professores; Villa-Lobos, cond;
     9/7/1932                                              W306

**Rêverie**
   Six part mixed a cappella chorus; 3 min.
   Melody by Robert Schumann
   Premiere: Rio; Orfeão de Professores; Villa-Lobos, cond;
     6/23/1933
   V. Vitale                                               W307

**O Rio**
   Four part mixed a cappella chorus; 2 min.
   Melody by G. Dogliani
   Premiere: Rio; Orfeão de Professores; Villa-Lobos, cond;
     6/23/1933
   V. Vitale                                             W308

**A roseira**
   Saxophone quintet; 14 min.
   Two soprano, 1 alto, 1 tenor and 1 baritone saxophone
   Based on a popular children's theme                W309

**Rudepoema**
   Orchestra; 30 min.
   Two pic, 2 fl, 2 ob, eng hn, 2 cl, E-flat cl, bass cl,
     s sax, a sax, 2 bn, cbn, 4 hn, 4 tpt, 4 trbn, tuba,
     timp, t-t, bomb, cymb, mat, reco, cho (metal), ca, cax,
     tambor surdo, tamb, glock, xyl, cel, harps, pf and str
   Original for piano (*See*: W184)
   Premiere: Rio; Orquestra do Teatro Municipal; Villa-
     Lobos, cond; 7/15/1942
   Eschig                                                  W310

**A sementinha**
Two part a cappella chorus; 1 min.
Melody and text by Julieta M.S. Miranda and J.B. Melo e
  Souza W311

**O tamborzinho**
Four part female a cappella chorus; 2 min.
Melody by A. Leça
Also for four part mixed a cappella chorus (*See*:
  Collections, C.O. v.2 #42) W312

**Terra natal**
Four part female a cappella chorus; 1 min.
Theme by Mozart
Poetry adapted by Honorato Faustino
Also for mixed a cappella chorus, (*See:* Collections,
  C.O., v.2, #43)
Premiere: Rio; Orfeão de Professores; Villa-Lobos, cond;
  9/14/1932 W313

**Teresinha de Jesus**
Band; 1 min.
Pic, fl, E-flat cl, cl, sax, B-flat cor, bug, sax, bar,
  trbn, bomb, Eb and Bb contrabass trbn
Also for two part a cappella chorus (*See*: Collections,
  G.P. #123)
Published by the Conservatório de Canto Orfeônico as
  *Partituras de banda* W314

**Valsa**
Six part mixed a cappella chorus; 4 min.
Choral adaptation of a Waltz by Chopin
Premiere: Rio; Orfeão de Professores; Villa-Lobos, cond;
  9/7/1932 W315

**Valsa da dor**
Piano; 5 min.
Dedicated to Julieta d'Almeida Strutt
Premiere: Rio; José Vieira Brandão, pf; 11/27/1939
Eschig W316

**Vem cá, siriri**
Band

Pic, fl, E-flat cl, cl, B-flat cor, sax, bug, trbn, bar,
   bomb, Eb and Bb contrabass trbn, ca, cymb and bomb
Also for unison chorus, voice with piano, instrumental
   ensemble or piano solo (*See*: Collections, G.P. #130)
Published by the Conservatório de Canto Orfeônico as
   *Partituras de banda*                                            W317

*1933*

**Acalentando**
   Three part a cappella chorus; 2 min.
   Melody and text by Sylvio Salema, arranged by Villa-
   Lobos                                                            W318

**Ave Maria** (Moteto)
   Four part mixed a cappella chorus; 2 min.
   Melody by F. Franceschini, inspired by Gregorian Chant
   Text in Latin
   Premiere: Rio; Orfeão de Professores; Villa-Lobos, cond;
   8/9/1933;                                                        W319

**Boris Godunov** (Coronation scene, Monologue of act I)
   Baritone and orchestra; 6 min.
   Adaptation of the original for voice and piano by
   Mussorgsky
   Premiere: Rio; Orchestra of the Teatro Municipal; Felipe
   Romito, Bar; Villa-Lobos, cond; 10/16/1936                      W320

**Canção a José de Alencar**
   Two part chorus; 1 min.
   Poetry by C. Paula Barros                                       W321

**Canção da saudade**
   Four part a cappella chorus; 3 min.
   Poetry by Sodré Viana
   Premiere: Rio; Orfeão de Professores do Distrito Federal;
   Villa-Lobos, cond; 10/10/1933
   V. Vitale                                                       W322

**A canção do barqueiro do Volga**
   Voice and orchestra; 3 min.
   Orchestral version of the original for voice and piano by
   E. Koenneman

Based on a popular Russian theme
Also transcribed for six part mixed chorus (*See*: W356)
Premiere: Rio, Teatro Municipal; A. Rappaport, v;
  Orchestra Villa-Lobos; Villa-Lobos, cond; 5/13/1933        W323

**Canto do pajé** (Marcha-Rancho)
  Band; 3 min.
  Pic, fl, E-flat cl, sax, hn, tpt, bug, eup, E-flat and
    B-flat contrabass trbn, drums and tamb
  Also for four part female chorus (*See*: Collections, C.O.
    v.1, #19)
  Published by the Conservatório de Canto Orfeônico as
    *Partituras de banda*        W324

**Ciranda das sete notas**
  Bassoon and string orchestra; 12 min.
  Transcribed for bassoon and piano (*See*: W548)
  Dedicated to Mindinha
  Peer        W325

**Concerto brasileiro**
  Two pianos and mixed chorus; 14 min.
  Based on *Atrevido* and *Odeon* by Ernesto Nazareth (lost)
  Premiere: Rio, Teatro João Caetano; Orfeão de Professores
    do Distrito Federal; José Vieira Brandão, pf 1; Villa-
    Lobos, pf 2; Orlando Frederico, cond; 6/20/1934        W326

**O contra- baixo**
  Three part childrens a cappella chorus; 1 min.
  Melody and text by Sylvio Salema, arranged by Villa-Lobos
  Premiere: Rio; Orfeão da Escola Argentina; Villa-Lobos,
    cond; 10/10/1933        W327

**Corrupio**
  Bassoon and string quintet; 3 min.        W328

**As costureiras** (Embolada)
  Four part female a cappella chorus; 4 min.
  Poetry by Villa-Lobos
  Also printed in Collections (C.O., v.2, #33)
  Premiere: Rio; Orfeão de Professores do Distrito Federal;
    Villa-Lobos, cond; 9/7/1932
  G. Schirmer        W329

**Ena-Môkôcê** (Canção de rede) (Hammock song)
Soloist, five part mixed chorus and percussion; 2 min.
Theme from the Pareci Indians (from the state of Mato
Grosso) collected by E. Roquette Pinto
Premiere: Rio; Orfeão de Professores do Distrito Federal
and percussion; Julieta Teles de Menezes, soloist;
Villa-Lobos, cond; 6/20/1934
V. Vitale        W330

**Estrela é lua nova**
Voice, clarinet in A, bassoon, 2 horns and strings
From *Canções típicas brasileiras* (*See*: W158 & W159)
Also for five part mixed a cappella chorus, (*See*:
Collections, C.O., v. 2; #37)        W331

**Invocação à cruz**
Four part mixed a cappella chorus; 2 min.
Melody by A. Nepomuceno, text by Osorio Duque Estrada
Premiere: Orfeão de Professores; Villa-Lobos, cond;
6/23/1933        W332

**Maria**
Voice and orchestra; 2 min.
Two fl, 2 ob, 2 cl, 2 bn, 2 hn, timp, harp and str
Original for voice and piano by Araújo Vianna
Premiere: Rio, Teatro Municipal; Abigail Parecis,
soloist; Orquestra Villa-Lobos; Villa-Lobos, cond;
4/24/1933        W333

**Noite de insônia**
Voice and orchestra; 3 min.
Original for voice and piano by Tschaikovsky
Premiere: Rio, Teatro Municipal; Orchestra Villa-Lobos;
A. Rappaport, v; Villa-Lobos, cond; 5/13/1933        W334

**O felix anima**
Four part chorus, 2 min.
Themed by G. Carissimi, arranged by Villa-Lobos        W335

**Papai curumiassú** (Canção de rede)
Soloist and mixed a cappella chorus; 1 min.
Theme from the caboclos of Pará
Premiere: Rio, Teatro João Caetano; Orfeão de Professores

and percussion; Julieta Teles de Menezes, v;
Villa-Lobos, cond; 6/20/1934                                    W336

**Prólogo do Mefistofle**
Mixed a cappella chorus; 2 min.
Choral adaptation of *Prólogo de Mefistofle* by A. Boito
Premiere: Rio; Orfeão de Professores; Villa-Lobos, cond;
6/23/1933                                                       W337

**Pedra bonita** (Ballet)
Orchestra; 10 min.
Premiere: Rio; Orchestra and ballet corps of the Teatro
Municipal; Valery Oeser, choreographer; Villa-Lobos,
cond; 1933                                                      W338

**Serenata**
Six part mixed a cappella chorus; 4 min.
Transcription of the Serenade by Franz Schubert
V. Vitale                                                       W339

**Trenzinho**
Three part a cappella chorus; 3 min.
Poetry by Catarina Santoro
Also for four part female chorus in Collections, *See*:
C.O. v. 2, #31
Premiere: Orfeão da Escola Argentina; Villa-Lobos, cond;
10/10/1939
V. Vitale                                                       W340

**A vrgem dos santos**
Two part female a cappella chorus; 2 min.
Adaptation of *La Forza del destino* by Verdi
Premiere: Rio; Orfeão de Professores; Villa-Lobos, cond;
April 1933                                                      W341


*1934*

**Abelhinha, A**
Three part chorus; 1 min.
Melody by J. Baptista Julião, text by A. Peixoto               W342

**Brincadeira de pegar**
Two part a cappella chorus; 1 min.

Dedicated to the children of Recife
Poetry by Ernâni Braga
V. Vitale                                                    W343

**Dança de roda**
Two part chorus, string quintet and bassoon; 3 min.
Based on a popular theme                    W344

**Gavião de penacho**
Mixed a cappella chorus; 2 min.
Choral adaptation by Francisco Braga, arranged by Villa-
Lobos
Poetry by Afonso Arinos                         W345

**A infância** (Hino escolar)
Two part a cappella chorus; 1 min.
Music by Francisco Braga
Poetry by Azevedo Júnior                       W346

**Kyrie**
Mixed chorus; 2 min.
Text in Latin
Adaptation of the Kyrie from the *Requiem Mass* by Padre
José Maurício Nunes Garcia               W347

**Pátria**
Mixed chorus and orchestra; 4 min.
Pic, 2 fl, 2 ob, 2 cl, 2 bn, 4 hn, 3 tpt, 3 trbn, tuba,
tim, t-t, bomb, harp and str
Dedicated to the Orfeão de Professores do Distrito
Federal
Also for six part mixed a cappella chorus, and for four
part female a cappella chorus (*See*: Collections, C.O.
v.2 #34 and #35)                                    W348

**Prelúdio**
Six part mixed a cappella chorus; 2 min.
Choral arrangement of a prelude by Rachmaninoff
Premiere: Rio; Orfeão de Professores; Villa-Lobos, cond;
6/26/1935                                                W349

**Prelúdio no.4**
Four part mixed a cappella chorus; 3 min.
Transcribed from *The Well-Tempered Clavier* of J.S. Bach    W350

**Tico-tico**
Two part a cappella chorus; 1 min.
Music by P.J.B. Lehmann
Poetry by Afonso Celso    W351

*1935*

**À praia**
Two part chorus; 2 min.
Based on a popular theme    W352

**Argentina**
Three part chorus; 2 min.
Melody from an Indian dance, collected by Isabel
  Etchensary
Premiere: Rio; Orfeão de Professores; Villa-Lobos, cond;
  12/14/1934    W353

**Ay-ay-ay**
Six part mixed a cappella chorus; 3 min.
Based on a popular Chilean theme    W354

**Canarinho**
Two part chorus; 1 min.
Music and text by Sylvio Salema    W355

**A canção do barqueiro do Volga**
Six part mixed a cappella chorus; 3 min.
Based on a popular Russian theme
Poetry by Sodré Viana
Also for voice and orchestra (*See*: W319)
Premiere: Rio; Orfeão de Professores; Villa-Lobos, cond;
  6/26/1935    W356

**Cânones perpétuos**
Four part a cappella chorus; 2 min.
  *Alegria de viver*
  *Companheiros, companheiros*
Based on a popular French theme
Poetry by M. Capistrano    W357

**Guia prático** Album 8
  Piano; 12 min.
  *O limão*
  *Carambola*
  *Pobre cega*
  *Pai Francisco*
  *Xô! Passarinho!*
  *Sinh 'Aninha*
  *Vestidinho branco*
  Based on popular childrens themes
  CMP                                                           W358

**Guia prático** Album 9
  Piano; 12 min.
  *Laranjeira pequenina*
  *Pombinha rolinha*
  *O ciranda, O cirandinha*
  *A velha que tinha nove filhos*
  *Constante*
  *O castelo*
  Based on popular childrens themes
  Premiere: (nos. 1, 4, & 6) Rio; 11/27/1939
    (nos. 2 & 5) Rio; José Vieira Brandão, pf; 11/13/1941
  CMP                                                           W359

**Hino escolar**
  Two part a cappella chorus; 1 min.
  Melody by Custódio Goes
  Poetry by Jacques Raymundo
  V. Vitale                                                     W360

**O pião**
  Band; 2 min.
  Pic, fl, E-flat cl, ob, cl, bn, sax, B-flat cor, bug
    saxhn, hn, trbn, bar, bomb, E-flat and B-flat
    contrabass trbn, tarol, cymb, bomb and coco
  Based on a popular childrens theme
  Peer                                                          W361

**A roseira**
  Wind quintet; 2 min.
  Pic, fl, cl, sax, B-flat contrabass sax
  Based on a popular childrens theme
  Premiere: Rio; Antenor Guimarães, Indalécio Fonseca,

Romeu Malta, Arlindo da Ponte, and Acyr Figueiredo;
6/24/1935                                                                W362

**Tão doce luz**
Three part a cappella childrens chorus; 1 min.
Music and poetry by Sylvio Salema                              W363

**Vocalismo no.11**
Four part chorus; 1 min.                                            W364

*1935-1943*

**Modinhas e canções** (Album No.1)
Voice and piano; 18 min.
*No.1 Canção do marinheiro*, 1936
In the Iberian manner, text by Gil Vicente (ca. 1470-
ca. 1536)
*No.2 Lundu da Marquesa de Santos*, 1938
To evoke memories of 1822, and the play *Marquesa de
Santos* by Viriato Correa
*No.3 Cantilena* (*Um canto que saiu das senzalas*), 1936
Based on a song of blacks from Bahia, collected by
Sodré Viana
*No.4 A gatinha parda* (popular infantil), 1941
*No.5 Remeiro de São Francisco*
On a theme of natives of the São Francisco River area
of Bahia
*No.6 Nhapopê*, 1935
On a poem by Alberto Deodato
*No.7 Evocação*, 1943
Poetry by Sylvia Salema
Also for voice and orchestra (*See*: W406)
Premiere: No.1  Salão Leopoldo Miguez of the Escola
Nacional de Música; 7/25/1942
No.2 Sung by Dulcina de Moraes in the play *Marquesa
de Santos*; 1958
Eschig                                                                  W365

*1936*

**Abertura**
Orchestra: 4 min.
Written for the commemoration of the centennial of the
birth of Carlos Gomes

Based on themes from *Colombo*, an opera by Carlos Gomes
Premiere: Rio; Orchestra of the Teatro Municipal; Villa-
Lobos, cond; 10/24/1936                                      W366

**Desfile aos heróis do Brasil**
Band; 2 min.
Pic, fl, ob, E-flat cl, 2 cl, a sax, t sax, bar sax, 2
   hn, 2 tpt, bug, 3 trbn, eup, B-flat contrabass trbn,
   bar, ca, bomb and cymb
Also for three part chorus of female voices, *See* :
   Collections, C.O. v. 1, #21                              W367

**Hino acadêmico** (Ao Estado)
Two part chorus and band; 1 min.
Music by Carlos Gomes
Poetry by Bittencourt Sampaio
Premiere: Rio; 30,000 students and 1,000 band
   instrumentalists; Villa-Lobos, cond; 9/7/1937            W368

**Hino escolar** (Cultura e afeto as nações)
Two part a cappella chorus; 1 min.
Music by E. Nazareth, arranged by Villa-Lobos
Poetry by M. M. Teixeira
Premiere: Rio; Orfeão de Professores; Villa-Lobos, cond;
   4/14/1935                                                W369

**Quadrilha brasileira**
Three part a cappella childrens chorus; 2 min.
Poetry by J. P. Baptista
Also in Collections, *See*: C.O. v. 2, #29-2
Dedicated to Júlio Cesar d'Almeida Dutra
                                                            W370

**Redemoinho**
Two part a cappella chorus
Text by Sylvio Salema                                       W371

**Rumo a escola**
Two part chorus; 1 min.
Melody by Paulo Jardi                                       W372

**Valsa sentimental**
Guitar; 1 min.                                              W373

*1936-37*

**Ciclo brasileiro**
Piano; 21 min.
  *Plantio do caboclo*
  *Impressões seresteiras*
  *Festa no sertão*
  *Dança do índio branco*
Dedicated to Arminda Neves d'Almeida
Premiere: (*Impressões seresteiras* and *Dança do índio
  branco*) Rio; Julieta Neves d'Almeida, pf; 1938
  (*Plantio do caboclo* and *Festa no sertão*) José Vieira
  Brandão, pf; 11/27/1939
V. Vitale and CMP                                                        W374

*1937*

**A gaita de fole**
English horn and harmonium;2 min.
Composed for the film *Descobrimento do Brasil*, directed
  by Humberto Mauro
Premiere: Rio; 1937                                                     W375

**Currupira** (Poema sinfônico)
Orchestra; 8 min.
Premiere: Paris; 1949                                                   W376

**Descobrimento do Brasil** (1st suite)
Orchestra; 12 min.
  *Introdução* (Largo)
  *Alegria*
Pic, 2 fl, 2 ob, eng hn, 2 cl, b cl, alto sax, 2 bn, cbn,
  4 hn, 3 trumpets, 3 trbn, tuba, timp, bomb, xyl, cel,
  harp, pf and str
Comissioned by the Brazilian Cacao Institute of Bahia for
  a film directed by Humberto Mauro with the technical
  assistance of Roquette Pinto. The score was expanded
  into four suites. The recording of the four suites won
  the "Prix des Relations Culturelles" in France
Premiere: Rio, Teatro Municipal; orchestra of the Teatro
  Municipal; Villa-Lobos, cond; 11/19/1939
Eschig                                                                 W377

**Descobrimento do Brasil** (2nd suite)
  Orchestra; 14 min.
  *Impressão moura* (Canção) (Moorish impressions - song)
  *Adágio sentimental*
  *Cascavel*
  Pic, 2 fl, 2 ob, eng hn, 2 cl, bass cl, a sax, 2 bn, cbn,
    4 hn, 3 tpt, 3 trbn, tuba, timp, cymb, reco, cho,
    tambor, surdo, sinos, mat, harp, pf and str
  Comissioned by the Brazilian Cacao Institute (*See*: W377)
  Premiere: Rio, Teatro Municipal; Orchestra of the Teatro
    Municipal; Villa-Lobos, cond; 10/11/1946
  Eschig                                                    W378

**Descobrimento do Brasil** (3rd suite)
  Orchestra; 13 min.
  *Impressão ibérica*
  *Festa nas selvas*
  *Ulalocê* (Visão dos navegantes)
  Pic, 2 fl, 2 ob, eng hn, 2 cl, b cl, a sax, 2 bn, cbn, 4
    hn, 4 tpt, 4 trbn, tuba, timp, tam-tam, pan,
    castanets, Indian drum, cho, tambor surdo, cymb,
    coco (large and small), bomb, ca, xyl, cel, 2 harps, pf
    and str
  Comissioned by the Brazilian Cacao Institute (*See*: W377)
  Premiere: 1942
  Significant performance: Rio, Teatro Municipal; Orchestra of the Teatro
    Municipal; Villa-Lobos, cond; October 10/11/1946
  Eschig                                                    W379

**Descobrimento do Brasil** (4th suite)
  Orchestra; 15 min.
  *Procissão da cruz*
  *Primeira missa no Brasil*
  Two pic, 2 fl, 2 ob, eng hn, 2 cl, b cl, 2 bn, cbn, 4 hn,
    4 tpt, 4 trbn, tuba, timp, tam-tam, reco, cho (metal
    and wood), cymb, coco, tambor surdo, Indian drum,
    pio, trocano, gong, pan, folha de flandres (tin plate
    sheet), xyl, cel, 2 harps, pf and str
  Dedicated to Mindinha
  Comissioned by the Brazilian Cacao Institute (*See*: W377)
  Premiere: (4 suites) Paris, Theatre Champs Elysées;
    Orchestre Nationale and choir of the Radiodiffusion
    Française; 2/28/1952
  Eschig                                                    W380

**Distribuição de flores**
Flute and guitar; 3 min.
Eschig
W381

**Luar do sertão** (Canção sertaneja)
Four part mixed a cappella chorus; 3 min.
Melody by J. F. Guimarães known as José Pernambuco
Poetry by Catulo da Paixão Cearense
W382

**Missa São Sebastião**
Three part a cappella chorus; 25 min.
*Kyrie* (Sebastião! O virtuoso)
*Gloria* (Sebastião! Soldado romano)
*Credo* (Sebastião! Defensor da igreja)
*Sanctus* (Sebastião! O mártir!)
*Benedictus* (Sebastião! O santo)
*Agnus Dei* (Sebastião! Protetor do Brasil!)
Dedicated to Friar Pedro Zinzig
Premiere: Rio, Teatro Municipal; chorus made up from
teachers and students of the technical schools: Paulo
de Frontin and João Alfredo; Villa-Lobos, cond;
11/13/1937
Associated and Napoleão
W383

**Primeira missa no Brasil**
Mixed chorus, children's chorus and instrumental ensemble
Cl, bass cl, bn, cbn, cho, reco, tambor surdo
In this work the clarinet is played without a mouthpiece
Composed for the film *Descobrimento do Brasil* directed
by Humberto Mauro (*See*: W377)
W384

**Procissão da cruz**
Four part chorus; 3 min.
In this work the clarinet is played without a mouthpiece
Composed for the film *Descobrimento do Brasil* directed
by Humberto Mauro (*See*: W377)
W385

**Redondilha**
Three part a cappella chorus, 2 min.
Text by Padre José de Anchieta
Premiere: Rio; 5/18/1950
W386

**Regozijo de uma raça**
Mixed chorus, tenor soloist and percussion; 5 min.

*Abolição* (Bailado)
  *Canto africano*
  *Canto místico*
Timp, pan, tamborete, tambor surdo (metal), cuíca, coco,
  cho, tamborim de samba, reco, garrafa (bottle),
  trocano, latinha (small can)
Text by J. P. Baptista
Dedicated to Julio César d'Almeida Dutra
Melodies from 2nd and 3rd movements published in
  Collections, *See*: C. O. v. 1 # 16
Premiere: 1,000 pupils; Canuto Roque Regis, soloist;
  Villa-Lobos, cond; 12/15/1937                          W387

## 1938

## Bachianas brasileiras no.3
Piano and orchestra; 24 min.
  *Prelúdio* (Ponteio)
  *Fantasia* (Devaneio)
  *Ária* (Modinha)
  *Tocata* (Picapau)
Pic, 2 fl, 2 ob, eng hn, 2 cl, b cl, 2 bn, cbn, 4 hn, 2
  tpt, 4 trbn, tuba, timp, t-t, bass drum, xyl, and str
Dedicated to Mindinha
Premiere: New York; CBS Orchestra; José Vieira Brandão,
  pf, Villa-Lobos, cond; 2/19/1947
G. Ricordi                                                W388

## 1938-1945

## Bachianas brasileiras no.5
Voice and orchestra of cellos, 8 min.
  *Ária* (Cantilena) 1938
  *Dança* (Martelo) 1945
Dedicated to Mindinha
Poetry by Ruth Valadares Correa and Manuel Bandeira
Also for and voice and piano (*See*: W390)
*Ária* transcribed for voice and guitar (*See*: W391)
Premiere: (*Aria*) Rio; 8 cellos; Ruth Valladares Correa,
  S, Villa-Lobos, cond; 3/25/1939
  (Complete) Paris; Hilda Ohlin, Sop; 10/10/1947
Associated                                                W389

**Bachianas brasileiras no. 5**
 Voice and piano 8 min.
 *Ária* (Cantilena)
 *Dança* (Martelo)
 Original for voice and orchestra of cellos (*See*: W389)
 Transcribed for voice and guitar (*See*: W391)
 Associated                                                                W390

*1938*

**Bachianas brasileiras no.5**
 Voice and guitar, 3 min.
 *Ária*
 Transcription made at the request of Olga Praguer Coelho
 Original for voice and orchestra of cellos (*See*: W389)
 Transcribed for voice and piano (*See*: W390)
 Premiere: New York, Town Hall; Olga Praguer Coelho,
  soloist, 12/2/1951
 Associated                                                                W391

**Bachianas brasileiras no. 6**
 Flute and bassoon, 6 min.
 *Ária* (choro)
 *Fantasia* (Allegro)
 Dedicated to Alfredo Martins Lage and Evandro Moreira
  Pequeno
 Premiere: 9/24/1945
 Associated                                                                W392

**Chile-Brasil** (Canção sertaneja)
 Three part a cappella chorus, 1 min.
 Premiere: Rio; Orpheonic Chorus of Escola Primária Chile,
  Villa-Lobos cond; 5/25/1938                                W393

**Fantasia e fuga no. 6**
 Orchestra, 4 min.
 Pic, 2 fl, 2 ob, eng hn, 2 cl, b cl, 2 bn, cbn, 4 hn, 2
  tpt, 2 trbn, tuba, timp, and str
 Transcription of a Fantasy and Fugue for organ by J.S.
 Bach                                                                        W394

**Marquesa de Santos** (Suíte)
 Orchestra; 7 min.
 *Lundu*

*Valsinha brasileira*
*Gavota-choro*
Fl, ob, cl, bn, hn, tpt, trbn, timp, cymb, bass drum,
   harp and str
Written for the play *Marquesa de Santos* by Viriato
   Correa
*Valsinha brasileira* and *Gavota-choro* transcribed for
   piano (*See*: W396)
Premiere: Rio, Theater of the Dulcina de Moraes Company
   1938                                                                            W395

**Marquesa de Santos** (Suíte)
Piano, 5 min.
   *Valsinha brasileira* (À maneira antiga)
   *Gavota-choro*
Transcribed from incidental music for the play by Viriato
   Correa (*See:* W395)                                                    W396

**Prelúdio e fuga no. 4**
Orchestra, 4 min.
Transcription of a Prelude and Fugue from *The Well-
Tempered Clavier* of J.S. Bach                                      W397

**Prelúdio e fuga no. 6**
Orchestra; 5 min.
Two fl, 2 ob, 2 cl, 2 bn, 3 hn, 2 tpt, 2 trbn, tuba,
   timp, harp and str
Transcription of a Prelude and Fugue for organ by J.S.
Bach                                                                               W398

**Quarteto de cordas no. 6**
Two violins, viola and cello, 22 min.
Dedicated to Orlando Frederico
Subtitled II Quarteto brasileiro
Premiere: Rio; Haydn Quartet; 11/30/1943
Associated                                                                      W399

**Saudação a Getúlio Vargas**
Chorus and orchestra; 1 min.
Also for four part a cappella chorus See: Collections,
   C.O., v.1 #40
V. Vitale                                                                          W400

**Sertanejo do Brasil**
Chorus and Band; 3 min.
Fl, cl in E-flat, sax, cor, bug, sax hn, bn, hn, trbn,
bar, eup, cont (E-flat & B-flat), ca, tarol (side
drum), bombo, cymb, tri, cho, reco, and pan
Melody and text by Clóvis Carneiro
Original for two part a cappella chorus, *See:*
Collections, C.O. v. 1 #27                          W401

**Sinos**
Three part a cappella chorus; 1 min.
Theme by A. Lessa
Premiere: Rio, Orfeão de Professores, Villa-Lobos cond;
9/3/1932                                            W402

**Tiradentes**
Chorus and orchestra; 2 min.
Written under the pseudonym Epaminondas Villalba Filho
Poetry by Viriato Correa
Also arranged for soloist and five part mixed chorus
(*See*: Collections, C.O. v.1 #25); voice and piano (*See*:
W409); voice, mixed chorus and harpsichord (*See*: W410)
Premiere: Rio; Teatro Municipal Orchestra; Orfeão de
Professores, Villa-Lobos, cond; 11/14/1930          W403

**Tocata e fuga no. 3**
Orchestra, 5 min.
Two fl, 2 ob, eng hn, cl, b cl, 2 bn, cbn, 4 hn, 2 tpt,
2 trbn, timp, and str
Transcription of an organ Toccata and Fugue by J.S. Bach
Premiere: Rio; Villa-Lobos, cond; 3/4/1944          W404

*1939*

**Canção do operário brasileiro** (Canção de Ofício)
Chorus and band, 2 min.
Pic in D Flat, fl, ob, cl in E Flat, cl, b cl, sop sax, bar sax, hn in
E Flat, sax hn, cor, bug, trbn, bar, eup, cont (E-Flat & B-Flat),
trbn, drums, cymb, bass drum, and cor (ad libitum)
Written under the pseudonym Epaminondas Villalba Filho
Poetry by Paulino Santos
Also for a cappella voices, *See*: Collections, C.O.
v. 1 #30                                            W405

**Modinhas e canções** (Album no.1)
  Voice and orchestra; 15 min.
  *Canção do marinheiro*
    Melody in the manner of the Iberian style of the 16th
    century.  Poetry from the same period.
  *Lundu da Marquesa de Santos*
    An evocation of the period of 1822, based on the play
    of Viriato Correa, *Marquesa de Santos*
  *Cantilena* (*Um canto que saiu das senzalas*)
    Chant from the House of Slaves.  Gathered among the
    blacks of the "Recôncavo" of the state of Bahia by
    Sodré Viana
  *Remeiro de São Francisco*
    Song of the natives of the river São Francisco of the
    state of Bahia
  *Nhapopê*
    Based on a popular theme
  *Evocação* (Rio/1933)
    Essay on a popular song
  *A gatinha parda* (Rio/1937)
    Based on the melody of a popular children's song of
    the 19th century
  Pic, 2 fl, 2 ob, eng hn, 2 cl in B-flat, 2 cl in A,
  a sax, 2 bn, cbn, 4 hn, tpt, 2 trbn, tuba, timp, cel,
  harp and str
  Also for voice and piano (*See*: W365)
  Eschig                                                    W406

**New York Skyline Melody**
  Piano, 6 min.
  The melodic outline of the composition was taken from a
    photograph of Manhattan in a procedure adopted in
    *Melodia das Montanhas* (Millimetrization), a musical
    game for students. This was done to satisfy the
    curiosity of an American reporter.
  Transcribed for orchestra, (*See*: W408)
  Eschig                                                    W407

**New York Skyline Melody**
  Orchestra, 6 min.
  Two fl, ob, eng hn, cl, a sax, bn, 3 hn, tpt in C, trbn,
    timp, tam-tam, wood block, cymb, tri, xyl, vibraphone,
    cel, harp and str
  Dedicated to William Morris

Based on a procedure called "millimetrization"
Original for piano (*See*: W407)
Eschig                                                                      W408

### Tiradentes
Voice and piano; 2 min.
Composed under the pseudonym Epaminondas Villalba Filho
Text by Viriato Correa
Also arranged for soloist and five part mixed chorus
  (*See*: Collections C.O. v.1, #25); chorus and orchestra
  (*See*: W403); voice, mixed chorus and harpsichord
  (*See*: W410)                                                             W409

### Tiradentes
Voice, mixed chorus and harpsichord, 2 min.
Composed under the pseudonym Epaminondas Villalba Filho
Text by Viriato Correa
Also arranged for soloist and five part mixed chorus
  (*See*: Collections C.O, v.1, #25); chorus and orchestra
  (*See*: W403); voice and piano (*See*: W409)                             W410

### As três Marias
Piano, 4 min.
  *Alnitah*
  *Alnilam*
  *Mintika*
Dedicated to Arminda Neves de Almeida
Three pieces on children's subjects, written at the
  request of Edgar Varèse
Premiere: Rio; José Vieira Brandão, pf; 11/27/1939
Carl Fischer                                                               W411


## 1940

### Canção da imprensa (Canção de ofício)
Band; 3 min.
Pic, fl, cl in E-flat, cl, sax, saxhn, tpt, eup, trbn,
  bar, eup, cont (E-flat & B-flat), tarol (side drum),
  and bomb
Poetry by Murillo Araújo
Transcribed for chorus and orchestra (*See*: W413)
Also for two part a cappella chorus, *See*: Collections,
  C.O. v. 1 #34

Published by the Conservatório de Canto Orfeônico as
*Partituras de banda*                                    W412

**Canção da imprensa** (Canção de ofício)
   Chorus and orchestra; 4 min.
   Pic, fl, 2 ob, eng hn, 2 cl, b cl, 2 bn, 4 hn, 2 tpt,
   2 trbn, tuba, timp, military drum, tamborin, cho, reco
   and str
   Hymn of the Associação Brasileira de Imprensa
   Poetry by Murilo Araújo
   Transcribed for band (*See*: W412)
   Also for two part a cappella chorus, *See*: Collections,
   C.O. v.1 #34                                           W413

**Canção dos caçadores de esmeraldas** (In the style of the
   seventeenth century)
   Two part chorus; 2 min.
   Written under the pseudonym of Epaminondas Villalba Filho
   Poetry by Viriato Correa                               W414

**Canta, canta, passarinho**
   Two part chorus; 1 min.
   Melody and text by Murillo Araújo                      W415

**Canto orfeônico** (Volume 1)
   A collection of choral compositions, both a cappella and
   accompanied (*See*: Collections for a description of
   contents)                                              W416

**Mandu çarará** (Secular Cantata)
   Orchestra, mixed chorus and children's choir,  13 min.
   Pic, 2 fl, 2 ob, eng hn, 2 cl, b cl, 2 bn, cbn, 4 hn,
   3 tpt, 4 trbn, tuba, timp, t-t, reco, cho, pan, bass
   drums (3 different sizes and shapes), chimes, dinner
   plate, xyl, cel, 2 harps, piano and str
   Based on an Indian legend collected by Barbosa Rodrigues
   Dedicated to Mindinha
   Also for piano, mixed chorus and children's choir, *See*:
   W418
   Premiere: Rio; Orchestra and chorus of the Teatro
   Municipal; chorus of Colégio Pedro II; Villa-Lobos,
   cond; 11/10/1946
   Eschig                                                 W417

**Mandu çarará** (Secular Cantata)
  Piano, mixed chorus and children's choir, 13 min. (piano
    reduction)
  Based on an Indian legend collected by Barbosa Rodrigues
  Dedicated to Mindinha
  Also for orchestra, mixed chorus, and children's choir,
    *See*: W 417
  Premiere: New York; Schola Cantorum of New York; Hugh
    Ross, cond; 1/23/1948                                    W418

**Prelúdios**
  Guitar, 25 min.
  Six preludes, the sixth has been lost
  Dedicated to Mindinha
  Transcribed for piano by José Vieira Brandão
  Premiere: Montevideu, Uruguay; Abel Carlevaro; 12/11/1943
  Eschig                                                     W419

**Saudade da juventude** (Suite no. 1)
  Orchestra; 18 min.
    *Vida formosa*
    *O ciranda, ó cirandinha*
    *A gatinha parda*
    *O sim*
    *Mando tiro, tiro lá*
    *Condessa*
    *Nésta rua*
    *A cotia*
    *Na corda da viola*
    *De flor em flor*
  Pic, 2 fl, 2 ob, eng hn, 2 cl, a sax, 2 bn, 4 hn, 2 tpt
    in C, 2 trbn, tuba, timp, reco, bass drum, tri, dinner
    plates, drum, dry coconut shells, pan, cho, str
  Based on popular children's melodies
  Premiere: Recife, Pernambuco, Brazil, Teatro Santa
    Isabel; Orquestra Sinfônica de Recife, Villa-Lobos,
    cond; 6/18/1950
  Associated                                                 W420

**Solfejos** (Volume 1)
  A collection of 1 and 2 part melodies used for
    instruction in "Orpheonic singing" (*See*: Collections
    for a description of contents)                           W421

## Uruguai-Brasil
Mixed chorus; 2 min.
Composed on board the ship Pedro I when Villa-Lobos was
in charge of an artistic-educational mission to
Montevideo, Uruguay
Premiere: Montevideo, Uruguay, Teatro Sodré; chorus of
300 children; Villa-Lobos, cond;
V. Vitale                                                              W422

## Vocalismo
Four part chorus; one min.                                             W423


## 1941

## Bachianas brasileiras no. 4
Orchestra; 24 min.
  Prelúdio (Introdução)
  Coral (Canto do sertão)
  Ária (Cantiga)
  Dansa (Miudinho)
Pic, 2 fl, 2 ob, 2 cl, b cl, 2 bn, cbn, 4 hn, 3 tpt,
  2 trbn, tuba, timp, t-t, bass drum, cel, xyl, and str
Original for piano solo (See: W264)
Premiere: Rio; Orchestra of the Teatro Municipal; Villa-
  Lobos, cond; 7/15/1942
G. Ricordi                                                             W424

## Cântico do Pará
Three part a cappella chorus; 1 min.
Also in Collections, See: C.O. v. 2 #17
V. Vitale                                                              W425

## Fugas nos. 1, 8, & 21
Orchestra of cellos, 12 min. (minimum of 8 cellos)
Transcribed from The Well-Tempered Clavier of J. S. Bach
Premiere: Edoardo  Guarnieri, cond; 10/27/1941
Eschig                                                                 W426

## Gondoleiro (Modinha antiga)
Two part chorus and band; 2 min.
Based on a popular theme
Poetry by Castro Alves, adapted by David Nasser
Premiere: Rio, Vasco da Gama stadium; 30,000 students and

500 band instrumentalists; Sylvio Caldas, soloist;
Villa-Lobos, cond; 9/7/1941                                              W427

**Hino à vitória**
Chorus and band; 2 min.
Also arranged for four part a cappella chorus (*See*:
Collections, C.O. v.2, #36); chorus and orchestra (*See*:
W429); voice and piano (*See*: W430)                           W428

**Hino à vitória**
Chorus and orchestra; 2 min.
Pic, 2 fl, 2 ob, eng hn, 2 cl, b cl, 2 bn, cbn, 4 hn,
3 tpt, 4 trbn, tuba, timp, t-t, bass drum and str
Poetry by Gustavo Capanema
Also arranged for four part a cappella chorus (*See*:
Collections, C.O. v.2, #36); chorus and band (*See*:
W428); voice and piano (*See*: W430)                           W429

**Hino à vitória**
Voice and piano; 2 min.
Also arranged for four part a cappella chorus (*See*:
Collections, C.O. v.2, #36); chorus and band (*See*:
W428); chorus and orchestra (*See*: W429)                  W430

**Prelúdios 8, 14, and 22**
Orchestra of cellos (minimum of 8); 18 min.
Transcribed from *The Well-Tempered Clavier* of J. S. Bach
No. 8 transcribed for cello and piano (*See*: W261)
No.14 transcribed for cello and piano (*See*: W262)
Premiere: Edoardo de Guarnieri, cond; 10/27/1944
Eschig                                                                        W431

*1942*

**Bachianas brasileiras no. 7**
Orchestra; 25 min.
  *Prelúdio* (Ponteio)
  *Giga* (Quadrilha caipira)
  *Tocata* (Desafio)
  *Fuga* (Conversa)
Pic, 2 fl, 2 ob, eng hn, 2 cl, b cl, 2 bn, cbn, 4 hn,
3 tpt, 4 trbn, tuba, timp, dry coconut hulls, bass
drum, t-t, xyl, cel, harp and str

Dedicated to Gustavo Capanema, Minister of Education
Premiere: Rio; Orchestra of the Teatro Municipal; Villa-
  Lobos, cond; 3/13/1944
Eschig                                                    W432

**Nossa América**
Two part chorus; 1 min.
Poetry by Ofelia Fontes                                   W433

**Poema singelo**
Piano, 6 min.
Dedicated to Arminda Neves d'Almeida
Premiere: Rio; José Vieira Brandão, pf; 1943
CMP, V. Vitale                                            W434

**Quarteto de cordas no.7**
Two violins, viola and cello; 30 min.
Dedicated to the Quarteto Borgerth
Premiere: Rio, Teatro Municipal; Quarteto Borgerth;
  5/30/1945
Associated                                                W435

**Voz do povo** (Grito de Guerra)
Voice and piano, 2 min.
Poem by Villa-Lobos under the pseudonym Epaminondas
  Villalba Filho                                          W436


**1943**

**Dança da terra** (Ballet)
Mixed chorus and percussion; 6 min.
Bass drum, cho, reco, cymb, drum, dinner plate, t-t
  played by hand, various types of native bass drums,
  pan, t-t
Premiere: Rio; sung and danced by children in public
  schools; Villa-Lobos, cond; 9/7/1943                   W437

**Hino da juventude brasileira**
Four part mixed a cappella chorus; 2 min.
Melody by Pedro da Costa
Poetry by Abgar Renault                                   W438

**Invocação em defesa da pátria** (Civic-religious song)
    Soloist, chorus, and orchestra; 8 min.
    Pic, 2 fl, 2 ob, eng hn, 2 cl, b cl, 2 bn, cbn, 4 hn
     3 tpt, 2 trbn, tuba, timp, harp and str
    Text by Villa-Lobos and Manuel Bandeira
    Dedicated to Violeta C.N. Freitas
    Also for four part female a cappella chorus, *See*:
    Collections, C.O. v. 2 #45
    Premiere: Rio; Orchestra and chorus of the Teatro
     Municipal; Violeta Coelho Neto de Freitas, soloist,
     Villa-Lobos cond; 1943
    Eschig                                           W439

**Minha terra**
    Three part a cappella chorus; 2 min.
    Melody by H. Vogeler
    Poetry by Ciro Vieira da Cunha                       W440

**Modinhas e canções** (Album no. 2)
    Voice and piano, 15 min.
     *Pobre peregrino*
     *Vida formosa*
     *Nésta rua*
     *Manda tiro, tiro lá*
     *João Cambuête*
     *Na corda da viola*
    Based on popular children's songs
    Eschig                                           W441

**Poema de Itabira** (Viagem na família)
    Voice and orchestra, 15 min.
    Pic, 2 fl, 2 ob, eng hn, 2 cl, b cl, 2 bn, cbn, 4 hn,
     2 tpt, 4 trbn, tuba, timp, t-t, bass drum, cymb, cel,
     harp, pf and str
    Poetry by Carlos Drummond de Andrade
    Dedicated to Marian Anderson
    Arranged for voice and piano (*See*: W443)
    Premiere: Rio, Orchestra of the Teatro Municipal;
     Asdrubal Lima, v; Villa-Lobos, cond; 12/30/46
    Eschig                                           W442

**Poema de Itabira** (Viagem na família)
    Voice and piano, 15 min.
    Original for voice and orchestra (*See*: W442)

Poem by Carlos Drummond de Andrade
Dedicated to Marian Anderson
Eschig                                                                    W443

## 1944

### Bachianas brasileiras no.8
Orchestra; 22 min.
  *Prelúdio*
  *Ária* (Modinha)
  *Tocata* (Catira batida)
  *Fuga*
Pic, 2 fl, 2 ob, eng hn, 2 cl, b cl, 2 bn, cbn, 4 hn,
  4 tpt, 4 trbn, tuba, timp, t-t, bass drum, side drum,
  wood block (played with wooden stick, high, medium, and
  low pitches) xyl, cel and str
Dedicated to Mindinha
*Fuga* arranged for four part a cappella chorus (*See*: W445)
Premiere: Rome; Orchestra of the Academy of Santa Cecilia
  de Roma; Villa-Lobos, cond; 8/6/1947
Eschig                                                                    W444

### Fuga
Four part a cappella chorus; 3 min.
Arrangement of the fugue from *Bachianas brasileiras
  no. 8* (*See*: W444)                                              W445

### Quarteto de cordas no.8
Two violins, viola and cello; 30 min.
Dedicated to the Quarteto Iacovino
Premiere: Rio; Quarteto Iacovino; 9/5/1946
Ricordi                                                                   W446

### Sinfonia no.6 (Sobre a linha das montanhas do Brasil)
Orchestra, 20 min.
Two pic, 3 fl, 2 ob, eng hn, 2 cl, b cl, 2 bn, cbn, 4 hn,
  4 tpt,  4 trbn, tuba, timp, t-t, bass drum, big snare
  drum, Indian drum, side drum, cymb, vibraphone, cel,
  2 harps and str
Dedicated to Mindinha
Premiere: Rio; Orchestra of the Teatro Municipal; Villa-
  Lobos, cond; 4/29/1950                                         W447

## Uirapuru
Mixed a cappella chorus; 1 min.
Premiere: Rio; Chorus of the Conservatório Nacional de
Canto Orfeônico; José Vieira Brandão, cond; 12/10/1944
Original for orchestra(*See*: W133)                                      W448

## 1945

## Bachianas brasileiras no.9
Orchestra of strings or human voices; 12 min.
*Prelúdio* (Vagoroso e místico)
*Fuga* (Poco apressado)
Premiere: Rio, Teatro Municipal; String Quintet and
Orquestra Sinfônica Brasileira; Eleazar de Carvalho,
cond; 11/17/1948
Eschig                                                                   W449

## Canções de cordialidade
Orchestra; 5 min.
*Feliz aniversário* (Happy Birthday)
*Boas -festas* (Best Wishes)
*Feliz natal* (Merry Christmas)
*Feliz ano novo* (Happy New Year)
*Boas -vindas* (Welcome)
Fl, cl, 3 sax (a and t), 3 hn, 3 trbn, timp, tri, chimes,
cymb, bass drum and str
Published for two, three and four part a cappella chorus
in Collections, *See*: C.O. v.2, #8, #9, #10, #11, and
#12; also transcribed for voice and orchestra (*See*:
W451) and voice and piano (*See*: W452)                                  W450

## Canções de cordialidade
Voice and orchestra; 6 min.
*Feliz aniversário* (Happy Birthday)
*Boas -festas* (Best Wishes)
*Feliz ano novo* (Happy New Year)
*Boas -vindas* (Welcome)
Fl, cl, 3 sax, a sax, t sax, 3 tpts, 3 trbn, timp, tri,
chimes, cymb, bomb and str
Text by Manuel Bandeira with collaboration by Villa-Lobos
Published for two, three and four part a cappella chorus
in Collections, *See*: C.O. v.2, #8, #9, #10, #11, and
#12; also for orchestra (*See*: W450) and voice and
piano (*See*: W452)

Premiere: Rio; Orchestra of Rádio Tupi; Cristina
Maristany, soloist; Milton Calazans, cond; 12/18/1946          W451

## Canções de cordialidade
Voice and piano; 8 min.
*Feliz aniversário* (Happy Birthday)
*Boas -festas* (Best Wishes)
*Feliz natal* (Merry Christmas)
*Feliz ano novo* (Happy New Year)
*Boas -vindas* (Welcome)
Text by Manuel Bandeira with collaboration by Villa-Lobos
Published for two, three and four part a cappella chorus
  in Collections, *See*: C.O. v.2, #8, #9, #10, #11, and
  #12; also for orchestra (*See*: W450) and voice and
  orchestra (*See*: W451)
Premiere: Rio; Cristina Maristany, v; Alceu Bocchino, pf;
  12/18/1946          W452

## Concerto no. 1
Piano and orchestra; 28 min.
Pic, 2 fl, 2 ob, eng hn, 2 cl, b cl, 2 bn, cbn, 4 hn,
  3 tpt, 4 trbn, tuba, timp, t-t, tri, bass drum, harp,
  and str
Commissioned by Ellen Ballon
Reduction for 2 pianos
Premiere: Rio; Orchestra of the Teatro Municipal; Ellen
  Ballon, pf; Villa-Lobos, cond
Eschig          W453

## Fantasia
Cello and orchestra; 18 min.
Pic, 2 fl, 2 ob, eng hn, 2 cl, b cl, 2 bn, cbn, 4 hn,
  2 tpt, 3 trbn, tuba, timp, novachordion, xyl, cymb,
  cel, harp, and str
Reduction for cello and piano
Written at the request of Walter Burle Marx
Dedicated to Serge Koussevitsky
Premiere: Rio; Orchestra of the Teatro Municipal; Iberê
  Gomes Grosso, vc; Villa-Lobos, cond; 10/8/1946
Associated          W454

## José (Quadrilha caipira)
Four part male a cappella chorus; 5 min.
Text by Carlos Drummond de Andrade

Dedicated to the Yale Glee Club "after a fine performance
of *O trenzinho*" (from *Bachianas brasileiras no.2, See*:
W247)                                                                          W455

**Madona** (Symphonic Poem)
  Orchestra, 14 min.
  Two pic, 3 flutes, 3 ob, eng hn, 3 cl, b cl, 3 bn, cbn,
    6 hn, 4 tpt, 4 trbn, tuba, timp, cymb, t-t, bass drum,
    xyl, glock, novachordion, cel, 2 harps, pf and str
  Commissioned by the Koussevitsky Foundation
  Dedicated to Natalie Koussevitsky
  Premiere: Rio; Orchestra of the Teatro Municipal, Villa-
    Lobos, cond; 10/8/1946
  Eschig                                                                       W456

**Quarteto de cordas no. 9** (composed in Rio)
  Two violins, viola and cello; 20 min.
  Dedicated to Mindinha
  Premiere: London; 1947
  Peer                                                                         W457

**Sinfonia no. 7**
  Orchestra, 30 min.
  Two pic, 3 fl, 3 ob, eng hn, 3 cl, 2 b cl, 3 bn, 2 cbn,
    6 hn, 4 tpt, 4 trbn, tuba, timp, t-t, cymb, tri, pan,
    cho, glock, reco, side drum, big snare drum, bass drum,
    novachordion, xyl, vibraphone, cel, 2 harps, pf and str
  Written for a competition in Detroit under the pseudonym
    of A. Caramurú
  Premiere: London; London Symphony Orchestra, Villa-Lobos,
    cond; 3/27/1949
  G. Ricordi                                                                   W458

**Solfejos** (Volume 2)
  Melodies in 1, 2, 3, 4 and 6 parts used for instruction
    in "Orpheonic singing" (*See*: Collections for a
    description of contents)                                                   W459

**Trio**
  Violin, viola and cello, 30 min.
  Commissioned by and dedicated to the Coolidge Foundation
  Premiere: The Albenieri Trio; 10/30/1945
  Eschig                                                                       W460

## 1946

### Divagação
Cello, piano, and drum, 3 min.
Premiere: Rio; Iberê Gomes Grosso, vc; Alceu Bocchino,
pf; 10/27/1951
Eschig                                                                              W461

### Duas paisagens (Deux Paysages)
Voice and piano; 2 min.
  *Manhã na praia*
  *Tarde na Glória*
Poetry by Carlos de Sá
Premiere: Rio; Studio of Rádio Tupi; Cristina Maristany,
  v; 1947
Eschig                                                                              W462

### Duo
Violin and viola; 10 min.
Dedicated to and written at the suggestion of Paulina
  d'Ambrozio
Premiere: New York; Mr. & Mrs. Fuchs, vn and va;
  February 1948                                                                      W463

### El libro brasileño (School song)
Chorus in two parts; 2 min.                                                          W464

### Meu jardim
Four part a cappella chorus; 2 min.
Arranged for chorus and band (*See*: W466)
Melody by Ernesto dos Santos, known as Donga
Poetry by David Nasser                                                              W465

### Meu jardim
Chorus and band; 2 min.
Melody by Ernesto dos Santos, popularly known as Donga
Poetry by David Nasser
Arranged for four part a cappella chorus (*See*: W465)
Premiere: Rio, Vasco da Gama Stadium; 40,000 students,
  and a band of 1,000  band instrumentalists; Francisco
  Alves, soloist; Villa-Lobos, cond; 9/7/1940                                        W466

**Prelúdio em ré maior**
 Six part mixed a cappella chorus; 2 min.
 Melody by João Alberto                                     W467

**Quarteto de cordas no. 10**
 Two violins, viola and cello; 20 min.
 Dedicated to Mindinha
 Premiere: Paris; Quarteto de São Paulo; 2/12/1950
 Peer                                                        W468

**Quero amar-te**
 Three part a cappella chorus
 Based on folklore of the state of Santa Catarina            W469

**Ratoeira**
 Three part a cappella chorus
 Based on folklore of the state of Santa Catarina            W470


**1947**

**The Emerald Song**
 Voice and piano; 2 min.
 Excerpted from Magdalena (*See*: W476)
 Poetry in English, by G. Forrest and R. Wright
 CMP                                                         W471

**Food for Thought**
 Voice and guitar; 3 min.
 Excerpted from Magdalena (*See*: W476)
 Poetry in English, by G. Forrest and R. Wright
 CMP                                                         W472


**Guia prático**  Album no.11
 Piano, 10 min.
  *O anel*
  *Nigue ninhas*
  *Pobre cega* (1st version)
  *A cotia*
  *Vida formosa*
  *Viva o carnaval*
 Popular children's melodies
 Dedicated to Mieczyslaw Horszoswki

Premiere: Rio; Noemi Bittencourt, pf; 10/12/1949
Peer                                                                                      W473

**Hommage à Chopin** (Homenagem a Chopin)
Piano, 8 min.
  *Noturno*
  *Ballada*
Written for UNESCO observances of the death of Chopin
Premiere: Arnaldo Estrela, pf; 8/29/1949
Eschig                                                                                    W474

**Il pleut, il pleut, bergère**
Three part a cappella chorus, 1 min.
Based on a French melody
Premiere: Rio; chorus of Colégio Andrews; Julieta Strutt,
  cond; November 1947                                                      W475

**Magdalena** (Musical Adventure in 2 acts)
  Soloists, chorus and orchestra, 90 min.
  Pic, 2 fl, 2 ob, eng hn, 2 cl in B-flat, 2 cl in A, b cl,
    a sax, s sax, 2 bn, 3 hn, 2 tpt in B-flat, 2 tpt in A,
    2 trbn, tuba, timp, t-t, castanets, bass drum, reco,
    Indian drum, big snare drum, tambourine, ca, wooden
    rattle, pio, dry cocunut hulls, chimes, cho, cymb, tri,
    pan, glock, cel, xyl, harp, pf  and str
  Commissioned by E. Lester, President of the Los Angeles
    Civic Light Opera Association
  Libretto by F.H. Brennan and H. Curran
  Poetry by R. Wright and G. Forrest
  Music from this work arranged for: voice and piano (*See*:
    W471, 479, 480 & 482); voice and guitar (*See*: W472);
    orchestra, soloists, and chorus (*See*: W477 & W478)
  Premiere: Los Angeles; Irra Petina, Dorothy Sarnoff, John
    Raitt, Hugh Haas, Gerhard Pechner, A. Garcia, M. Niles,
    H. Reese, F. Hilt, J. Arthur, B. Huff, C. Matsios, L.
    Morganthaler, J. Schickling, L. Miller, G. Curtainger,
    P. Kirk, B. Brusher, and Jack Cole, soloists; Jack
    Cole, choreographer; chorus prepared by R. Zeller;
    Jules Dassin, General Director; A. Kay, cond;
    7/26/1947                                                                        W476

**Magdalena** (First Suite)
  Orchestra, soloists and mixed chorus, 8 min.
  *My Bus and I*

*Scene of Paris*
*Food for Thought*
Excerpted from *Magdalena* (See: W476)
Poetry by G. Forrest and R. Wright
Pic, 2 fl, 2 ob, eng hn, 2 cl, a sax, 2 bn, 4 hn, 2 tpt,
3 trbn, tuba, timp, cymb, reco, tambor surdo, t-t, tri,
pan, mat, cho, glock, xyl, cel, harp and str                    W477

**Magdalena** (Second Suite)
Orchestra, soloists, and mixed chorus, 8 min.
*The Singing Tree*
*The Emerald Song*
*Valse d'Espagne*
Excerpted from *Magdalena* (*See*: W476)
Pic, 2 fl, 2 ob, eng hn, 2 cl in B-flat, 2 cl in A,
a sax, 2 bn, 4 hn, 2 tpt, 3 trbn, tuba, timp, t-t,
bells, cymb, castanets, pan, bass drum, vibraphone,
cel, harp, pf and str                                           W478

**Magdalena**
Voice and piano; 2 min.
Excerpted from *Magdalena* (*See*: W476)
Poetry in English by G. Forrest and R. Wright
Napoleão                                                        W479

**My Bus and I**
Voice and piano, 2 min.
Popular children's song, from *Magdalena* (*See*: W476)
Text by G. Forrest and R. Wright
CMP                                                             W480

**Quarteto de cordas no. 11**
Two violins, viola and cello; 15 min.
Dedicated to Mindinha
Premiere: Rio; Quarteto Iacovino; 1953
Peer                                                            W481

**Scène de Paris**
Voice and piano, 2 min.
Excerpted from *Magdalena* (*See*: W476)
CMP                                                             W482

**Sinfonieta no. 2**
Orchestra, 15 min.

Pic, fl, ob, eng hn, cl, b cl, a sax, bn, 3 hn, 2 tpt,
2 trbn, tuba, timp, t-t, dinner plates, bass drum, xyl,
cel, harp and str
Written for the Philharmonic Academy of Rome
Premiere: Rome; Orchestra of the Philharmonic Academy;
Villa-Lobos, cond; 3/15/1948
Peer                                                                           W483

## 1948

**Big Ben** (London poem)
Voice and piano; 3 min.
Written under the pseudonym Epaminondas Villalba Filho
Dedicated to Frederick Fuller
Arranged for voice and orchestra (*See*: W485)
Premiere: London; Frederick Fuller, soloist; 1958
Southern                                                                       W484

**Big Ben** (London poem)
Voice and orchestra; 3 min.
Fl, 2 ob, eng hn, 2 cl, 2 bn, 2 hn, tpt, 2 trbn, tuba,
timp, t-t, sin, cel, harp, pf and str
Written under the pseudonym of Epaminondas Villalba Filho
Dedicated to Frederick Fuller
Arranged for voice and piano (*See*: W484)
Southern                                                                       W485

**Canção do poeta do século XVIII**
Voice and piano; 2 min.
Text by Alfredo Ferreira
Dedicated to Cristina Maristany
Southern                                                                       W486

**Concerto no. 2**
Piano and orchestra; 22 min.
Pic, 2 fl, 2 ob, eng hn, 2 cl, b cl, 2 bn, cbn, 4 hn,
3 tpt, 4 trbn, tuba, timp, t-t, cymb, bass drum, cel,
harp and str
The third movement (Cadência) dedicated to João de Souza
Lima
Reduction for 2 pianos
Premiere: Rio; Orchestra of the Teatro Municipal; João de
Souza Lima, pf; Villa-Lobos, cond; 4/21/1953
Eschig                                                                         W487

**Conselhos**
Voice and piano; 1 min.
Text written by Villa-Lobos under the pseudonym
Epaminondas Villalba Filho                                    W488

**Coração inquieto**
Voice and piano; 2 min.
Poetry by Silvio Moreaux                                      W489

**Fantasia para saxophone**
Soprano or tenor saxophone, 2 horns and strings; 15 min.
Dedicated to Marcel Mule
Reduction for saxophone and piano
Premiere: Rio, Auditório do Ministério da Educação e
Cultura; Chamber orchestra; Waldemar Szilman, soloist;
Villa-Lobos, cond; 11/17/1951
Peer                                                         W490

**1949**

**Cortejo nupcial**
Orchestra and organ; 5 min.
Composed at the request of Ambassador Carlos Martins de
Souza for the wedding of his daughter
Premiere: Paris; 1949                                        W491

**Dinga-donga** (Poema realista)
Voice and piano; 2 min.
Music and text written in Barcelona at the residence of
soprano Conxita Badia, at her request
Dedicated to Conxita Badia
Premiere: Magdalena Lebeis, v; Fritz Jank, pf; 6/14/1955
Southern                                                     W492

**1950**

**Assobio a jato** (The Jet Whistle)
Flute and cello; 12 min.
*Allegro non troppo*
*Adagio*
*Vivo - Poco meno*
*Prestissimo*
*Prestissimo* dedicated to Elizabeth and Carleton Sprague Smith

The player is instructed to blow inside the mouthpiece to
produce a whistling sound beginning with a low pitch of
d and gradually ascending, which creates a sound
similar to a player warming up his flute on a cold day
Premiere: Rio, Auditório do Ministério da Educação e
Cultura; Ary Ferreira, fl; Iberê Gomes Grosso, vc;
3/13/1950
Peer                                                                    W493

### Canção de cristal
Voice and piano; 3 min.
Poetry by Murillo Araújo
Eschig                                                                  W494

### Erosão (Sorimão Uipirunauá)
Indian Legend no. 1 of the origin of the Amazon  River
Orchestra; 14 min.
Two pic, 2 fl, 2 ob, eng hn, 3 cl, bass cl, 2 bn, cbn,
    4 hn, 4 tpt, 4 trbn, tuba, timp, t-t, cymb, bass drum,
    pan, xyl, harp, cel, pf and str
Based on the Indian legend, "The Sun and the Moon" as
    related by Barbosa Rodrigues
Commissioned by the Louisville Orchestra
Premiere: Louisville, KY; Robert Whitney, cond; 11/7/1951
Eschig                                                                  W495

### Quarteto de cordas no. 12
2 violins, viola and cello, 20 min.
Dedicated to Mindinha
Premiere: Rio; Haydn Quartet; 11/9/1951
Associated                                                             W496

### Samba clássico (Ode)
Voice and orchestra, 2 min.
Two fl, 2 ob, 2 cl, bass cl, 2 bn, 4 hn, 3 tpt, 4 trbn,
    tuba, timp, cho, tamb, bass drum, reco, harp and str
Poem by Villa-Lobos written under the pseudonym of
    Epaminondas Villalba Filho
Also for voice and piano (See: W498)
Premiere: Montreal; Canadian Broadcasting Company;
    Maria Kareska, v;, Villa-Lobos, cond; 2/28/1958
Eschig                                                                  W497

**Samba clássico** (Ode)
Voice and piano, 2 min.
Poem by Villa-Lobos written under the pseudonym of
Epaminondas Villalba Filho
A homage to composers of popular music
Also for voice and orchestra (*See*: W497)
Eschig                                                                                    W498

**Sinfonia no. 8**
Orchestra; 22 min.
Two pic, 3 fl, 2 ob, eng hn, 2 cl, b cl, 2 bn, cbn, 4 hn,
    4 tpt, 4 trbn, tuba, timp, t-t, cymb, xyl, cel,
    2 harps, pf and str
Dedicated to Olin Downes
Premiere: Philadelphia; Philadelphia Symphony Orchestra;
    Villa-Lobos, cond; 1/14/1955
G. Ricordi                                                                               W499

**1951**

**Canto orfeônico** (Volume 2)
A collection of compositions used for instruction in
    "Orpheonic singing" (*See*: Collections for a description
    of contents)                                                                     W500

**Concerto para violão**
Guitar and orchestra; 18 min.
Fl, ob, cl, bn, hn, trbn and str
Dedicated to Andres Segovia
Reduction for guitar and piano (*See*: W502)
Premiere: Houston; Houston Symphony Orchestra; Andres
    Segovia, guitar; Villa-Lobos cond; 2/6/1956
Eschig                                                                                    W501

**Concerto para violão**
Guitar and piano; 18 min.
Dedicated to Andres Segovia
Arranged from the original orchestration (*See*: W501)
Eschig                                                                                    W502

## Quarteto de cordas no. 13
2 violins, viola and cello; 20 min.
Dedicated to the Quarteto Municipal, São Paulo
Eschig                                                                    W503

## Rudá (Dio d'amore) (Bailado ameríndio)
Orchestra; 35 min.
  *Os maias*
  *Os aztecas*
  *Os incas*
  *Os marajoaras*
  *La vittoria dell' amore nel tropico*
  *Epílogo*
Two pic, 4 fl, 2 ob, eng hn, 2 cl, b cl, sonovox,
  sopranino sax, s sax, 2 bn, cbn, 4 hn, 4 tpt, 4 trbn,
  tuba, timp, t-t, bass drum,  small drum, large drum,
  Indian drum, dry cocunut hulls, wooden rattle, glock,
  tri, cho, reco, caisse claire, dinner plates, pan, xyl,
  vibraphone, cel, two harps, pf, and str
A story of pre-European America, ordered by La Scala,
  Milan, Italy; choreography by Walmann
Dedicated to Mindinha
Premiere: Paris, Theatre Champs Elysées; Orchestre
  National de la Radiodiffusion Française; Villa-Lobos,
  cond; 8/30/1954
Eschig                                                                    W504

## 1952

## Concerto no. 4
Piano and orchestra; 24 min.
Pic, 2 fl, 2 ob, eng hn, 2 cl, b cl, 2 bn, cbn, 4 hn,
  2 tpt, 2 trbn, tuba, timp, t-t, cymb, dry coconut
  hulls, chimes and str
Commissioned by pianist Bernardo Segal
Reduction for 2 pianos
Premiere: Pittsburgh; Pittsburgh Symphony Orchestra;
  Bernardo Segal, pf; Villa-Lobos cond; 1/9/1953
Eschig                                                                    W505

## Duas lendas ameríndias
Four part a cappella mixed chorus; 3 min.
  *O iurupari e o menino*
  *O iurupari e o caçador*

Dedicated to Mindinha
Premiere: Rio; Coral Ars Nova; Carlos Alberto Pinto da
Fonseca, cond; 11/20/1967
Eschig                                                                    W506

**Música sacra** (Volume 1)
Choral compositions of 2,3,4, and more voices,
   a cappella, and with accompaniments; a collection of 23
   sacred works both original and arrangments of works by
   other composers
*See*: Collections
Dedications to Mindinha, Julieta Strutt and Frei Antonio
   Garciandia Gamboa
V. Vitale                                                                  W507

**Ouverture de l'homme tel**
Orchestra; 4 min.
Pic, fl, ob, eng hn, cl in A, bn, hn, tpt in B-flat, tpt
   in A, trbn, timp, t-t, dinner plate, bass drum, cel, pf
   and str
Based on suíte sugestiva (no. 1) (*See*: W242 and W243)
Dedicated to Madame Frederico Moreau
Premiere: Lisbon, Portugal; Orquestra Sinfônica Nacional;
   Villa-Lobos, cond; 6/25/1952
Eschig                                                                    W508

**Panis angelicus**
Four part mixed a cappella chorus, 3 min.
Latin Text
Premiere: Rio, Teatro Municipal; Coral Ars Nova of the
   Federal University of Minas Gerais, Carlos Alberto Pinto da
   Fonseca, cond; 11/20/1967
V.Vitale                                                                  W509

**Sinfonia no. 9**
Orchestra; 20 min.
Pic, 3 fl, 2 ob, eng hn, 2 cl, bass cl, 2 bn, cbn, 4 hn,
   4 tpt, 4 trbn, tuba, timp, t-t, cymb, dry coconut
   hulls, bass drum, xyl, vibraphone, cel, harp and str
Dedicated to Mindinha
Premiere: Philadelphia Symphony Orchestra; Eugene
   Ormandy, cond
Eschig                                                                    W510

**Sinfonia amerĩndia no. 10** (Sume Pater Patrium - Oratorio)
Orchestra, mixed chorus, tenor, baritone and bass
soloists; 60 min.
Two pic, 4 fl, 2 ob, eng hn, 3 cl, b cl, 2 bn, cbn, 4 hn,
4 tpt, 4 trbn, tuba, timp, t-t, cymb, chu, coco, pio,
gong, chimes, sleigh bells, pan, bomb, org, xyl,
marimba, cel, 2 harps, pf and str
An adaptation of the verses of Padre José de Anchieta's
*Beata Virgem*
Written for the four hundredth anniversary of the city of
São Paulo
Dedicated to Mindinha
Premiere: Paris, Theatre Champs Elysées; Orchestre
National and Choeur de la  Radiodiffusion Française;
Villa-Lobos, cond; 4/4/1957
Eschig                                                                        W511

**1952-1957**

**Concerto no.3**
Piano and orchestra; 22 min.
Pic, 2 fl, 2 ob, eng hn, 2 cl, b cl, 2 bn, cbn, 4 hn,
2 tpt, 2 trbn, tuba, timp, t-t, cymb, vibraphone, xyl,
cel, harp and str
Work begun in 1952 as a commission, but completed only in
1957
Dedicated to pianist Arnaldo Estrella
Reduction for 2 pianos
Premiere: Rio; Orquestra Sinfônica Brasileira; Arnaldo
Estrella, pf; Eleazar de Carvalho, cond; 8/24/1957
Eschig                                                                        W512

**1953**

**Alvorada na floresta tropical** (Dawn in a Tropical Forest,
Overture)
Orchestra; 12 min.
Pic, 2 fl, 2 ob, eng hn, 2 cl, b cl, 2 bn, cbn, 4 hn,
3 tpt, 3 trbn, tuba, timp, t-t, cymb, cho, tri, bass
drum, coco, cel, harp, pf and str
Commissioned by the Louisville Symphony Orchestra
Premiere: Louisville (KY); Louisville Orchestra; Robert
Whitney, cond; 1953                                                  W513

**Canção do poeta do século XVIII**
Voice and guitar; 2 min.
Poetry by Alfredo Ferreira
Premiere: Rio, Auditório do Ministério da Educação e
 Cultura; Cristina Maristany and Jodacil Damasceno;
 1 ı/10/1962
Southern                                                    W514

**Concerto para harpa e orquestra**
Harp and orchestra; 23 min.
Pic, 2 fl, 2 ob, eng hn, 2 cl, bass cl, 2 bn, cbn, 4 hn,
 3 tpt, 2 trbn, tuba, timp, cymb, xyl, marimba, cel, and
 str
Commissioned by and dedicated to Nicanor Zabaleta
Premiere: Philadelphia; Philadelphia Symphony Orchestra;
 Nicanor Zabaleta, harp, Villa-Lobos, cond; 1/14/1955
Eschig                                                      W515

**Concerto para violoncelo e orquestra no. 2**
Cello and orchestra; 20 min.
Pic, 2 fl, 2 ob, eng hn, 2 cl, b cl, 2 bn, cbn, 4 hn,
 2 tpt, 3 trbn, tuba, timp, t-t, cel, side drum, pan,
 cymb, harp and str
Commissioned by and dedicated to Aldo Parisot
Reduction for cello and piano
Premiere: New York; Philharmonic Society of New York;
 Aldo Parisot, vc; Walter Hendl, cond; 2/5/1955;
Eschig                                                      W516

**Fantasia concertante**
Piano, clarinet and bassoon; 15 min.
Dedicated to and commissioned by Eugene Liszt
Premiere: Rio, Sala Cecília Meireles; Ivy Improta, pf;
 José Botelho, cl; Noël Devos, bn; 11/19/1968
Eschig                                                      W517

**Odisséia de uma raça**
Orchestra, 14 min.
Pic, 2 fl, 2 ob, eng hn, 2 cl, b cl, 2 bn, cbn, 4 hn,
 3 tpt, 3 trbn, tuba, timp, t-t, dinner plate, xyl, cel,
 2 harps, pf and str
Dedicated to Israel, all performing rights signed over to
 the nation of Israel
Premiere: (At the opening of the 28th World Music

Festival of the International Society of Contemporary
Music) Haifa, Israel; Israel Philharmonic Orchestra;
Michael Taube, cond; 5/30/1954
Israeli Music Publications, Tel Aviv                                    W518

## Quarteto de cordas no.14
2 violins, viola and cello; 22 min.
Commissioned by the Stanley Quartet
Premiere: The Stanley Quartet; 8/11/1954
Eschig                                                                 W519

## 1954

## Cantilena da paz
Six part a cappella chorus
At the end of the manuscript, the inscription appears: "A
work without beginning and without end"                                W520

## Concerto no. 5
Piano and orchestra; 20 min.
Pic, 2 fl, 2 ob, eng hn, 2 cl, bass cl, 2 bn, cbn, 4 hn,
2 tpt, 3 trbn, tuba, timp, bass drum, cel, xyl, harp
and str
Reduction for 2 pianos
Commissioned by and dedicated to Felicia Blumental
Premiere: London; London Symphony Orchestra; Felicia
Blumental, pf; Jean Martinon, cond; 5/8/1955
Eschig                                                                 W521

## Gênesis (Symphonic poem and ballet)
Orchestra; 16 min.
Pic, 2 fl, 2 ob, eng hn, 2 cl, b cl, 2 bn, cbn, 4 hn,
2 tpt, 3 trbn, tuba, timp, t-t, bomb, woods, tri, gong,
ca, drum, tambor surdo, Indian drum, cymb, cho (metal),
glock, xyl, cel, harp, pf and str
Commissioned by dancer Janet Collins
Premiere: Rio, Teatro Municipal; Orchestra of the Teatro
Municipal; Mário Tavares, cond; 11/21/1969
Eschig                                                                 W522

## Quarteto de cordas No.15
2 violins, viola and cello; 20 min.
Dedicated to the New Music String Quartet
Premiere: Washington, D.C.; The Juilliard String Quartet;

April 1958
Eschig                                                                    W523

**1955**

**Concerto para harmônica e orquestra**
Harmonica and orchestra; 20 min.
Fl, ob, cl, bn, 2 hn, trbn, timp, tri, cymb, cel, harp
 and str
Commissioned by and dedicated to John Sebastian
Reduction for harmonica and piano
Premiere: U.S. Air Force Orchestra; John Sebastian,
 harmonica; Guillermo Espinoza, cond;
Associated                                                                W524

**Jardim fanado** (Jardim Fané)
Voice and piano; 2 min.
Poem by Amarylio de Albuquerque
Dedicated to Mindinha
Eschig                                                                    W525

**Quarteto de cordas no.16**
2 violins, viola and cello; 22 min.
Dedicated to Mindinha
Premiere: Rio; Quarteto Rio de Janeiro; 9/13/1958
Eschig                                                                    W526

**Sinfonia no.11**
Orchestra, 22 min.
Two pic, 4 fl, 2 ob, eng hn, 2 cl, b cl, 2 bn, cbn, 4 hn,
 4 tpt, 4 trbn, tuba, timp, t-t, cymb, tri, wooden
 rattle, bomb, xyl, vibraphone, cel, 2 harps, pf and str
Dedicated to Natalie and Serge Koussevitsky
Commissioned for the 75th anniversary of the Boston
 Symphony Orchestra
Premiere: Boston; Boston Symphony Orchestra; Villa-Lobos,
 cond; 3/2/1956
Eschig                                                                    W527

**1955-1956**

**Yerma** (Opera in 3 acts)
Soloists, chorus and orchestra; 90 min.
Pic, 2 fl, 2 ob, eng hn, 2 cl in B-flat, b cl, 2 bn, cbn,

a sax, s sax, t sax, 2 hn, 2 tpt, 3 trbn, tuba, timp,
t-t, gong, Tambor de Provence, tambor surdo, chimes,
sonovox, cymb, bombo, pan, castanets, sleigh bells,
mat, xyl, vibraphone, cho, glock, cel, harp, pf and str
Commissioned by J. Blankenship
Original written in Spanish, by Federico Garcia Lorca
Dedicated to Hermenegilda Neves d'Almeida on Mother's
Day
Premiere: Santa Fe, New Mexico; Santa Fe Opera Orchestra;
Christopher Keene, cond; Basil Longton, producer; José
Limon, choreographer; scenery by Allen Charles Klein;
original paintings by Giorgio de Chirico; 8/12/1971
Eschig                                                                          W528

## 1956

### Canção das águas claras
Voice and orchestra, 10 min.
Pic, 2 fl, 2 ob, eng hn, 2 cl, b cl, 2 bn, cbn, 4 hn,
2 tpt, 2 trbn, tuba, timp, t-t, dinner plates, xyl,
vibraphone, cel, harp and str
Poetry by Gilberto Amado
Dedicated to Mindinha
Premiere: London; London Symphony Orchestra; Carmem
Prietto, soloist; Villa-Lobos, cond; 4/28/1957
Eschig                                                                          W529

### Canção das águas claras
Voice and piano; 8 min.
Text by Gilberto Amado
Dedicated to Mindinha
Eschig                                                                          W530

### The Emperor Jones
(Incidental music for a play by Eugene O'Neill)
Orchestra with alto and baritone solos (ad libitum);
18 min.
Pic, 2 fl, 2 ob, eng hn, 2 cl, b cl, 2 bn, cbn, 4 hn,
4 tpt, 4 trbn, tuba, timp, t-t, tambor surdo, Indian
drum, medium sized drum, coco, ca, mat, gong, sleigh
bells (large), cho, cymb, glock, bomb, xyl, cel, harp,
solovox, pf and str
Commissioned by and dedicated to The Empire Music
Festival

Reduction for piano
  Premiere: (Empire Music Festival) Ellenville, New
    York; choreography and dance by José Limon and Company;
    José Limon and Lucas Hoving, soloists; Symphony of the
    Air; Villa-Lobos, cond;
  Eschig                                                        W531

**Eu te amo**
  Voice and orchestra; 4 min.
  Pic, 2 fl, 2 ob, eng hn, 2 cl, b cl, 2 bn, cbn, 4 hn,
    2 tpt, 2 trb, tuba, timp, t-t, cel, harp and str
  Text by Dora Vasconcellos
  Dedicated to Mindinha
  Also for voice and piano (*See*: W533)
  Eschig                                                        W532

**Eu te amo**
  Voice and piano; 4 min.
  Text by Dora Vasconcellos
  Dedicated to Mindinha
  Also for voice and orchestra (*See*: W532)
  Eschig                                                        W533

**Modinha** (Seresta no.5)
  Voice and guitar; 3 min.
  Text by Manuel Bandeira
  Transcription made at the request of Olga Praguer Coelho
  Premiere: Rio, Auditório do Palácio da Cultura MEC;
    Cristina Maristany, v; Jodacil Damasceno, guitar;
    11/12/1962
  Eschig                                                        W534

**1957**

**Duo**
  Oboe and bassoon; 18 min.
  Dedicated to Mindinha
  Premiere: Rio; Paolo Nardi, ob; Noel Devos, bn;
    11/19/1967
  Eschig                                                        W535

## Izi
Orchestra
Based on an Indian legend as told by Barbosa Rodrigues
(Incomplete)                                                W536

## Quarteto de cordas no.17
2 violins, viola and cello; 22 min.
Dedicated to Mindinha
Premiere: Washington, D.C.; Budapest String Quartet;
10/16/1959
Eschig                                                      W537

## Quinteto instrumental
Flute, violin, viola, cello and harp; 20 min.
Written at the suggestion of the Instrumental Quintet of
the Radiodiffusion Française
Premiere: Rio; 11/16/1962
Eschig                                                      W538

## Sinfonia no.12
Orchestra; 20 min.
Pic, 3 fl, 2 ob, eng hn, 2 cl, b cl, 2 bn, cbn, 4 hn,
4 tpt, 4 trbn, tuba, timp, t-t, cymb, coco (large,
medium and small), xyl, cel, harp and str
Completed on the 70th birthday of Villa-Lobos
Dedicated to Mindinha
Premiere: Washington, D.C.; National Symphony Orchestra;
Howard Mitchell, cond; 1958
Eschig                                                      W539

## 1957-1958

## Menina nas nuvens, A (Musical Adventure in 3 Acts)
Soloists, chorus and orchestra; 90 min.
Pic, 2 fl, ob, eng hn, 2 cl, a sax, bn, 3 hn, tpt, trbn,
tuba, timp, t-t, bass drum, ca, tambor de provence,
tambourine, tin plate sheet, cho (metal), tri, pan,
cymb, xyl, cel, vibraphone, harp, pf and str
Libretto by Lucia Benedetti
Dedicated to Mindinha
Premiere: Rio; Orchestra, chorus and ballet of the Teatro
Municipal; Aracy Belas Campos, Assis Pacheco, Edson de
Castilho, Paulo Fortes, G. Damiano, Lísia Demoro, G.
Queiroz, I. Camino, M. Henrique, and M. Mucelli,

soloists; choreography by Eugenia Teodorova; Santiago
Guerra, director of the chorus; Gianni Ratto,
director; Edoardo de Guarnieri,cond; 11/29/1960      W540

## Poema de palavras
Voice and piano; 3 min.
Poem taken from *Historietas* by Dora Vasconcellos
Dedicated to Mindinha
Also for voice and orchestra (*See*: W542)
Eschig      W541

## Poema de palavras
Voice and orchestra; 3 min.
Pic, 2 fl, 2 ob, eng hn, 2 cl, b cl, 2 bn, cbn, 3 hn,
  tpt, 2 trbn, tuba, timp, cel, harp and str
Poem taken from *Historietas* by Dora Vasconcellos
Dedicated to Mindinha
Also for voice and piano (*See*: W541)
Eschig      W542

## 1958

## Bendita sabedoria
Six part a cappella chorus; 10 min.
Six Chorales:
  *Adagio* (Sapientia foris predicat)
  *Andantino* (Vao pretiosum)
  *Quasi allegretto* (Principium sapientiae)
  *Allegro* (Vir Sapiens fortis est)
  *Andante* (Beatus homo)
  *Largo* (Imponente)
  *Dexteram tuam*
Biblical texts
Written at the suggestion of Carleton Sprague Smith
Dedicated to New York University
Premiere: New York, Vanderbilt Hall and Washington
  Square; New York University College Chorus; Maurice
  Paress, cond; 12/2/1958
Eschig      W543

## Cair da tarde
Voice and piano, 2 min.
From *Floresta do Amazonas* (Music for the film *Green
  Mansions*) (*See*: W551)

Poetry by Dora Vasconcellos
Dedicated to Mindinha
Also for voice and orchestra (*See*: W545)
P. Robbins                                                    W544


## Cair da tarde
Voice and orchestra; 2 min.
Two fl, 2 ob, eng hn, 2 cl, b cl, s sax, 2 bn, cbn, 4 hn,
  2 tpt, 3 trbn, tuba, timp, solovox, harp and str
From *Floresta do Amazonas* (Music for the film *Green
  Mansions*) (*See*: W551)
Poetry by Dora Vasconcellos
Dedicated to Mindinha
Also for voice and piano (*See*: W544)
Premiere: (Empire Music Festival) (This was Villa-Lobos
  last public appearance as a conductor prior to his
  death on 11/17/1959) Symphony of the Air; Elinor Ross,
  v; Villa-Lobos, cond; 7/12/1959
P. Robbins                                                    W545

## Canção do amor
Voice and orchestra; 5 min.
Two fl, eng hn, cl, b cl, s sax, 2 bn, cbn, 3 hn, timp,
  cel, guitar, solovox, harp and str
From *Floresta do Amazonas* (Music for the film *Green
  Mansions*) (*See*: W551)
Poetry by Dora Vasconcellos
Dedicated to Mindinha
Premiere: (Empire Music Festival) (This was Villa-Lobos
  last public appearance as a conductor prior to his
  death on 11/17/1959) Symphony of the Air; Elinor Ross,
  v; Villa-Lobos, cond; 7/12/1959
P. Robbins                                                    W546

## Cântico do Colégio Santo André
Voice and piano; 2 min.
Written at the request of Manuel Bandeira, author of the
  poem                                                       W547

## Ciranda das sete notas
Bassoon and piano; 12 min.
Dedicated to Mindinha
Original version for bassoon and string quintet (*See*:

W325)
Peer                                                              W548

## Fantasia concertante
Orchestra of cellos; 22 min.
To be performed by a minimum of 32 cellos
Written for the Violoncello Society
Premiere: New York, Town Hall; The Violoncello Society
  (32 cellists); Villa-Lobos, cond; December 1958
Eschig                                                           W549

## Fantasia em três movimentos (em forma de choros)
Orchestra; 20 min.
Two pic, 6 fl, 6 ob, 2 eng hn, s E-flat cl, a E-flat cl,
  6 cl in B-flat, b cl, contrabass cl, 6 bn, 2 cbn, 6 hn,
  3 tpt in B-flat, 2 tpt in C, Flugelhorn, 4 trbn, 2 bass
  trbn, tuba, timp, t-t, cymbals, cho, pan, basque drum,
  province drum, castanets, coco, ca clara, tri, mat,
  bomb, xyl, vibraphone, cel, harp, pf (ad libitum) and
  two db
Commissioned by the American Wind Symphony
Dedicated to Mindinha
Premiere: Pittsburgh, PA; American Wind Symphony;
  R. Boudreau, cond; 2/26/1958                                   W550

## Floresta do Amazonas
Orchestra, soloist, and male chorus; 90 min.
Pic, 2 fl, 2 ob, eng hn, 2 cl, b cl, a sax, s sax, 2 bn,
  cbn, 4 hn, 4 tpt, 4 trbn, tuba, timp, t-t, cho, tri,
  cymb, reco, pan, coco, t-t, bomb, mat, tamb, Indian
  drum, ca clara, sleigh bells, small bells, marimba,
  xyl, vibraphone, cel, harp, guitar, solovox, pf and str
Ordered by M.G.M. for the film *Green Mansions*, based on
  a novel by W.H. Hudson. The film included excerpts from
  the original work. The original includes songs with
  poems by Dora Vasconcellos: *Cair da tarde, Canção do
  amor, Melodia sentimental,* and *Veleiros*
*Cair da tarde* arranged for voice and piano (*See*: W544),
  and voice and orchestra (*See*: W545)
*Canção do amor* arranged for voice and orchestra (*See*:
  W546)
*Melodia sentimental* arranged for voice and piano (*See*:
  W556) and voice and orchestra (*See*: W555)
*Veleiros* arranged for voice and piano (*See*: W560), voice

and orchestra (See: W561) and voice and 2 guitars (See:
W562)
Premiere: (excerpts) Rio, Teatro Municipal; Orchestra and
Chorus of the Teatro Municipal; Maria Lúcia Godoy, s;
Mário Tavares, cond; 11/21/1969                                    W551

**Francette e Piá**
Orchestra; 22 min.
Pic, fl, ob, cl, bn, 2 hn, tpt, trbn, timp, coco, t-t,
   basque drum, provence drum, reco, bomb, ca clara, cymb,
   mat, tri, small bells, cho, cel, harp and str
Story of a small Indian boy who went to France and met a
   little French girl
*Piá veio a Franca* (Piá came to France)
*Piá viu Francette* (Piá saw Francette)
*Piá falou a Francette* (Piá spoke to Francette)
*Piá e Francette brincam* (Piá and Francette play
   together)
*Francette ficou zangada* (Francette is angry)
*Francette ficou triste* (Francette is sad)
*Piá voltou da guerra* (Piá returns from the war)
*Francette ficou contente* (Francette is happy)
*Francette e Piá brincam para sempre* (Francette and Piá
   play together for ever)
Original for piano (See: W237)
Dedicated to the precocious students of Marguerite Long
Premiere: Rio; Orquestra Sinfônica Nacional of the Rádio
   Ministério da Educação e Cultura; Alceu Bocchino, cond;
   11/23/1961
Eschig                                                             W552

**Magnificat aleluia**
Soloist, mixed choir and orchestra; 12 min.
Pic, 2 fl, 2 ob, 2 cl, 2 bn, cbn, 2 hn, tpt, trbn, tuba,
   timp, org and str
Also for soloist, mixed choir and organ (See: W554)
Premiere: Rio, Teatro Municipal; Associação de Canto
   Coral; Orquestra Sinfônica Brasileira; Edoardo de
   Guarnieri, cond; 11/8/1958
Eschig                                                             W553

**Magnificat aleluia**
Soloist, mixed choir and organ;12 min.
Written at the invitation of the Italian Association of

Santa Cecilia
Offered to Pope Pius XII in honor of the year of Lourdes
Original for soloist, mixed choir and orchestra (*See*: W553)
Eschig                                                                 W554

## Melodia sentimental
Voice and orchestra; 3 min.
Pic, 2 fl, 2 ob, eng hn, 2 cl, sax, b cl, 2 bn, cbn,
  4 hn, 3 tpt, 4 trbn, tuba, timp, harp and str
From *Floresta do Amazonas* (Music for the film *Green
  Mansions*) (*See*: W551)
Poetry by Dora Vasconcellos
Dedicated to Mindinha
Arranged for voice and piano (*See*: W556)
Premiere: (Empire Music Festival) (This was Villa-Lobos
  last public appearance as a conductor prior to his
  death on 11/17/1959) Symphony of the Air; Elinor Ross,
  v; Villa-Lobos, cond; 7/12/1959
P. Robbins                                                          W555

## Melodia sentimental
Voice and piano; 3 min.
From *Floresta do Amazonas* (*See*: W551)
Poetry by Dora Vasconcellos
Dedicated to Mindinha
Also for voice and orchestra (*See*: W555)
P. Robbins                                                          W556

## Sete vezes
Voice and orchestra; 2 min.
Two fl, 2 ob, eng hn, 2 cl, b cl, 2 bn, cbn, 2 hn, 2 tpt,
  2 trbn, tuba, timp, harp and str
Poetry by Dora Vasconcellos
Dedicated to Blanca Bouças
Premiere: Rio; Orquestra da Rádio Nacional, Cristina
  Maristany, v; R. Vareto, cond; 1/29/1962
Eschig                                                                 W557

## Sete vezes
Voice and piano; 2 min.
Poetry by Dora Vasconcellos
Dedicated to Blanca Bouças
Premiere: Rio; Assis Pacheco, v; 6/2/1960
Eschig                                                                 W558

**Terezinha de Jesus**
Guitar; 2 min.
Transcription by E. Pujol
Original for piano (from *Cirandas, See*: W220)
Eschig                                                                                    W559

**Veleiros**
Voice and piano; 2 min.
From *Floresta do Amazonas* (Music for the film *Green
Mansions*) (*See*: W551)
Poetry by Dora Vasconcellos
Dedicated to Mindinha
Also for voice and orchestra (*See*: W561) and voice
and 2 guitars (*See*: W562)                                                      W560

**Veleiros**
Voice and orchestra; 2 min.
Pic, 2 fl, ob, eng hn, 2 cl, b cl, s sax, 2 bn, cbn,
4 hn, 4 tpt, 4 trbn, tuba, timp, xyl, cel, harp, pf,
and str
From *Floresta do Amazonas* (Music for the film *Green
Mansions*) (*See*: W551)
Poetry by Dora Vasconcellos
Dedicated to Mindinha
Arranged for voice and piano (*See*: W560) and voice and
2 guitars (*See*: W562)
Premiere: (Empire Music Festival) (This was Villa-Lobos
last public appearance as a conductor prior to his
death on 11/17/1959) Symphony of the Air; Elinor Ross,
v; Villa-Lobos, cond; 7/12/1959                                              W561

**Veleiros**
Voice and two guitars; 2 min.
From *Floresta do Amazonas* (Music for the film *Green
Mansions*) (*See*: W551)
Poetry by Dora Vasconcellos
Dedicated to Mindinha
Also for voice and piano (*See*: W560) and voice and
orchestra  (*See*: W561)                                                         W562

**1958-1959**

**Modinhas e canções** (Album no. 2)
Voice and orchestra; 4 min.

*Pobre peregrino*
*Nésta rua*
*Manda tiro, tiro lá*
Pic, 2 fl, 2 ob, eng hn, 2 cl, b cl, 2 bn, cbn, 2 hn, 2
tpt, trbn, tuba, timp, cymbals, triangle, harp and str
Based on popular children's themes
Eschig                                                          W563

## 1959

**Canção do poeta do século XVIII**
Voice and orchestra; 2 min.
Two fl, 2 cl, 2 bn, 3 hn, 2 trbn, tuba, timp, harp and
str
Poetry by Alfredo Ferreira
Dedicated to Cristina Maristany
Premiere: Rio, Teatro Municipal, Orquestra Sinfônica
Brasileira; Cristina Maristany, soloist; Eleazar de
Carvalho, cond; 11/10/1962
Southern                                                        W564

**Concerto grosso**
Woodwind ensemble; 22 min.
(Concertino) fl, ob, cl, bn; (Ripieno) 2 pic, 5 fl, 5 ob,
6 eng hn, 5 cl, a cl, 2 b cl, contrabass cl, 5 bn, 2
cbn, 6 hn, 3 tpt in B-flat, 2 tpt in C, 2 fluegelhorns,
4 trbn, 2 bass trbn, tuba, timp, t-t, cho, reco, drum,
tri, tamb, cymb, xyl, cel, harp and 2 db
Commissioned by the American Wind Symphony
Dedicated to Mindinha
Premiere: Pittsburgh; American Wind Symphony; R.
Boudreau, cond; 7/4/1959
Peters                                                          W565

**I Suite for Chamber Orchestra**
Chamber Orchestra; 14 min.
*Abertura* (Allegro)
*Pitoresco* (Poco andantino, quasi animato)
*Uma fuga para brincar* (Allegro)
*Pastoral*
*Dança*
Two fl, 2 ob, 2 cl, 2 bn, 2 hn, 2 tpt, 2 trbn, tuba,
timp, and str
Written at the suggestion of an American editor for

American university students as an exercise in writing
for different solo instruments
Dedicated to Mindinha
Premiere: Rio, Teatro Municipal; Orquestra Sinfônica
Brasileira; João de Souza Lima, cond; 11/21/1960
Eschig                                                    W566

**II Suite for Chamber Orchestra**
Chamber orchestra; 16 min.
  *Lamento* (Andante cantabile)
  *Scherzo* (Vivace)
  *Passeio* (Promenade) Andantino quasi Allegretto
  *Canção lírica* (Poco Moderato)
  *Macumba* (Evocation of the spirits)
Two fl, 2 ob, 2 cl, 2 bn, 2 hn, 2 tpt, 2 trbn, tuba, timp
  and str
Written at the suggestion of an American editor for
  American university students as an exercise in writing
  for solo instruments
Premiere: Rio, Teatro Municipal; Orquestra Sinfônica
  Brasileira; João de Souza Lima, cond; 11/21/1960
Eschig                                                    W567

# Additional Works

Villa Lobos' lifestyle made it difficult if not impossible for scholars to make a complete list of his works. He wrote music "by necessity", at a feverish pace, leaving many works incomplete. Friends have said that he frequently would begin a composition, write a few measures, and subsequently begin a totally new work, leaving the earlier composition unfinished. An added difficulty to any attempt to compile a complete list of works is the fact that many fragments and completed compositions have been lost. Even works which were planned but never written seem to have found their way into various lists of works. The most common solution to this problem is for scholars to provide a "representative" rather than complete list of works. The works listed under Works and Performances in this book are works which were either published, or works in manuscript for which there is reliable confirmation that the works were completed. Works listed in this section are representative of a large body of incomplete, fragmentary works, or works for which no date could be established.

**Bachianas brasileiras no.2**
Cello and piano
  *Prelúdio*
  *Ária*
  *Dansa*
Dedicated to Mindinha
Original for orchestra (*See*: W247)                                W568

**Bachianas brasileiras no.2**
Piano
  *Dansa*
Original for orchestra (*See*: W247)                                W569

**Cabocla do Caxangá** (Embolada do Norte)
  Soloist and four part mixed chorus
  From *Canções típicas brasileiras* (*See*: W159)
  Melody and text by Catulo da Paixão Cearense                 W570

**Canção da folha morta**
  Chorus and orchestra
  Fl, ob, cl in A, a sax, bn, 3 hn, trbn, timp, t-t, bass
    drum, piano, and strings                                   W571

**Canção dos caçadores de esmeraldas**
  Voice and piano; 3 min.
  Original version for two part chorus written in 1940
    (*See*: W414)                                              W572

**Cantiga boêmia**
  Orchestral transcription by Villa-Lobos
  Premiere 8/19/1921                                           W573

**Ciranda das sete notas**
  Voice and piano
  Original for bassoon and string quintet (*See*: W325)        W574

**Distribuição de flores**
  Transcription for female chorus
  Also for flute and guitar (*See*: W381)                      W575

**Gueixas**
  This title appears in several catalogs as a result of
    the fact that *Japonesa* W15 was frequently referred to
    by the composer as Gueixas                                 W576

**Izaht**
  Oratorio version of the opera (*See*: W055)
  Preformed in 1940                                            W577

**Lenda árabe**
  This title appears in several catalogs, and is the
    original title given by Villa-Lobos for *Canção
    árabe* W73                                                 W578

**Marcha religiosa no. 6** (1918)
  Premiere  12/5/1925                                          W579

**Motivos gregos**
Flute, guitar, and female chorus
Premiere: Rio, Teatro Municipal, Antonio Maria Passos,
Passos, fl; João Teixeira Guimarães, guitar;
Chorus of the Technical High School of Paulo de
Frontim; and choreography by Mario Queiroz, 11/13/1937    W580

**Na Bahia tem**
Four part male chorus; 3 min.
Also for band (*See*: W297); chorus and band (*See*: W577)
and voice with piano or instrumental accompaniment
(*See*: Collections, G.P. #12)
Published by the Conservatório de Canto Orfeônico as
*Partituras de banda*    W581

**Na Bahia tem**
Chorus and band, 3 min.
Also for band (*See*: W297); four part male chorus (*See*:
W576) and voice with piano or instrumental
accompaniment (*See*: Collections, G.P. #12)
Published by the Conservatório de Canto Orfeônico as
*Partituras de banda*    W582

**Oração ao diabo**
Orchestral transcription by Villa-Lobos
Premiere 8/19/1921    W583

**Pierrot**
Orchestral transcription by Villa-Lobos    W584

**Quadrilha de roça**
Piano; 10 minutes
Original version possibly for other instruments
Based on popular children's songs    W585

**Redondilhas de Anchieta**
Three part chorus; 2 min.    W586

**Suíte oriental**
This title appears in several catalogs. Villa-Lobos
wrote a *Canto oriental* (W124) which he either expanded
to a suite and the manuscript was lost, or else was
never written    W587

**Suíte pitoresca**
   (Fragment only)
   Piano and orchestra
   Two fl, 2 ob, 2 b cl, 2 bn, 2 hn, 2 tpt, 2 trbn, tuba,
      timp, ca, harp and str                                    W588

**Trovas**
   Orchestral transcription by Villa-Lobos                      W589

**Viva a nossa América**
   Two part a cappella chorus; 1 min.                           W590

**Xangô**
   Voice, eng hn, bn, 2 hn, tpt, trbn, timp, bomb, pf (or
      harp) and str
   From *Canções típicas brasileiras* (*See*: W158 & W159)      W591

**Yerma** (Opera)
   Voice, chorus and piano reduction
   Original for soloist, chorus, and orchestra (*See*: 528)     W592

ERRATA

During the preparation of this book, research into the life and works of Villa-Lobos continues, and the following information arrived too late for inclusion in the original Works and Performances list:

**Louco**
   The original score is an orchestral version of 1917. The
   dates 1913 and 1914 are incorrect in the Works and
   Performances list                                           W060 and
                                                               W079

**Grande concerto para violoncello e orquestra**
   First performance in 1919, not 1918                         W095

**Sonata no. 2 for cello and piano**
   First performance in 1916, not 1918                         W103

**Descobrimento do Brasil** (3d Suite)
   First performance in 1942, not 1946                         W379

# Collections

Villa-Lobos at one point indicated his intention to publish all melodies which he had collected during his travels in a six volume orpheonic collection entitled: *Guia prático* (A Practical Guide). The collections was planned for the purpose of providing a complete guide to musical and artistic education in the public schools in a nation-wide program of musical education. His plan of organization for the collections was as follows:

> Volume One (in two parts):  Musical Entertainment
> (Popular children's songs to be sung by Brazilian
> children)
>
> Volume Two:  Civic-Musical Songs
> (National, foreign, school,and patriotic songs)
>
> Volume Three:  Artistic Entertainment
> (National and foreign school songs)
>
> Volume Four:  Folk Music
> (Indian melodies, melodies of mixed racial origin,
> African melodies, American melodies, common
> universal melodies)
>
> Volume Five:  For free choice of students
> (Music selected with the goal of permitting observation
> of progress in temperament and artistic taste as
> demonstrated in the choices made by the student, or
> music used for this type of educational purpose)

Volume Six:  Artistic-Musical
(Liturgical, classic and secular, foreign, national and
other available types of music)

Villa-Lobos never completed the ambitious six-volume collection he had outlined. One volume of children's songs with the title *Guia prático* (First Volume) was published with 137 melodies collected mostly in the public schools. Two published volumes with the title *Canto orfeônico,* contained 86 additional arrangements by Villa-Lobos of  marches, and songs of civic, and folk character for use in public school music instruction. Two volumes of solfeggios and one volume of simple religious songs, *Música sacra*, complete the published collections of songs for "orpheonic singing."

Eleven volumes of published piano pieces, also entitled *Guia prático*, represent a selection of piano pieces based on the melodies in the orpheonic collections. The melodies in the orpheonic  collections were also a rich source of inspiration for Villa-Lobos in many of his later works. The contents of the published orpheonic collections is as follows:

**GUIA PRATICO** (1932)
*ESTUDO FOLCLORICO MUSICAL*
Volume I
FIRST PART

No.1    **Acordei de madrugada** (1st version)
        Two voices

No.2    **Acordei de madrugada** (2nd version)
        Piano solo

No.3    **A agulha**
        Two voices

No.4    **Ainda não comprei**
        Three part chorus

No.5    **Anda à roda** (1st version)
        Two voices

No.6    **Anda à roda** (2nd version)
        Two voices

No.7    **Anda à roda** (3rd version)
        Piano solo

No.8    **O anel**
        Two part chorus

No.9    **Anquinhas**
        Two voices
        In the rhythm of a Habanera

No.10   **Atché**
        Two part chorus
        Chorus and piano or instrumental group

No.11   **Ba-be-bi-bo-bu**
        Text with piano accompaniment

No.12   **Na Bahia tem**
        Two or three part chorus with piano or
            instrumental group

No.13   **Bam-ba-la-lão** (Senhor Capitão) (Oferta da criança à lua)
        Two voices

No.14   **O bastão ou Mia gato**
        Voice with piano or instrumental group, or piano solo

No.15   **Bela pastora**
        Voice with piano or instrumental group, or piano solo

No.16   **Besuntão da lagoa**
        Two part chorus

No.17   **Brinquedo** (Olhe aquela menina)
        Voice with piano or instrumental group, or piano solo

No.18   **Cachorrinho**
        Voice with piano or instrumental group, or piano solo

No.19   **Cai, cai, balão** (Vem ca, Bitu)
        Two part chorus

No.20   **O café**
Two part chorus

No.21   **Canário**
Two part chorus

No.22   **Candieiro**
Two part chorus

No.23   **A canoa virou**
Two voices

No.24   **Canoinha nova**
Two part chorus

No.25   **A cantiga de ninar**
Two voices

No.26   **A cantiga de roda** (As bonecas)
Two part chorus

No.27   **Capelinha de melão**
Two part chorus, also voice with piano or
instrumental group

No.28   **Carambola**
Voice with piano, instrumental group, or piano solo

No.29   **Carangueijo** (The Crab, 1st version)
Voice with piano, instrumental group, or piano solo

No.30   **Carangueijo** (The Crab, 2nd version)
Two part chorus

No.31   **Carneirinho, carneirão**
Voice with piano, instrumental group, or piano solo

No.32   **O castelo**
Unison chorus; also voice with piano or
instrumental group, or piano solo

No.33   **A praia** (Chamados para brinquedos de roda)
(Calls for round dance games)

No.34    **Chora, menina, chora**
         Three part chorus; voice with piano or
         instrumental group; or piano solo

No.35    **Ó ciranda, ó cirandinha**
         Voice with piano, instrumental group, or piano solo

No.36    **A cobra e a rolinha**
         Two voices

No.37    **Có-có-có**
         Three part chorus

No.38    **As conchinhas**
         Two voices

No.39    **Condessa**
         Voice with piano or instrumental group

No.40    **Constante**
         Voice with piano or instrumental group, or piano solo

No.41    **Constância**
         Voice with piano or instrumental group, or piano solo

No.42    **O corcunda**
         Voice with piano or instrumental group, or piano solo

No.43    **Na corda da viola**
         Voice with piano or instrumental group, or piano solo

No.44    **A cotia**
         Voice with piano or instrumental group

No.45    **O cravo brigou com a rosa** (1st version)
         Two part chorus ad libitum; voice with
         piano or instrumental group

No.46    **O cravo brigou com a rosa** (2nd version)
         Two part chorus

No.47    **A dansa da carranquinha** (1st version of the Anquinhas)
         Unison chorus

No.48   **De flor em flor**
Three part chorus; voice with piano or
instrumental group, or piano solo

No.49   **Entrei na roda**
Two part chorus

No.50   **Os escravos de Jó**
Three part chorus

No.51   **Ficarás sózinha** (Fui no Itoróró)
Voice

No.52   **Formiguinhas**
Two part chorus

No.53   **A freira**
Voice with piano or instrumental group

No.54   **Fui no Itoróró** (1st version)
One or two part chorus; also for voice with piano
or instrumental group

No.55   **Fui no Itoróró** (2nd version)
Voice with piano; instrumental group or piano solo

No.56   **Fui passar na ponte** (Na Baia tem) (2nd version)
Two part chorus

No.57   **No fundo do meu quintal**
Voice with piano accompaniment

No.58   **Garibaldi foi à missa**
Voice with piano or instrumental group or piano solo

No.59   **A gatinha parda** (Popular childrens song) (1st version)
Two part chorus

No.60   **A gatinha parda** (2nd version)
Two voices

No.61   **O gato**
Voice with piano or instrumental group

No.62    **Hei de namorar**
           Four voices

No.63    **Espanha**
           Voice with piano or instrumental group or piano solo

No.64    **Higiene**
           Two part chorus

No.65    **No jardim celestial**
           Two part chorus
           Voice with piano, instrumental ensemble or piano solo

No.66    **João Cambuête**
           Voice with piano or instrumental group

No.67    **Laranjeira pequenina**
           Voice with piano or instrumental group or piano solo

No.68    **O limão** (1st version)
           Voice with piano or instrumental group or piano solo

No.69    **O limão** (2nd version)
           Three part chorus; also voice with piano or
             instrumental group

No.70    **Lindas laranjas**
           Two part chorus

No.71    **Machadinha**
           Voice with piano or instrumental group or piano solo

No.72    **A Mamãe estava doente**
           Voice with piano or instrumental group

No.73    **Manda tiro, tiro lá**
           Voice with piano or instrumental group or piano solo

No.74    **Manquinha**
           Voice with piano or instrumental group or piano solo

No.75    **Na mão direita** (2nd version)
           Three voices

No.76    **A maré encheu**
Voice with piano or instrumental group or piano solo

No.76a   **A maré encheu**
Unison chorus

No.77    **Margarida**
Two part chorus; also for voice with piano or
instrumental group, or piano solo

No.78    **Mariquita muchacha** (or As Mariquitas)
Voice with piano or instrumental group or piano solo

No.79    **Meninas, o' meninas**
Voice with piano or instrumental group or piano solo

No.80    **Meu benzinho**
Three part chorus

No.81    **Meu pai amarrou meus olhos**
Piano (text included)

No.82    **Nésta rua** (Esta noite)
Two part chorus

No.83    **Nigue ninhas**
Two voices

No.84    **Olha o bicho**
Two or three part chorus; also for voice with
piano or instrumental group, or piano solo

No.85    **Olha o passarinho domine**
Piano (text included)

No.86    **Padre Francisco**
Four part chorus

No.87    **Pai Francisco** (1st version)
Voice with piano or instrumental group

No.88    **Pai Francisco** (2nd version)
Voice with piano or instrumental group or piano solo

No.89    **Passe, passe gavião** (Lá na ponte de Vinhaça)
Voice with piano or instrumental group or piano solo

No.90    **Passarás, não passarás**
Voice with piano, instrumental ensemble or
piano solo

No.91    **O pastorzinho**
Two part chorus ad libitum; also for voice with
piano, instrumental ensemble or piano solo

No.92    **O pescador da barquinha**
Two voices or two part chorus

No.93    **O pião**
Voice with piano or instrumental group or piano solo

No.94    **Pintor de Cannahy**
Two part chorus

No.95    **Pirolito** (or Fiorito)
Voice with piano or instrumental group

No.96    **Pobre cega** (1st version)
Three part chorus

No.97    **Pobre cega** (2nd version)
Two part chorus

No.98    **O pobre e o rico**
Voice with piano or instrumental group or piano solo

No.99    **Pobre peregrino**
Voice with piano or instrumental group

No.100    **Pombinha, rolinha** (Brinquedo de roda)
Voice with piano or instrumental group

No.101    **Os pombinhos**
Two part chorus

No.102    **Os pombinhos** (2nd version)
Voice with piano or instrumental group or piano solo

No.103   **A pombinha voou**
   Voice with piano or instrumental group or piano solo

No.104   **Lá na ponte da vinhaça** (Passa, passa gavião)
   Two part chorus

No.105   **Quando eu era pequenino**
   Voice and piano, instrumental ensemble or piano solo

No.106   **Quantos dias tem o mês?**
   Two part chorus

No.107   **Que lindos olhos**
   One or two part chorus; also for voice with piano
      or instrumental group

No.108   **Rosa amarela** (1st version)
   Voice with piano or instrumental group or piano solo

No.109   **Rosa amarela** (2nd version)
   Two part chorus; also for voice with piano or
      instrumental group

No.110   **A roseira** (1st version)
   Three part a cappella chorus

No.111   **A roseira** (2nd version)
   Wind quintet or piano solo

No.112   **Samba-le-lê**
   Voice with piano or instrumental group or piano solo

No.113   **Sapo jururú**
   Two part chorus

No.114   **Senhora Dona Sancha** (1st version)
   Voice with piano or instrumental group or piano solo

No.115   **Senhora Dona Sancha** (2nd version)
   Unison a cappella chorus

No.116   **Senhora Dona Sancha** (3rd version)
   Unison a cappellachorus

No.117 **Senhora Dona Viúva** (2nd version)
Two part chorus; also for voice with piano or
instrumental group

No.118 **Senhora Dona Viúva** (Viuvinha)
Three voices

No.119 **O sim**
One or two part chorus; voice with piano or
instrumental group or piano solo

No.120 **Sinh' Aninha**
Voice with piano or instrumental group

No.121 **Sôdade**
Two voices

No.122 **Sonho de uma criança**
Voice with piano or instrumental group or piano solo

No.123 **Terezinha de Jesus**
Two part chorus

No.124 **Uma, duas angolinhas**
Three part chorus

No.125 **Vai abóbora!**
Voice with piano or instrumental group or piano solo

No.126 **Vamos atrás da serra, Oh! Calunga!**
Three part chorus; also for voice with piano or
instrumental group, or piano solo

No.127 **Vamos, maninha** (2nd version)
Two part chorus

No.128 **Vamos, Maruca**
Three part chorus; also for voice with piano or
instrumental group, or piano solo

No.129 **A velha que tinha nove filhas**
Voice with piano or instrumental group or piano solo

No.130 **Vem cá, siriri**
One part chorus; also for voice with piano or
instrumental group, or piano solo

No.131 **Vestidinho branco**
Voice with piano or instrumental group or piano solo

No.132 **Vida formosa**
Voice with piano or instrumental group

No.133 **Vitú**
Two part chorus; also for voice with piano, or
popular instrumental group

No.134 **Viuvinha da banda d'além**
Two part chorus

No.135 **Viva o carnaval**
Two voices with rhythmic effects

No.136 **Você diz que sabe tudo**
Voice with piano or instrumental group

No.137 **Xô! Passarinho**
Voice with piano or instrumental group

**CANTO ORFEONICO**
Volume One
(1937)

No.1 **Meus brinquedos** (School song) (1935)
Two part children's voices; 1 minute
Music by Júlia Dickie, arranged by Villa-Lobos
Anonymous text

No.2 **Vamos crianças** (1932)
Three part children's voices; 1 minute
Popular theme arranged by Villa-Lobos

No.3 **Vamos companheiros** (March) (1935)
Two part children's voices; 1 minute
School song, arranged by Villa-Lobos
Text from the book *Alvorada* by Fabiano Lozano

No.4    **Carneirinho de algodão** (Kindergarden song) (1934)
        Two part children's voices; 1 minute
        Music by Villa-Lobos
        Text by Sylvio Salema

No.5    **Soldadinhos** (March movement, School song) (1935)
        Two part children's voices; 1 minute
        Music by Sylvio Salema, arranged by Villa-Lobos
        Text by Narbal Fontes

No.6    **A jangada** (March movement) (1941)
        Two part children's voices; 1 minute
        Melody and text by Henriqueta M. de Abreu
        Arranged by Villa-Lobos

No.7    **Marcha escolar** (Cantiga, My Little Frog) (1933)
        Two part children's voices; 1 minute
        Melody and text by Sylvio Salema
        Arranged by Villa-Lobos

No.8    **Marcha escolar** (Returning from Recess) (1933)
        Two part a cappella chorus; 1 minute
        Music by Villa-Lobos under the pseudonym E. Villalba Filho
        Text by Catarina Santoro

No.9    **Marcha escolar** (Going to Recess)
        Two part children's voices; 1 minute
        Anonymous music and text
        Arranged by Villa-Lobos

No.10   **Marcha escolar** (A Walk)
        Two part children's voices; 1 minute
        Anonymous music and text
        Arranged by Villa-Lobos

No.11   **Marcha escolar** (Vocalization) (1940)
        Two part children's voices; 1 minute
        Vocalization to develop march rhythms in different meters

No.12   **Canção escolar**
        Two part children's voices; 1 minute
        Music by Assis Pacheco
        Dedicated to Alberto Barth
        Anonymous text

No.13    **Canção cívica do Rio de Janeiro**
         Three voice children's voices
         Music by Ernesto Nazareth
         Text by Leoncio Corrêa

No.14    **Meu Brasil** (Samba,1935)
         Unison voices, piano and percussion; 2 minutes
         Melody by Ernani Silva, seller of newspapers,
             popular samba school composer, music arranged by
             Villa-Lobos
         Text by Alberto Ribero
         Premiere: Rio de Janeiro; chorus of 25,000 school
             children accompanied by bands from Fire
             Dept., Navy, Police and Army bands.
             Percussionist from various Samba schools
             (Escolas de samba) 7/7/1935;

No.15    **Brasil unido** (Patriotic song)
         Two part children's voices
         Music by Plinio de Brito
         Text by Domingos Magarinos

No.16    **Regozijo de uma raça** (1937)
             *I. Canto africano*
             *II. Canto mestiço*
         Unison a cappella voices
         Transcribed for mixed chorus, tenor soloist and
             percussion (*See*: W387)

No.17    **Canção do norte** (to Ceará) (1932)
         Two part children's voices; 2 minutes
         Music by A. Nepomuceno, arranged by Villa-Lobos
         Text by Thomas Lopes

No.18    **Brasil novo** (1922)
         Four part mixed chorus, piano and percussion
         3 minutes
         Transcribed for chorus and orchestra (*See*: W185),
             and band (*See*: W186)

No.19    **O canto do pagé** (1933)
         Four part female or children's a cappella voices;
             3 minutes
         Text by C. Paula Barros

Based on primitive music of aborigenal Brazilians
with rhythmical fragments of Spanish popular
music
Also for band (*See*: W324)

No.20 **Cantar para viver** (1933)
Two part children's voices; 1 minute
Text by Sylvio Salema
Music by Villa-Lobos

No.21 **Desfile aos heróis do Brasil** (1936)
Three part children's voices; 3 minutes
Text by C. Paula Barros
Music by Villa-Lobos
Also for band (*See*: W367)

No.22 **Dia de alegria** (1933)
Two part children's voices ; 2 minutes .
Text by Catarina Santoro

No.23 **Heranças de nossa raça** (March song) (1934)
Two part children's voices; 3 minutes
Text by C. Paula Barros
Dedicated to Joaquim Francisco d'Almeida

No.24 **Meu país** (Brazilian Patriotic Song) (1919)
Soloist, five part mixed chorus; 2 minutes
Transcribed for chorus and orchestra (*See*: W149),
and chorus and band (*See*: W258)
Premiere: Rio de Janeiro, Teatro Municipal; chorus
and orchestra; Villa-Lobos, conductor

No.25 **Tiradentes** (Patriotic Song) (1938)
Soloist and five part mixed chorus; 2 minutes
Music by Villa-Lobos under the pseudonym E. Vilalba Filho
Text by Viriato Corrêa
Transcribed for chorus and orchestra (*See*: W403),
voice and piano (*See*: W409) and soloist, mixed
chorus and harpsichord (*See*: W410)

No.26 **Verde pátria** (Civic Song)
Five part mixed a cappella voices
Music by Francisco Braga
Text by Humberto de Campos

No.27    **Sertanejo do Brasil** (Samba Song) (1935)
Two part a cappella chorus; 3 minutes
Music and text by Clovis Carneiro, arranged by
Villa-Lobos
Transcribed for chorus and band (*See*: W401)
Premiere: Rio de Janeiro, Vasco da Gama stadium,
September 7, 1939; 30,000 students and 1,000
band musicians; Villa-Lobos, conductor

No.28    **O ferreiro** (Work Song) (1932)
(Canção de oficio - "Scherzo" for 2 voices)
Two part male a cappella voices; 1 minute
Music by D. R. Antolisei, arranged by Villa-Lobos

No.29    **Canto do lavrador** (1933)
Four part male, female, or mixed voices
Text by C. Paula Barros

No.30    **Canção do operário brasileiro** (1939)
Four part a cappella chorus; 2 minutes
Music by Villa-Lobos under the pseudonym E.
Villalba Filho
Text by Paulino Santos
Transcribed for chorus and band (*See*: W405)

No.31    **Canção do trabalho** (1932)
Four part a cappella chorus of male, female or
mixed voices; 2 minutes
Melody by Duque Bicalho, arranged by Villa-Lobos
Text by José Rangel
Premiere: Rio de Janeiro, September 3, 1932;
Orfeão de Professores do Distrito Federal;
Villa-Lobos, conductor

No.32    **Nozani-ná**
Solo voice or unison voices; 1 minute
Song of the Parecis Indians
Theme collected by Roquette Pinto, also included
in *Canções típicas brasileiras* (*See*: W158, W159)
Premiere: Rio de Janeiro, Teatro João Caetano,
June 20, 1934; Orfeão de Professores and
percussion; Julieta T. de Menezes, soloist

No.33    **Canção do marcineiro** (Work Song) (1932)
Two part male a cappella voices; 1 minute
Text by Villa-Lobos under pseudonym E. Vilalba
Filho
Written especially for the Brazilian professional
technical schools
Premiere: Rio de Janeiro, September 7, 1932;
Orfeão de Professores do Distrito Federal;
Villa-Lobos, conductor

No.34    **Canção da imprensa** (1940)
(Official song of the Brazilian Press Association)
Two part a cappella voices; 3 minutes
Text by Murillo Araújo
Transcribed for chorus and orchestra (*See*:
W413); and for band (*See*: W412)
Premiere: Rio de Janeiro, April 25, 1940; Orfeão
de Professores; Villa-Lobos, conductor

No.35    **Duque de Caxias** (Patriotic Song)
Solo or unison a cappella voices
Music by Fransisco de Paula Gomes
Text by D. Aquino Corrêa

No.36    **Deodoro** (Military Song)
Music by Francisco Braga
Text by Leôncio Corrêa

No.37    **Canção do artilheiro de costa**
Two part a cappella voices; 2 minutes
Music by Lieutenant Herminio P. Souza, arranged by
Villa-Lobos
Text by Colonel Luiz Lobo

No.38    **Mar do Brasil** (1938)
Unison voices with piano accompaniment; 2 minutes
Text by Sylvio Salema

No.39    **Alerta!** (Rataplan!)  (Boy Scout Song) (1937)
Two part a cappella chorus; 1 minute
Music and text by B. Cellini,
Arranged by Villa-Lobos

No.40   **Saudação a Getúlio Vargas** (1938)
Four part voices with accompaniment; 1 minute
Transcribed for chorus and orchestra (*See*: W400)
Premiere: Rio de Janeiro, September 7, 1939;
30,000 voices and 1,000 band musicians; Villa-
Lobos, conductor

No.41   **Canção dos artistas** (1919)
Five part mixed voices with piano accompaniment; 3
minutes
Text by Raul Pederneiras
Song of the Casa dos artistas, also called Hino do
Artista
Also for voice and piano under the title of Hino
dos Artistas (*See*: W147)

### CANTO ORFEONICO
Volume Two
(1951)

No.1   **Brincadeira de pegar** (1934)
Two part a cappella children's voices
Dedicated to Ernâni Braga and for the children of
Recife (*See*: W343)

No.2   **Esperança da mãe pobre** (1933)
Two part a cappella children's voices
Anonymous text
From an idea by Lygia P. Leite
Music by Heitor Villa-Lobos

No.3   **O balão do Bitu**
Two part a cappella children's voices
Text from popular songs
From the folk-melody "Vem cá Bitú"

No.4   **Repiu-piu-piu**
Two part a cappella chorus; 1 minute
Melody  by Tomas Borba, arranged by Villa-Lobos
Text by Affonso Lopes Vieira

No.5   **Minha terra tem palmeiras** (1935)
Two part a cappella chorus; 1 minute

Popular melody arranged by Villa-Lobos
Text by Gonçalves Dias

No.6    **O gaturamo** (1934)
Three part a cappella chorus; 1 minute
Melody by J. Carlos Dias, arranged by Villa-Lobos
Text by J. Pinto e Silva

No.7    **Cantiga de rede**
Three part children's voices
Music and text by A. Cardoso Machado, arranged by
Villa-Lobos
Can be performed in two parts

No.8    **Feliz aniversário** (Canção de cordialidade) (1945)
Three part a cappella children's voices
Text by Manuel Bandeira, music by Villa-Lobos
Also for orchestra (*See*: W450); voice and
orchestra (See: W451); and voice and piano (*See*:
W452)

No.9    **Boas-festas** (Canção de cordialidade) (1945)
Three part a cappella children's voices
Text by Manuel Bandeira, music by Villa-Lobos
Also for orchestra (*See*: W450); voice and
orchestra (See: W451); and voice and piano (*See*:
W452)

No.10   **Feliz natal** (Canção de cordialidade) (1945)
Two part a cappella children's voices
Text by Manuel Bandeira, music by Villa-Lobos
Also for orchestra (*See*: W450); voice and
orchestra (See: W451); and voice and piano (*See*:
W452)

No.11   **Feliz ano novo** (Canção de cordialidade) (1945)
Three part a cappella children's voices
Text by Manuel Bandeira
Also for orchestra (*See*: W450); voice and
orchestra (See: W451); and voice and piano (*See*:
W452)

No.12   **Boas-vindas** (Canção de cordialidade) (1945)
Four part mixed a cappella children's voices

Text by Manuel Bandeira, music by Villa-Lobos
Also for orchestra (*See*: W450); voice and
   orchestra (See: W451); and voice and piano (*See*:
   W452)

No.13   **Brasil** (Marcha)
Two part a cappella children's voices
Music by Thiers Cardoso, arranged by Villa-Lobos

No.14   **Canção do marinheiro** (1937)
Four part a cappella chorus; 2 minutes
Music by Antônio M. de Espirito Santo, arranged by
   Villa-Lobos
Text by Benidito Xavier de Macedo
*See*: W365, W406

No.15   **Mês de Junho** (1950)
Three part a cappella chorus; 1 minute
Popular children's melody (*Pobre céga,*
   Collections, GP #96), arranged by Villa-Lobos
Text by Thomé Brandão

No.16   **Aboios** (1935)
Two part a cappella chorus; 1 minute
Based on melodies  of the Amerindios-mestiços of
   the Amazon River area
Collected and adapted by Villa-Lobos

No.17   **Cântico do Pará** (War Song) (1935)
Three part a cappella chorus
Anonymous text
Collected and adapted by Villa-Lobos
*See*: W425

No.18   **Cantos do Çairé** No.1 (1941)
Two part a cappella female voices; 1 minute
Theme from Amazonian folklore
Arranged by Villa-Lobos

No.19   **Cantos do Çairé** No.2 (1941)
Three part female a cappella voices; 1 minute
Theme from Amazonian folklore

No.20     **Cantos do Çairé** No.3 (1941)
         Two part a cappella voices; 1 minute
         Theme from Amazonian folklore

No.21     **Evocação** (1941)
         Two part a cappella chorus, 1 minute
         Based on Indian themes of the Amazon River area

No.22     **Canidé Ioune-Sabath** (1933)
         (Ave Amarela) (Canto elegíaco)
         Six part mixed a cappella chorus; 2 minutes
         Based on an Brazilian Indian melody collected
         by Jean de Léry in the sixteenth century (*See*:
         W223, and W224)
         Premiere: Rio de Janeiro, June 20, 1934; Orfeão de
         Professores do Distrito Federal; Villa-Lobos,
         conductor

No.23     **Um canto que saiu das senzalas** (1933)
         Two part a cappella voices; 2 minutes
         Melody by blacks of the reconcavo baiano area,
         collected by Sodré Viana

No.24     **Xangô**(1933)
         Five part a cappella chorus; 2 minutes
         Macumba melody of an earlier epoch
         Premiere: Rio de Janeiro, June 20, 1934; Orfeão de
         Professores do Distrito Federal; Julieta Teles
         de Menezes, soloist; Villa-Lobos, conductor

No.25     **Santos Dumont** (The Conquest of Airspace)(1944)
         Three part a cappella voices; 1 minutes
         Music and text by Eduardo das Neves, arranged by
         Villa-Lobos

No.26     **Canção do pescador brasileiro** (1935)
         Three part a cappella voices; 1 minute
         Music by Eduardo Souto, arranged by Villa-Lobos
         Text by Bastos Tigre

No.27     **Marcha para oeste** (1937)
         Three part a cappella voices; 1 minute
         Music by Vicente Paiva, arranged by Villa-Lobos
         Text by J. Sá Roris

No.28      **A sanfona** (Cateretê à moda paulista)
           Four part a cappella chorus
           Music and text by Henriqueta M. d'Abreu, arranged
           by Villa-Lobos

No.29      **Quadrilha das estrelas no céu do Brasil** (Bailado
           cívico-artístico-folclórico) (1944)
           *No.1 Introdução*
           *No.2 Quadrilha brasileira*
           *No.3 Fui no Itoróró*
           *No.4 Cantiga de roda*
           *No.5 Anda à roda*
           Three (Two) part a cappella voices; 2 minutes
           Text by Manuel Bandeira
           Premiere: Rio de Janeiro, September 7, 1944;
           Villa-Lobos, conductor

No.30      **Juramento** (1942)
           Three soloists and four part a cappella chorus; 4
           minutes
           Text by Murilo de Araújo
           Premiere: Rio de Janeiro, Estádio Clube de Regatas
           Vasco da Gama, September 7, 1944; 25,000
           students, 500 instrumentalists; Villa-Lobos,
           conductor

No.31      **O trenzinho**
           Four part a cappella chorus
           Text by Catharina Santoro
           Also for three part a cappella chorus (*See*: W340)

No.32      **Pra frente, ó Brasil**  (Canção marcial) (1931)
           Four part female a cappella chorus; 3 minutes
           Text by Villa-Lobos under the pseudonym Zé Povo
           Premiere: São Paulo, May 24, 1931; 10,000 voices
           and 400 instrumentalists; Villa-Lobos, conductor

No.33      **As costureiras** (Embolada) (1932)
           Four part female a cappella chorus
           *See*: W329

No.34      **Pátria** (1932)
           Four part a cappella female voices; 4 minutes
           Text by F. Haroldo

Also  for male chorus and military drums (*See*:
W303) and mixed chorus and orchestra (*See*:
W348)

No.35   **Pátria** (Hino Orfeônico brasileiro) (1932)
Six part mixed a cappella chorus; 1 minute
Text by F. Haroldo
Dedicated to Orfeão de Professores do Distrito
Federal
Also  for male chorus and military drums (*See*:
W303) and mixed chorus and orchestra (*See*:
W348)
Premiere: Rio de Janeiro, Teatro João Caetano,
September 7, 1932; Orfeão de Professores do
Distrito Federal; Villa-Lobos, conductor

No.36   **Hino à vitória** (1941)
Four part a cappella chorus; 2 minutes
Text by Gustavo Capanema
Transcribed for chorus and band (*See*: W428)
and chorus and orchestra (*See*: W429)
Premiere: Rio de Janeiro, Estádio do Clube Regatas
do Vasco da Gama, September 7, 1943; 15,000
students; Villa-Lobos, conductor

No.37   **Estrela é lua nova** (1933)
Soloists and five part mixed a cappella chorus; 2
minutes
Macumba melody (*See*: W156 and W157)
Premiere: Rio de Janeiro, June 20, 1934; Orfeão de
Professores

No.38   **Jaquibáu** (1933)
Mezzo-soprano and tenor soloists, and six part
mixed a cappella voices; 3 minutes
Theme from Minas Gerais, during the era of slavery

No.39   **Bazzum** (1936)
Five part male a cappella chorus; 4 minutes
Text by Domingos Magarinos
Dedicated to Arminda Neves d'Almeida
Premiere: Rio de Janeiro, December 18, 1937;
Orfeão de Professores do Distrito Federal;
Villa-Lobos, conductor

No.40    **Vira** (1945)
Five part a cappella chorus; 4 minutes
Popular Portuguese melody
Collected and arranged by Villa-Lobos

No.41    **Na risonha madrugada** (1933)
Four or five part mixed a cappella chorus;
2 minutes
Music by Haydn, arranged by Villa-Lobos
Text by F. Haroldo
Also for four part female a cappella chorus
(*See*: W298)
Premiere: Rio de Janeiro, September 14, 1932;
Orfeão de Professores; Villa-Lobos, conductor

No.42    **O tamborzinho** (1932)
Four part mixed a cappella chorus; 2 minutes
Music by Rameau, arranged by Villa-Lobos
Portuguese text adapted by F. Haroldo
Also arranged for four part female a cappella
chorus (*See*: W312)

No.43    **Terra natal** (1932)
Four part mixed a cappella chorus; 1 minute
Music by Mozart, arranged by Villa-Lobos
Portuguese text adapted by Honorato Faustino
Also arranged for four part female a cappella
chorus (*See*: W313)

No.44    **Remeiro de São Francisco** (1934)
Soloist and six part mixed a cappella chorus with
optional piano accompaniment; 2 minutes
Song of mestiços of the São Francisco River area
of Bahia (*See*: W360)
Collected by Sodré Viana

No.45    **Invocação em defesa da pátria** (1943)
Soloist and four part a cappella chorus; 2
minutes
Text by Manuel Bandeira
Dedicated to Violeta Coelho Netto de Freitas
Also for soloist, chorus and orchestra (*See*:
W439)
Premiere: Rio de Janeiro, Estádio do Clube de

Regatas Vasco da Gama, September 7, 1943; 15,000
students; Violeta Coelho Netto de Freitas,
soloist; Villa-Lobos, conductor

## SOLFEJOS
### Volume I
### (1940)

40 One-part melodies

163 Two-part melodies

## SOLFEJOS
### Volume II
### (1946)

30 One-part melodies

25 Two-part melodies

6 Three-part melodies

2 Four-part melodies

2 Six-part melodies

Arrangements of various short works by Villa-Lobos
and other composers. The arrangements include both
short pieces with and without texts.

## MUSICA SACRA
### Volume I
### (1952)

No.1  **Ave Maria** (1916)
Two part a cappella chorus; 2 minutes
Canon in two voices
Text in Latin

No.2    **Ave Maria** (1918)
        Four part mixed chorus
        Text in Latin
        Programmed as *Ave Maria* No. 17 in the first
          performance, Rio, Teatro Municipal, Coral
          Ars Nova of the Federal University of Minas
          Gerais, Carlos Alberto Fonseca, cond 11/20/67

No.3    **Ave Maria** (1917)
        Four part female voices
        Text in Portuguese

No.4    **Ave Maria** (Reza) (1917)
        Four part mixed chorus
        Text in Latin

No.5    **Ave Maria** (1938)
        Five part mixed chorus
        Text in Portuguese

No.6    **Ave Maria** (1914)
        Four part mixed chorus
        Text in Latin

No.7    **Ave Maria** (1948)
        Six part mixed chorus
        Text in Latin
        Composed in New York

No.8    **Ave Maria** (Reza) (1917)
        Voice with piano or organ
        Text in Latin

No.9    **Ave Maria** (1914)
        Voice and string quartet
        Text in Portuguese

No.10   **Padre nosso** (1910)
        Four part mixed a cappella chorus; 2 minutes
        Text in Portuguese
        Vitale

No.11   **Padre nosso** (Prece) (1914)
        Voice and string quartet

Text in Portuguese
Also reduction for voice and organ

No.12 **Pater noster** (1950)
Four part mixed chorus
Text in Latin
Premiere: Rio, Teatro Municipal; Coral Ars Nova
of the Federal University of Minas Gerais,
Carlos Alberto Fonseca, cond; 11/20/67

No.13 **Tantum ergo** (1910)
Four part a cappella chorus; 2 min.
Text in Latin
Premiere: Rio de Janeiro, Teatro Municipal,
November 11, 1922; Schola Cantorum Santa
Cecilia; Canon Alpheo Lopes de Araújo, conductor

No.14 **Ave verum** (1930)
Four part mixed chorus
Text in Latin

No.15 **Sub tuum** (1952)
Four part mixed a cappella chorus
Dedicated to Mindinha
Text in Latin

No.16 **O cor Jesu** (1952)
Four part chorus
Text in Latin

No.17 **O salutaris** (1916)
Four part mixed chorus
Dedicated to Conego Alpheu
Text in Latin

No.18 **Cor dulce, cor amabile** (1952)
Four part mixed a cappella chorus
Dedicated to Julieta d'Almeida Strutt
Text in Latin

No.19 **Panis angelicus** (1950)
Four part mixed a cappella chorus
Dedicated to Mindinha
Text in Latin

No.20    **Hino à Santo Agostinho** (1952)
        Mixed chorus
        Official hymn for the Colegio Santo Agostinho,
          Leblon, Rio
        Text by Agostinofilo

No.21    **Praesepe** (1952)
        Soloist and a cappella chorus
        Dedicated to Mindinha
        Based on a text by Padre José de Anchieta (1563)
        Text in Latin

No.22    **Canto de natal**
        Three part chorus
        Text by Manoel Bandeira
        Text in Portuguese

No.23    **Preces sem palavras**
        Male a cappella chorus
        Dedicated to Clovis Martins de Camargo

# Discography

## *Directory of Record Companies*

The recordings listed are for the purpose of providing the scholar and musician interested in the music of Villa-Lobos with representative recordings of his works. The list is selective and represents only a fraction of the recordings to be found in major collections such as the tape and recordings collection of the Museu Villa-Lobos in Rio de Janeiro, the Latin American Music Center at Indiana University, Bloomington, Indiana; and the tapes of the Radiodiffusion Française. The selective discography includes recordings currently available, unavailable recordings of good quality, and a number of recordings originally issued as LP's and currently being released for the Villa-Lobos Centennial year in new CD recordings. The reader will note that in this list spellings for various works appear as listed on the record, and record catalogs. Spellings for compositions in the Works and Performances (W) list appear in the language used by the composer. Therefore Symphony No. 4 (D406) appears in the W list as *Sinfonia No. 4* (A Vitória) W153, and many other titles of works used by record companies will differ from the original title.

ANGEL RECORDS
1750 N. Vine St.
Hollywood, CA 90028

BIS & CLAVES
Qualiton Imports, Ltd.
39-28 Crescent St.
Long Island City, NY 11101

CBS RECORDS
51 West 52nd St.
New York, NY 10019

CALLIG VERLAG GmbH,
Landsberger Str.77
8000 Muunchen 2
West Germany
US Dist.: Audio Source
Foster City, CA

CENTAUR RECORDS
Box 23764
Baton Rouge, LA  70893

COLUMBIA SPECIAL PRODUCTS
51 W. 52nd St.
New York, NY  10019

CRYSTAL RECORDS
2235 Willida Lane
Sedro Wooley, WA  98284

DA CAMERA
Disco-Center
Vereinigte Schallplatten
Vertriebsges. mbH
Postfach 10 1029
3500 Kassel
West Germany

DESTO RECORDS
c/o CMS Records Inc.
226 Washington St.
Mount Vernon, NY  10553

DEUTSCHE GRAMMOPHON
Polygram Classics, Inc.
810 Seventh Ave.
New York, Ny  10019

EMI ELECTROLA GmbH
Maarweg 149
5000 Köln 30
West Germany

EDUCO RECORDS
P.O. Box 3006
Ventura, CA  93006

ELEKTRA/ASYLUM/NONESUCH RECORDS
75 Rockefeller Plaza
New York, NY  10019

FIRST EDITION RECORDS
609 W. Main St.
Louisville, KY  40202

GC GOLDEN CREST RECORDS
220 Broadway
Huntington Station, NY  11746

GASPARO RECORDS
Box 120069
Nashville, TN 37212

INTER-AMERICAN MUSICAL EDITIONS
Organization of American States (OAS)
1889 F St. NW
Washington, DC  20006

LYRICHORD RECORDS
141 Perry St.
New York, NY  10014

MNEMOSYNE RECORDS
c/o Titanic Records
P.O. Box 204
Somerville, MA  02144-0204

MVL (MUSEU VILLA-LOBOS)
Rua Sorocaba 200
Botafogo, Rio de Janeiro
20.000 Rio de Janeiro, Brazil

PAN VERLAG VLEUGELS
German News Co., Inc.
218 East 86th Street
New York NY 10028

POLYGRAM CLASSICS, INC.
810 Seventh Ave.
New York, NY  10019

RCA RECORDS
1133 Ave. of the Americas
New York, NY  10036

RAVENNA RECORDS
University of Washington Press
Box 85569
Seattle, WA  98195

RICERCAR
Mr. Jerôme Lejeune
Burnaumont, 73
B-6912  ANLOY-LIBIN
Belgium

SCHWANN MUSICA MUNDI
German News Company
218 E. 86th St.
New York, NY  10028

SPECTRUM
Uni-Pro Recordings
Harriman, NY  10926

TURNABOUT RECORDS
Moss Music Group
48 W. 38th St.
New York, NY  10018

VANGUARD RECORDS
71 W. 23rd St.
New York, NY  10010

WERGO
Harmonia Mundi USA
3364 S. Robertson Blvd.
Los Angeles, CA  90034

ZEPHYR
Schott Frères
Rue Saint-Jean, 30
1000 Brussels
Belgium

## The Catalog

**A procura de uma agulha** (From *Cirandas*)
CARAVELLE CAR 43007
O piano de Villa-Lobos
Arnaldo Estrella, pf
Includes his *Tristorosa;* Teresinha de Jesus, Senhora Dona
Sancha, Pobre cega, Vamos atrás da serra, Calunga, and
Fui no tororó from *Cirandas*; Pobrezinha from *A prole do
bebê no.1*; O gatinho de papelão, and O boizinho de
chumbo from *A prole do bebê no.2*; *Valsa da dor; Choros
no.5*; O pastorzinho, João Cambuetê, A freira, Garibaldi
foi à missa, and O pião from *Guia prático Album 3*; A
gaita de um precoce fantasiado from *Carnaval das
crianças*; Aria from *Bachianas brasileiras no.4*; and
Dança do índio branco from *Ciclo brasileiro*
*See*: W220                                                    D001

**Adeus Ema**
CLAVES D 8401
Teresa Berganza, mezzo; Juan Antonio Alvarez Parejo, pf
Includes his Viola quebrada, *Canção do poeta do século
XVIII*, *Samba clássico*, Desejo, and Xangô; and works by
Ernâni Braga, and Carlos Guastavino
*See*: W159                                                    D002

**Amazonas** (Bailado indígena brasileiro)
EMI/LA VOIX DE SON MAITRE 2 C 165-16250/9
L'oeuvre de piano
Anna Stella Schic, pf
Includes his *Guia prático, Tristorosa, Petizada,
Brinquedo de roda*, 1st and 2nd *Suíte infantil, Valsa-
Scherzo*, O gato e o rato, *Ondulando, Ibericarabé,
Danças características africanas, Suíte floral, Simples*

coletânea, Amazonas, A prole do bebê nos. 1 and 2,
Histórias da carochinha, Carnaval das crianças, A lenda
do caboclo, Bailado infernal, A fiandeira, Rudepoema,
Choros nos.1, 2, and 5 "Alma Brasileira", Sul-
América, Saudades das selvas brasileiras, Cirandinhas,
Cirandas, Francette et Pià, Caixinha de música
quebrada, Valsa da dor, Ciclo brasileiro, Poema
singelo, Bachianas brasileiras no.4, New York Skyline
Melody, Hommage à Chopin, As três Marias, and five
Preludes for guitar (piano transcription)
See: W119                                                               D003

**Assobio a jato**
CHANTECLER 2-08-404-088
Obras cameristicas brasileiras
Includes works by Sergio O. Vasconcellos Correa
See: W493                                                               D004

**Assobio a jato**
CID MEC/MVL-007
Concurso internacional de Conjuntos Instrumentais 1972
Sexteto do Rio
Includes his Choros no.2, Fantasia concertante; and
   Guerra-Peixe, Duo
See: W493                                                               D005

**Ave Maria**
TAPECAR GRAVAÇÕES MEC/MVL 024
I Concurso Internacional de Coro Misto
University of Texas Chamber Singers; Morris J. Beachy,
   cond
Includes his Fuga, Bendita sabedoria, Duas lendas
   ameríndias, Estrela é lua nova, Bazzum, and Jaquibáu;
   and works by Breno Blauth, Murillo Santos, Sergio
   Vasconcelos Correa, Marlos Nobre, and Frederico Richter     D006

**Ave Maria** (1918)
ENIR ECL-002
Coral Ars Nova (da Universidade Federal de Minas Gerais);
   Carlos Alberto Pinto da Fonseca, cond
Includes his Padre nosso, Ave verum, Pater noster,
   Bendita sabedoria, Duas lendas amerindias, and Panis
   angelicus; and Francisco Mignone, Sexta Missa              D007

**Ave verum**
ENIR ECL-002
Coral Ars Nova (da Universidade Federal de Minas Gerais);
Carlos Alberto Pinto da Fonseca, cond
For complete listing of contents see *Ave Maria* D007   D008

**Bachianas brasileiras no. 1**
ANGEL CDC-47433
Cellists of the Royal Philharmonic Orchestra; Enrique
Batiz, cond
Includes his *Bachianas brasileiras nos. 5 & 7*
*See*: W246   D009

**Bachianas brasileiras no. 1**
EMI 2 C 153-14090/9
Villa-Lobos par lui-même
Orchestre National de la Radiodiffusion Française; Villa-
Lobos, cond
Includes his *Bachianas brasileiras nos.1-9, Choros
nos.2, 5, 10 & 11, Deux Chôros (bis), Invocação em
defesa da pátria, Descobrimento do Brasil* (Suites 1-4),
*Symphony no.4* (A Vitória), *Momoprecoce, Concerto
no.5* for piano, and *A prole do bebê nos.1 & 2*
*See*: W246   D010

**Bachianas brasileiras no. 1**
FJA - 112 (MVL 30)
II Concurso Internacional de Violoncelo
Mário Tavares, cond
Includes his *Pequena suite, O canto do capadocio, O
trenzinho do caipira, Capriccio*, and *O canto do cisne
negro*
*See*: W246   D011

**Bachianas brasileiras no. 1**
GASPARO GS-222CX
Members of the National Philharmonic of England; Morris
Hochberg, cond
Includes Joaquin Turina, *La oracion del torero*;
Charles Mills, *Prologue and Dithyramb*
*See*: W246   D012

**Bachianas brasileiras no. 1**
MEC/MVL/FUNARTE - 016/1976

Associação dos Violoncelistas do Brasil
Includes his *Fantasia concertante*
*See*: W246                                                                D013

**Bachianas brasileiras no. 1**
MGM E3105
Ensemble of cellists; Theodore Bloomfield, cond
Includes his *Bachianas brasileiras no.4*
*See*: W246                                                                D014

**Bachianas brasileiras no. 1**
RCA LCT1143
Brazilian Festival Orchestra; Walter Burle Marx, cond
Includes his *Nonetto*, Canção do carreiro, and various
   songs performed by Elsie Houston
*See*: W246                                                                D015

**Bachianas brasileiras no. 1**
TAPECAR GRAVAÇÕES MEC/MVL 016
Associação dos Violoncelistas do Brasil
Includes his *Fantasia concertante* for orchestra of
   violoncellos
*See*: W246                                                                D016

**Bachianas brasileiras no. 1** (Modinha)
EVEREST SDBR 3016
Stadium Symphony Orchestra of New York; Leopold
   Stokowski, cond
Includes his *Uirapuru*; Prokofiev, *Cinderella*
*See*: W246                                                                D017

**Bachianas brasileiras no.1** (Prelude)
LE CHANT DU MONDE LDX 78.644
Mistislav Rostropovitch, vc; ensemble of cellists
Includes his *Bachianas brasileiras nos. 2* and
   *5* (Aria), *Choros no. 4,* and *Ciranda das sete notas*
*See*: W246                                                                D018

**Bachianas brasileiras no.2**
ANGEL 35547
Orchestre National de la Radiodiffusion Française; Villa-
   Lobos, cond
Includes his *Bachianas brasileiras nos. 5, 6, & 9*
*See*: W247

**Bachianas brasileiras no. 2**
ANGEL 36979
Orchestre de Paris; Paul Capolongo, cond
Includes his *Bachianas brasileiras nos.5, 6, & 9*
*See*: W247

D020

**Bachianas brasileiras no. 2**
LE CHANT DU MONDE LDX 78.644
Orchestre Nationale de USSR; Vladimir Bakharev, cond
Includes his *Bachianas brasileiras nos. 1* and
*5* (A'ria), *Choros no. 4*, and *Ciranda das sete notas*
*See*: W247

D021

**Bachianas brasileiras no. 2**
EMI 2 C 153-14090/9
Villa-Lobos par lui-même
Orchestre National de la Radiodiffusion Française; Villa-
Lobos, cond
For complete listing of contents see *Bachianas
brasileiras no.1* D010
*See*: W247

D022

**Bachianas brasileiras no. 2**
KUARUP KLP BV1-4
Villa-Lobos 100 Anos
*Canto do capadócio*, and *Canto da nossa terra* (vc & pf),
*Lembrança do sertão* (pf), and *O trenzinho do caipira*
(vc & pf)
Alceu Reis, vc; João Carlos Assis Brasil, pf
Includes his *Bachianas brasileiras nos. 4 & 5* (A'ria), 12
*Etudes* (guitar), *Choros nos. 1, 2, 3, & 5*, and *Cirandas*
(complete)
*See*: W247

D023

**Bachianas brasileiras no. 3**
ANGEL 37439
Christina Ortiz, pf; New Philharmonia Orchestra; Vladimir
Ashkenazy, cond
Includes his *Momoprecoce*
*See*: W388

D024

**Bachianas brasileiras no. 3**
ANGEL S3CBX 493
Manoel Braune, pf; Orchestre National de la

Radiodiffusion Française; Villa-Lobos, cond
Includes his *Bachianas brasileiras no.4*
*See*: W388                                        D025

**Bachianas brasileiras no. 3**
EMI 2 C 153-14090/9
Villa-Lobos par lui-même
Orchestre National de la Radiodiffusion Française; Villa-
Lobos, cond
For complete listing of contents see *Bachianas
brasileiras no.1* D010
*See*: W388                                        D026

**Bachianas brasileiras no. 4**
ANGEL S3CBX 493
Orchestre National de la Radiodiffusion Française; Villa-
Lobos, cond
Includes his *Bachianas brasileiras* no.3
*See*: W424                                        D027

**Bachianas brasileiras no. 4**
CHANTECLER 2.08-404-080
Gilberto Tinetti, pf
Includes Brenno Blauth, *Trio* 1960
*See*: W264                                        D028

**Bachianas brasileiras no. 4**
EMI/LA VOIX DE SON MAITRE 2 C 165-16250/9
L'oeuvre de piano
Anna Stella Schic, pf
For complete listing of contents see *Amazonas* D003
*See*: W264                                        D029

**Bachianas brasileiras no. 4**
EMI 2 C 153-14090/9
Villa-Lobos par lui-même
Orchestre National de la Radiodiffusion Française; Villa-
Lobos, cond
For complete listing of contents see *Bachianas
brasileiras no.1* D010
*See*: W424                                        D030

**Bachianas brasileiras no. 4**
FERMATA 305.103

Isis Moreira, pf
Includes Almeida Prado, *Variações, recitativo e fuga,*
  and *Momentos*
*See*: W264                                  D031

**Bachianas brasileiras no. 4**
INTER AMERICAN OAS 002
Orquestra Sinfônica Brasileira; Isaac Karabtchevsky,
  cond
Includes works by Marlos Nobre and Claudio Santoro
*See*: W424                                  D032

**Bachianas brasileiras no. 4**
KUARUP KLP BV1-4
Villa-Lobos 100 Anos
Antonio Guedes Barbosa, pf
For complete listing of contents see *Bachianas*
  *brasileiras no.2* D023
*See*: W264                                  D033

**Bachianas brasileiras no. 4**
LOU 762
Louisville Orchestra; Jorge Mester, cond
Includes a work by McLean
*See*: W424                                  D034

**Bachianas brasileiras no. 4**
MGM E3105
Menahem Pressler, pf
*See*: W264                                  D035

**Bachianas brasileiras no. 4** (Aria)
CARAVELLE CAR 43007
O piano de Villa-Lobos
Arnaldo Estrella, pf
For complete listing of contents see *À procura de uma*
  *agulha* D001
*See*: W264                                  D036

**Bachianas brasileiras no. 4** (Prelúdio, Cantiga, and Dansa)
EMI 31C 064 422957
Trem Caipira
Egberto Gismonti, performer
Includes *O trenzinho do caipira, Bachianas*

*brasileiras no.5*, Desejo, Canção do carreiro, and Pobre cega
See: W424 and W264                                              D037

**Bachianas brasileiras no. 4** (Prelúdio)
LONDON LLB 1110
Ney Salgado, pf
Includes his *Choros no.5; Ciranda no.2:* A condessa, and *Ciranda no.7:* Xô, xô, passarinho; and Almeida Prado, *Cartas celestes*
See: W264                                                       D038

**Bachianas brasileiras no. 4** (Prelúdio)
SPECTRUM SR-198
Claudio Vasquez, pf
Includes his *A prole do bebê no.2, Chôros no.5, Poema singelo,* and *As três Marias*
See: W264                                                       D039

**Bachianas brasileiras no. 4** (Prelúdio)
TELEFUNKEN SAT 22547 6.41299
Nelson Freire, pf
Includes his *A prole do bebê no.1, As três Marias,* and *Rudepoema*
See: W264                                                       D040

**Bachianas brasileiras no. 4** (Preludio, arr. for strings)
FESTA LDR-5020
Chamber orchestra of Rádio Ministério de Educação e Cultura; Roberto Schnorrenberg, cond
Includes his *Magnificat-Allelluia,* and *Quarteto de cordas no.11*
See: W424                                                       D041

**Bachianas brasileiras no. 5**
ANGEL 35547
Victoria de los Angeles, S; Orchestre National de la Radiodiffusion Française; Villa-Lobos, cond
Includes his *Bachianas brasileiras nos. 2, 6, & 9*
See: W389                                                       D042

**Bachianas brasileiras no. 5**
ANGEL 36979
Mady Mesplé, S; Orchestre de Paris; Paul Capolongo, cond

Includes his *Bachianas brasileiras nos. 2, 6, & 9*
*See*: W389                                                          D043

**Bachianas brasileiras no. 5**
 ANGEL CDC-47433
 Barbara Hendricks, S; Royal Philharmonic Orchestra;
   Enrique Batíz, cond
 Includes his *Bachianas brasileiras nos. 1 & 7*
 *See*: W389                                                         D044

**Bachianas brasileiras no. 5** (Aria)
 CBS MK-42122
 Romances for Saxophone
 Branford Marsalis, soprano saxophone; English Chamber
   Orchestra; Andrew Litton, cond
 Includes works by Colombier, Debussy, Fauré, Mussorgsky,
   Rachmaninoff, Ravel, Satie, and Stravinsky
 *See*: W389                                                         D045

**Bachianas brasileiras no. 5**
 COMPANHIA BRASILEIRA DE PROJETOS E OBRAS  803.401
 Victoria de los Angeles, S; Orchestre de la
   Radiodiffusion Française; Villa-Lobos, cond
 Includes his *Choros no.1, Valsa-choro, Mazurka-choro,*
   *Gavota-choro, Preludio no.1, Etude no.1, Valsa da dor,*
   Impressões seresteiras, Festa no sertão, *Choros bis,*
   *Bachianas brasileiras no.9,* and 3 selections from
   *Cirandas*: O cravo brigou com a rosa, A condessa, Passa
   passa gavião
 *See*: W389                                                         D046

**Bachianas brasileiras no. 5**
 EMI 2 C 153-14090/9
 Villa-Lobos par lui-même
 Orchestre National de la Radiodiffusion Française; Villa-
   Lobos, cond
 For complete listing of contents see *Bachianas*
   *brasileiras no.1* D010
 *See*: W389                                                         D047

**Bachianas brasileiras no. 5**
 EMI 31C 064 422957
 Trem Caipira
 Egberto Gismonti, performer

For complete listing of contents see *Bachianas brasileiras no.4* D037
*See*: W389                                                                          D048

**Bachianas brasileiras no. 5 (Ária)**
KUARUP KLP BV1-4
Villa-Lobos 100 Anos
Lelia Guimarães, S; Turíbio Santos, guitar
For complete listing of contents see *Bachianas brasileiras no.2* D023
*See*: W389                                                                          D049

**Bachianas brasileiras no. 5**
LONDON 411 730
Kiri Te Kanawa, S; Lynn Harrell, vc; instrumental
  ensemble; English Chamber Orchestra; Jeffrey Tate, cond
Includes Canteloube - *Songs of the Auvergne*
*See*: W389                                                                          D050

**Bachianas brasileiras no. 5**
MNEMOSYNE Mn-5
PICAFLOR - Latin American Music for Guitar and Mandolin
Mair-Davis Duo: Marilynn Mair, mandolin; Mark Davis,
  guitar
Includes his *Five Songs of the Cuzco Indians* (arr.
  Mair/Davis)
*See*: W389                                                                          D051

**Bachianas brasileiras no. 5 (Ária)**
ODYSSEY 32 16 0377
Bidu Sayão, S; Leonard Rose, vc; ensemble of cellists,
  Villa-Lobos, cond
Includes works by Mozart, Bellini, Verdi and Massenet
*See*: W389                                                                          D052

**Bachianas brasileiras no. 5**
PHILIPS 6598 309  Serie de Luxo
Maria Lúcia Godoy,S; Sérgio Abreu, guitar, cello ensemble
Includes his Na paz do outono, Lundu da Marquesa de
  Santos, Desejo, Cantiga do viuvo, *Canção do amor,*
  Cantilena, Modinha, Remeiro de São Francisco, *Canção do
  poeta do século* XVIII, *Suíte para canto e violino*
  (arranged for voice and guitar)
*See*: W391                                                                          D053

**Bachianas brasileiras no. 5**
RCA LSC-2795(Stereo) LM-2795(Mono)
Anna Moffo, S; American Symphony Orchestra; Leopold
  Stokowski, cond
Includes Canteloube - *Songs of the Auvergne*; and
  Rachmaninoff - *Vocalise*
*See*: W389                                                      D054

**Bachianas brasileiras no. 5**
SFP 31024/5/6
L'Oeuvre pour Voix et Instruments
Anna-Maria Bondi, S, Françoise Petit, pf; les Solistes
  de Paris; Henri-Claude Fantapie, cond
Includes also his *Poème de l'enfant et de sa mère, Suíte
  para canto e violino, Duas paisagens, Jardim fanado,
  Canção de cristal,* Vôo *(Seresta no.14), Serestas,
  Canções típicas brasileiras, Modinhas e canções*
*See*: W389                                                      D055

**Bachianas brasileiras no. 5** (Ária)
ANGEL 36050
Duets with the Spanish Guitar
Laurindo Almeida, guitar; Salli Terri, voice
Includes works by Jacques Ibert, Emile Desportes, Jayme
  Ovalle, Frédéric Chopin, Laurindo Almeida, François
  Gossec, Waldemar Henrique, Gabriel Fauré, Paurillo
  Barroso, Maurice Ravel and Ernâni Braga
*See*: W391                                                      D056

**Bachianas brasileiras no. 5** (Ária)
ANGEL DS-37351
Kathleen Battle, S; Christopher Parkening, guitar
Includes works by Dowland, Bach/Gounod, Granados,
  Henrique, Ovalle, Barroso, Falla, and traditional
  Spirituals
*See*: W391                                                      D057

**Bachianas brasileiras no. 5** (Ária)
LE CHANT DU MONDE LDX 78.644
Galina Vishnievskaya, S; Mistislav Rostropovitch, vc;
  ensemble of cellists
Includes his *Bachianas brasileiras nos. 1 and 2,
  Choros no. 4,* and *Ciranda das sete notas*
*See*: W389                                                      D058

**Bachianas brasileiras no. 5** (Ária)
TURNABOUT TV 34726
Spanish Music for Voice & Guitar
Elizabeth Suderburg, S; David Starobin, guitar
Includes works by Rodrigo, Garcia-Lorca, Tarrago, and
  Falla
*See*: W391                                                          D059

**Bachianas brasileiras no. 5** (Ária)
VANGUARD VSD-79160
Joan Baez, S;  Maurice Abravanel, cond
Includes various popular and folk songs
*See*: W389                                                          D060

**Bachianas brasileiras no. 6**
ANGEL 35547
Fernand Dufrene, fl; René Plessier, bn
Includes his *Bachianas brasileiras nos. 2, 5, & 9*
*See*: W392                                                          D061

**Bachianas brasileiras no. 6**
ANGEL 36979
Orchestre de Paris; Paul Capolongo, cond
Includes his *Bachianas brasileiras nos.2, 5, & 9*
*See*: W392                                                          D062

**Bachianas brasileiras no. 6**
EMI 2 C 153-14090/9
Villa-Lobos par lui-même
Orchestre National de la Radiodiffusion Française; Villa-
  Lobos, cond
For complete listing of contents see *Bachianas
  brasileiras no.1* D010
*See*: W392                                                          D063

**Bachianas brasileiras no. 6**
NONESUCH 71030
Baron, fl; Garfield, bn
Includes his *Quintette en forme de choros* and works by
  Glazunov and Ibert
*See*: W392                                                          D064

**Bachianas brasileiras no. 6**
RAVENNA RAVE 702

Soni Ventorum Wind Quintet
Includes his *Choros no.2, Trio* (Ob, cl, and bn), and
*Quarteto* (Fl, ob, cl, and bn)
*See*: W392                                                                    D065

**Bachianas brasileiras no. 7**
ANGEL CDC-47433
Royal Philharmonic Orchestra; Enrique Batíz, cond
Includes his *Bachianas brasileiras nos. 1 and 5*
*See*: W432                                                                    D066

**Bachianas brasileiras no. 7**
EMI 2 C 153-14090/9
Villa-Lobos par lui-même
Orchestre National de la Radiodiffusion Française; Villa-
Lobos, cond
For complete listing of contents see *Bachianas
brasileiras no.1* D010
*See*: W432                                                                    D067

**Bachianas brasileiras no. 7**
VCD 47257
Orchestre R.I.A.S. de Berlin; Villa-Lobos, cond
Includes his *Choros no.6*, and Varèse, *Sarabande*
*See*: W432                                                                    D068

**Bachianas brasileiras no. 8**
ANGEL 35179
Magda Tagliaferro, pf; Orchestre National de la
Radiodiffusion Française; Villa-Lobos, cond
Includes his *Momoprecoce*
*See*: W444                                                                    D069

**Bachianas brasileiras no. 8**
EMI 2 C 153-14090/9
Villa-Lobos par lui-même
Orchestre National de la Radiodiffusion Française; Villa-
Lobos, cond
For complete listing of contents see *Bachianas
brasileiras no.1* D010
*See*: W444                                                                    D070

**Bachianas brasileiras no. 9**
ANGEL 35547

Orchestre National de la Radiodiffusion Française; Villa-
  Lobos, cond
Includes his *Bachianas brasileiras nos. 2, 5, & 6*
*See*: W449                                              D071

**Bachianas brasileiras no. 9**
  ANGEL 36979
  Orchestre de Paris; Paul Capolongo, conductor
  Includes his *Bachianas brasileiras nos.2, 5, & 6*
  *See*: W449                                            D072

**Bachianas brasileiras no. 9**
  COMPANHIA BRASILEIRA DE PROJETOS E OBRAS  803.401
  Orchestre National de la Radiodiffusion Française; Villa-
    Lobos, cond
  For complete listing of contents see *Bachianas
    brasileiras* no.5 D046
  *See*: W449                                            D073

**Bachianas brasileiras no. 9**
  EMI 2 C 153-14090/9
  Villa-Lobos par lui-même
  Orchestre National de la Radiodiffusion Française; Villa-
    Lobos, cond
  For complete listing of contents see *Bachianas
    brasileiras* no.1 D010
  *See*: W449                                            D074

**Bachianas brasileiras no. 9**
  MEC/DAC/MVL 022
  Associação de Canto Coral; Elza Lakshevitz, cond
  Includes his *Missa São Sebastião*
  *See*: W449                                            D075

**Bachianas brasileiras no. 9**
  PHILIPS 6598 308  Serie de Luxe
  Artis Canticum
  Chorus conducted by Nelson de Macedo
  Includes works by José Joaquim Emerico Lobo de Mesquita,
    Pe. José Mauricio Nunes Garcia, and Aylton Escobar
  *See*: W449                                            D076

**Bachianas brasileiras no. 9**
  SCHWANN MUSICA MUNDI CD-11611

Berlin Radio Symphony; Albrecht, cond
Includes works by Casella and Henze
*See*: W449                                                      D077

**Bailado infernal**
EMI/LA VOIX DE SON MAITRE 2 C 165-16250/9
L'oeuvre de piano
Anna Stella Schic, pf
For complete listing of contents see *Amazonas* D003
*See*: W160                                                      D078

**Bazzum**
TAPECAR GRAVAÇÕES MEC/MVL 024
I Concurso Internacional de Coro Misto
University of Texas Chamber Singers; Morris J. Beachy,
   cond
For complete listing of contents see *Ave Maria* D006
*See*: Collections, C.O. v2 #39                                 D079

**Bendita sabedoria**
ENIR ECL-002
Coral Ars Nova (da Universidade Federal de Minas Gerais);
   Carlos Alberto Pinto da Fonseca, cond
For complete listing of contents see *Ave Maria* D007
*See*: W543                                                      D080

**Bendita sabedoria**
TAPECAR GRAVAÇÕES MEC/MVL 024
I Concurso Internacional de Coro Misto
University of Texas Chamber Singers; Morris J. Beachy,
   cond
For complete listing of contents see *Ave Maria* D006
*See*: W543                                                      D081

**O boizinho de chumbo** (From *A prole do bebê no.2*)
CARAVELLE  CAR 43007
O piano de Villa-Lobos
Arnaldo Estrella, pf
For complete listing of contents see *À procura de uma
   agulha* D001
*See*: W180                                                      D082

**Brinquedo de roda**
EMI/LA VOIX DE SON MAITRE 2 C 165-16250/9

L'oeuvre de piano
Anna Stella Schic, pf
For complete listing of contents see *Amazonas* D003
*See*: W045

D083

**Caixinha de música quebrada**
EMI/LA VOIX DE SON MAITRE 2 C 165-16250/9
L'oeuvre de piano
Anna Stella Schic, pf
For complete listing of contents see *Amazonas* D003
*See*: W256

D084

**Canção de cristal**
EMI ODEON SC-10.114
Cristina Maristany, S; Alceu Bocchino, pf
Includes his *Jardim fanado, Canções típicas brasileiras,
Canção do poeta do século* XVII, Cantilena (no.3 from
*Modinhas e canções*, Album 1), and Vira português
*See*: W494

D085

**Canção de cristal**
SFP 31024/5/6
L'Oeuvre pour Voix et Instruments
Anna-Maria Bondi, S, Françoise Petit, pf; les Solistes
de Paris; Henri-Claude Fantapie, cond
For complete listing of contents see *Bachianas
Brasileiras no.5*, D055
*See*: W494

D086

**Canção do amor**
PHILIPS 6598 309  Série de Luxo
Maria Lúcia Godoy,S; Sérgio Abreu, guitar
For complete listing of contents see *Bachianas
brasileiras no.5,* D053
*See*: W546

D087

**Canção do carreiro**
EMI 31C 064 422957
Trem Caipira
Egberto Gismonti, performer
For complete listing of contents see *Bachianas
brasileiras no.4* D037
*See*: W215 and W216

D088

**Canção do carreiro**
RCA LCT1143
Elsie Houston, S
Includes various Brazilian songs performed by Elsie
Houston, and his *Bachianas brasileiras no.1*, and
*Nonetto*
*See*: W215 and W216                                    D089

**Canção do poeta do século XVIII**
CLAVES D 8401
Teresa Berganza, mezzo; Juan Antonio Alvarez Parejo, pf
For complete listing of contents see *Adeus Ema* D002
*See*: W486                                             D090

**Canção do poeta do século XVIII**
EMI ODEON SC-10.114
Cristina Maristany, S; Alceu Bocchino, pf
For complete listing of contents see *Canção de cristal*
D085
*See*: W486                                             D091

**Canção do poeta do século XVIII**
PHILIPS 6598 309 Série de Luxo
Maria Lucia Godoy,S; Sérgio Abreu, guitar
For complete listing of contents see *Bachianas
brasileiras no.5* D053
*See*: W514                                             D092

**Canções típicas brasileiras**
EMI ODEON SC-10.114
Cristina Maristany, S; Alceu Bocchino, pf
For complete listing of contents see *Canção de cristal*
D085
*See*: W486                                             D093

**Canções tipicas brasileiras**
SFP 31024/5/6
L'Oeuvre pour Voix et Instruments
Anna-Maria Bondi, S, Françoise Petit, pf; les Solistes
de Paris; Henri-Claude Fantapie, cond
For complete listing of contents see *Bachianas
brasileiras no.5*, D055
*See*: W159                                             D094

**Cantigo do viúvo**
PHILIPS 6598 309  Série de Luxo
Maria Lúcia Godoy,S; Sérgio Abreu, guitar
For complete listing of contents see *Bachianas brasileiras no.5* D053
*See*: W215 and W216                                                        D095

**Cantilena**
EMI ODEON SC-10.114
Cristina Maristany, S; Alceu Bocchino, pf
For complete listing of contents see *Canção de cristal* D085
*See*: W099                                                                  D096

**Cantilena**
PHILIPS 6598 309  Série de Luxo
Maria Lúcia Godoy,S; Sérgio Abreu, guitar
For complete listing of contents see *Bachianas brasileiras no.5* D053
*See*: W099                                                                  D097

**O canto da nossa terra**
TAPECAR GRAVAÇÕES MEC/MVL 019
Victor Addiego and Laurien Laufmann, vc; F. Eger, pf
Includes his *Pequena suite, O trenzinho do caipira, O canto do cisne negro*, and works by Guerra Vicente and Camargo Guarnieri
*See*: W250                                                                  D098

**O canto do capadócio**
FJA - 112 (MVL 30)
II Concurso Internacional de Violoncelo
Mário Tavares, cond
For complete listing of contents see *Bachianas brasileiras no.1*, D011
*See*: W251                                                                  D099

**O canto do cisne negro**
FJA - 112 (MVL 30)
II Concurso Internacional de Violoncelo
Mário Tavares, cond
For complete listing of contents see *Bachianas brasileiras no.1*, D011
*See*: W122                                                                  D100

**O canto do cisne negro**
TAPECAR GRAVAÇOES MEC/MVL 019
Victor Addiego and Laurien Laufmann, vc; F. Eger, pf
Includes his *Pequena suite*, O trenzinho do caipira, *O canto da nossa terra*, and works by Guerra Vicente and Camargo Guarnieri
*See*: W122                                                          D101

**Um canto que saiu das senzalas**
CARAVELLE MEC-MVL 002
Villa-Lobos, O Interprete
Beate Roseroiter, S; Villa-Lobos, pf and guitar
Includes his *Prelude* no.1, *Choros nos.1* and *5*, Nhapopê, Guriata do coqueiro, Xangô, *A lenda do caboclo*, and Polichinelo
*See*: Collections, C.O. v2 #23                                      D102

**Capriccio**
FJA - 112 (MVL 30)
II Concurso Internacional de Violoncelo
Mário Tavares, cond
For complete listing of contents see *Bachianas brasileiras no.1*, D011
*See*: W92                                                           D103

**Carnaval das crianças**
DEUTSCHE GRAMMOPHON 2530 634
Roberto Szidon, pf; with Richard Metzler, pf
Includes his *Rudepoêma, Saudades das selvas brasileiras, New York Skyline, A fiandeira, A lenda do caboclo*, and *Suíte floral*
*See*: W157                                                          D104

**Carnaval das crianças**
EMI/LA VOIX DE SON MAITRE 2 C 165-16250/9
L'oeuvre de piano
Anna Stella Schic, pf
For complete listing of contents see *Amazonas* D003
*See*: W157                                                          D105

**Choros bis**
CARAVELLE MEC/MVL 007
Quarteto Guanabara
Includes his string *Trio* W460
*See*: W227                                                    D106

**Choros bis**
CDM  78836
Les choros de chambre
Turíbio Santos, guitar; Carlos Rato, fl; José Botelho,
   cl; Paulo Moura, sax; Noël Devos, bn, Jesse Sadoc,
   trbn; Murillo Santos, pf; Mário Tavares, cond
Includes his *Choros nos. 1, 2, 3, 4, 5,* and *7, Choros
   bis,* and *Quintette en forme de choros*
*See*: W227                                                    D107

**Choros bis**
COMPANHIA BRASILEIRA DE PROJETOS E OBRAS  803.401
Giancarlo Pareschi, vn; Watson Clis, vc
For complete listing of contents see *Bachianas
   brasileiras no.5* D046
*See*: W227                                                    D108

**Choros no. 1**
ADES 14096-2
Anna-Stella Schic, pf
Includes his *Choros nos. 2 & 5, Ciclo brasileiro, A prole
   do bebê no.2*
*See*: W161                                                    D109

**Choros no. 1**
BIS  LP-233
Favourite Guitar Music
Diego Blanco, guitar
Includes his *Suite populaire brésilienne,* and works by
   Tárrega, Myers, Yocoh, and Albeniz
*See*: W161                                                    D110

**Choros no. 1**
CARAVELLE MEC-MVL 002
Villa-Lobos, O Interprete
Beate Roseroiter, S; Villa-Lobos, pf and guitar
For complete listing of contents see *Um canto que saiu
das senzalas*, D103
*See*: W161                                                    D111

**Choros no. 1**
CBS M-35123
Music from Japan, England, and Latin America
*See*: W161                                                    D112

**Choros no. 1**
CDM  78836
Les choros de chambre
For complete listing of performers and contents see
*Choros bis* D107
*See*: W161                                                    D113

**Choros no. 1**
COMPANHIA BRASILEIRA DE PROJETOS E OBRAS  803.401
Turibio Santos, guitar
For complete listing of contents see *Bachianas
brasileiras no.5* D046
*See*: W161                                                    D114

**Choros no. 1** (Típico)
EMI/LA VOIX DE SON MAITRE 2 C 165-16250/9
L'oeuvre de piano
Anna Stella Schic, pf
For complete listing of contents see *Amazonas* D003
*See*: W161                                                    D115

**Choros no. 1**
KUARUP KLP BV1-4
Villa-Lobos 100 Anos
Turibio Santos, guitar
For complete listing of contents see *Bachianas
brasileiras no.2* D023
*See*: W161                                                    D116

**Choros no. 1**
PAV ADW 7097

Oscar Cáceres, guitar
Includes his *Etudes nos. 5 & 10,, Preludes nos. 1, 3, &
4, Suite populaire brésilienne*, and a work by Marlos
Nobre
*See*: W161                                                    D117

**Choros no. 1**
RCA VCS-7057
Art of Spanish Guitar
Julian Bream, guitar
*See*: W161                                                    D118

**Choros no. 1** (Típico brasileiro)
WERGO WER 60 105
Guitar Music of our Time
Konrad Rgaossnig, guitar
Includes his Mazurka-choro, *Prelude no.4*, and *Etude
no.12*, and works by Vogel, Zehm, Mittergradnegger,
Brindle, and Dohl
*See*: W161                                                    D119

**Choros no. 2**
ADES 14096-2
Anna Stella Schic, pf
Includes his *Choros nos. 1 & 5, Ciclo brasileiro, A prole
do bebê no.2*
*See*: W197                                                    D120

**Choros no. 2**
CARAVELLE MEC/MVL 004
Quarteto Santiago; various soloists
Includes his *Choros no.4, Quarteto de cordas no.15*, and
*Quatuor* (fl, ob, cl and bn)
*See*: W197                                                    D121

**Choros no. 2**
CID MEC/MVL-007
Concurso Internacional de Conjuntos Instrumentais 1972
Sexteto do Rio
Includes his *Assobio a jato, Fantasia concertante*; and
Guerra-Peixe, *Duo*
*See*: W197                                                    D122

**Choros no. 2**
CDM 78836
Les choros de chambre
For complete listing of performers and contents see
  *Choros bis* D107
*See*: W197                                              D123

**Choros no. 2**
CID MEC/MVL-007
Sexteto do Rio
Includes his *Assobio a jato, Fantasia concertante*; and
  Guerra-Peixe, *Duo*
*See*: W197                                              D124

**Choros no. 2**
EMI/LA VOIX DE SON MAITRE 2 C 165-16250/9
L'oeuvre de piano
Anna Stella Schic, pf
For complete listing of contents see *Amazonas* D003
*See*: W198                                              D125

**Choros no. 2**
EMI 2 C 153-14090/9
Villa-Lobos par lui-même
Orchestre National de la Radiodiffusion Française; Villa-
  Lobos, cond
For complete listing of contents see *Bachianas
  brasileiras no.1* D010
*See*: W197                                              D126

**Choros no. 2**
KUARUP KLP BV1-4
Villa-Lobos 100 Anos
Carlos Rato, fl; José Botelho, cl
For complete listing of contents see *Bachianas
  brasileiras no.2* D023
*See*: W197                                              D127

**Choros no. 2**
RAVENNA RAVE 702
Soni Ventorum Wind Quintet
Includes his *Bachianas brasileiras no.6, Trio* (Ob, cl,
  and bn), and *Quarteto* (Fl, ob, cl, and bn)
*See*: W197                                              D128

**Choros no. 3**
CDM  78836
Les choros de chambre
For complete listing of performers and contents see
   *Choros bis* D107
*See*: W206                                                                    D129

**Choros no. 3** (Pica-pau)
ENIR ECL-001
Various instrumentalists; Mário Tavares, cond
Includes his *Choros no.7*, and *Fantasia concertante* (pf,
   cl, & bn)
*See*: W206                                                                    D130

**Choros no. 3**
KUARUP KLP BV1-4
Villa-Lobos 100 Anos
Instrumental ensemble; Mário Tavares, cond
For complete listing of contents see *Bachianas
   brasileiras no.2* D023
*See*: W206                                                                    D131

**Choros no. 4**
CARAVELLE MEC/MVL 004
Quarteto Santiago; various soloists
Includes his *Choros no.2*, *Quarteto de cordas no.15*, and
   *Quatuor* (fl, ob, cl and bn)
*See*: W218                                                                    D132

**Choros no. 4**
CDM  78836
Les choros de chambre
For complete listing of performers and contents see
   *Choros bis* D107
*See*: W218                                                                    D133

**Choros no. 4**
LE CHANT DU MONDE LDX 78.644
Bouianovski, Evstigneev, Soukoroukiv, Benglovski
Includes his *Bachianas brasileiras nos. 1* (Prelude), *2* &
   *5* (Ária); and *Ciranda das sete notas*
*See*: W218                                                                    D134

**Choros no. 4**
CRYSTAL RECORDS S 378
Gregory Hustis, hn; Lorin Larson, hn; William Scharnberg,
hn, and Daral Rauscher, trbn
Includes works by F. Strauss, Rossini, Faith, Francaix,
and Lefebvre
*See*: W218                                                      D135

**Choros no. 5**
ADES 14096-2
Anna Stella Schic, pf
Includes his *Choros nos. 1 & 2, Ciclo brasileiro, A prole
do bebê no.2*
*See*: W207                                                      D136

**Choros no. 5**
ANGEL S-37110
Cristina Ortiz, pf
Includes his Festa no sertão, *A prole do bebe no.1* and
Impressões seresteiras; and Fructuoso Viana, *Dansa
de negros, Jogos pueris*; Leopoldo Miguez, *Nocturne*;
Camargo Guarnieri, *Dansa negra, Dansa brasileira*; and
Oscar Lorenzo Fernandez, from *Suite brasileira no.2*:
Ponteio, Moda, and Cataretê
*See*: W207                                                      D137

**Choros no. 5**
ANGEL SBR-XLD-12.276
Magda Tagliaferro, pf
Includes his Rosa amarela, Festa no sertão, A maré
encheu, A gaita de um precoce fantasiado, Impressões
seresteiras, Farrapós, Vamos atrás da serra, O'
Calunga, and *A lenda do caboclo*
*See*: W207                                                      D138

**Choros no. 5**
CARAVELLE CAR 43007
O piano de Villa-Lobos
Arnaldo Estrella, pf
For complete listing of contents see *À procura de uma
agulha* D001
*See*: W207                                                      D139

**Choros no. 5**
CARAVELLE MEC-MVL 002
Villa-Lobos, O Interprete
Beate Roseroiter, S; Villa-Lobos, pf and guitar
For complete listing of contents see *Um canto que saiu
   das senzalas,* D103
*See*: W207                                                            D140

**Choros no. 5**
CDM  78836
Les choros de chambre
Murillo Santos, pf
For complete listing of performers and contents see
   *Choros bis* D107
*See*: W207                                                            D141

**Choros no. 5**
DENON OX-7113-ND
Arthur Moreira-Lima, pf
Includes his *A prole do bebê no.1, Valsa da dor,* and
   *Rudepoema*
*See*: W207                                                            D142

**Choros no. 5**
DESTO 6426
Hilda Somer, pf
Includes his Dança do indio branco, and works by Castro,
   Chavez, Ginastera and Revueltas
*See*: W207                                                            D143

**Choros no. 5**
EMI/LA VOIX DE SON MAITRE 2 C 165-16250/9
L'oeuvre de piano
Anna Stella Schic, pf
For complete listing of contents see *Amazonas* D003
*See*: W208                                                            D144

**Choros no. 5**
EMI 2 C 153-14090/9
Villa-Lobos par lui-même
Orchestre National de la Radiodiffusion Française; Villa-
Lobos, cond
For complete listing of contents see *Bachianas
brasileiras no.1* D010
*See*: W208                                                          D145

**Choros no. 5**
KUARUP KLP BV1-4
Villa-Lobos 100 Anos
Murilio Santos, pf
For complete listing of contents see *Bachianas
brasileiras no.2* D023
*See*: W208                                                          D146

**Choros no. 5**
LONDON LLB 1110
Ney Salgado, pf
For complete listing of contents see *Bachianas
brasileiras no.4* D038
*See*: W208                                                          D147

**Choros no. 5**
SPECTRUM SR-198
Claudio Vasquez, pf
Includes his *A prole do bebê* no.2, *Poema singelo*,
*As três Marias*, *Bachianas brasileiras no.4* (Prelude)
*See*: W208                                                          D148

**Choros no. 6**
PHILIPS 9500 120
Orquestra Sinfônica Brasileira; Isaac Karabtchewsky, cond
Includes works by César Guerra-Peixe, and Marlos Nobre
*See*: W219                                                          D149

**Choros no. 6**
VCD 47257
Orchestre R.I.A.S. de Berlin; Villa-Lobos, cond
Includes his *Bachianas brasileiras no.7* and Varèse,
*Sarabande*
*See*: W219                                                          D150

**Choros no. 7**
CDM 78836
Les choros de chambre
For complete listing of performers and contents see
  *Choros bis* D107
*See*: W199                                                D151

**Choros no. 7** (Settimino)
ENIR ECL-001
Various instrumentalists; Mário Tavares, cond
Includes his *Choros no.3,* and *Fantasia concertante* (pf,
  cl, & bn)
*See*: W199                                                D152

**Choros no. 7**
KUARUP KLP BV1-4
Villa-Lobos 100 Anos
Instrumental ensemble; Mário Tavares, cond
For complete listing of contents see *Bachianas
  brasileiras no.2* D023
*See*: W199                                                D153

**Choros no. 8**
RECORDS INTERNATIONAL 7002-2
Hong Kong Philharmonic Orchestra; Kenneth Schermerhorn, cond
Includes his *Choros no.9*
*See*: W208                                                D154

**Choros no. 9**
RECORDS INTERNATIONAL 7002-2
Hong Kong Philharmonic Orchestra; Kenneth Schermerhorn, cond
Includes his *Choros no.8*
*See*: W232                                                D155

**Chorus no. 10**
EMI 2 C 153-14090/9
Villa-Lobos par lui-même
Orchestre National de la Radiodiffusion Française; Villa-
  Lobos, cond
For complete listing of contents see *Bachianas
  brasileiras no.1* D010
*See*: W209                                                D156

**Choros no. 10**
TAPECAR GRAVAÇÕES MEC/MVL 014
Orchestra and chorus of the Teatro Municipal of Rio de
  Janeiro; Vladimir Verbitsky, cond
Also includes his *Descobrimento do Brasil* (4th suite) and
  *Noneto*
*See*: W209                                               D157

**Choros no. 11**
EMI 2 C 153-14090/9
Villa-Lobos par lui-même
Orchestre National de la Radiodiffusion Française; Villa-
  Lobos, cond
For complete listing of contents see *Bachianas
  brasileiras no.1* D010
*See*: W228                                               D158

**Choros no. 11**
RECERCAR RIC 007
Orchestre Philharmonique de Liège; Pierre Bartolomée,
  cond
*See*: W233                                               D159

**Ciclo brasileiro**
ADES 14096-2
Anna Stella Schic, pf
Includes his *Choros nos. 1, 2, & 5,* and *A prole do bebê
  no.2*
*See*: W374                                               D160

**Ciranda das sete notas**
LE CHANT DU MONDE LDX 78.644
Orchestre de chambre de Leningrad; Lazare Gozman, cond
Includes his *Bachianas brasileiras nos. 1* (Prelude), *2* &
  *5* (Ária); and *Choros no.4*
*See*: W325                                               D161

**Ciranda das sete notas**
CRYSTAL RECORDS Recital Series S 341
Joseph Polisi, bn; Ronald Roseman, ob; John Snow, eng hn;
  Thomas Schmidt, pf
Includes works by Matthews, Bitsch, and Noon
*See*: W548                                               D162

**Cirandas** (Complete)
ADES 14095-2
Anna Stella Schic, pf
Includes his *Preludes* and *A prole do bebê no.1*
*See*: W220                                                                D163

**Cirandas** (Complete)
EMI/LA VOIX DE SON MAITRE 2 C 165-16250/9
L'oeuvre de piano
Anna Stella Schic, pf
For complete listing of contents see *Amazonas* D003
*See*: W220                                                                D164

**Cirandas** (Complete)
FERMATA 308.0026
Isis Moreira, pf
Includes Dinorah de Carvalho, *Sonata no.2*
*See*: W220                                                                D165

**Cirandas** (Complete)
KUARUP KLP BV1-4
Villa-Lobos 100 Anos
Roberto Szidon, pf
For complete listing of contents see *Bachianas
  brasileiras no.3* D023
*See*: W220                                                                D166

**Cirandinhas**
EMI/LA VOIX DE SON MAITRE 2 C 165-16250/9
L'oeuvre de piano
Anna Stella Schic, pf
For complete listing of contents see *Amazonas* D003
*See*: W207                                                                D167

**Concerto no. 2** (Cello and orchestra)
ABC WESTMINSTER GOLD 6-30-404-004
Aldo Parisot, vc; Vienna State Opera Orchestra; Gustav
  Meier, cond
Includes Camargo Guarnieri, *Choro* for cello and
  orchestra
*See*: W516

**Concerto no. 5** (Piano and orchestra)
EMI 2 C 153-14090/9

Villa-Lobos par lui-même
Orchestre National de la Radiodiffusion Française; Villa-
Lobos, cond
For complete listing of contents see *Bachianas
brasileiras no.1* D010
*See*: W521                                                          D169

**Concerto para violão**
ANGEL DS-38126
Angel Romero, guitar; London Philharmonic Orchestra;
  Jesus Lopez-Cobos, cond
Includes Lalo Schifrin, *Concerto* for guitar and
  orchestra
*See*: W501                                                          D170

**Concerto para violão**
CBS MK-33208
John Williams, guitar; English Chamber Orchestra; Daniel
  Barenboim, cond
Includes Rodrigo, *Concerto de Aranjuez*
*See*: W501                                                          D171

**Concerto para violão**
DEUTSCHE GRAMMOPHON DG 2530718
Narciso Yepes, guitar; London Symphony Orchestra; Garcia
  Navarro, cond
*See*: W501                                                          D172

**Concerto para violão**
EMI-HMV 2703301
Alfonso Moreno, guitar; Philharmonic  Orchestra of
  Mexico; Enrique Batiz, cond
Includes Castelnuovo-Tedesco, *Concerto* pour guitare
*See*: W501                                                          D173

**Concerto para violão**
MEC/SEAC/FUNARTE/MVL - 025
II Concurso Internacional de Violão
Eduardo Castanera, guitar; Orquestra de Camara e Sexteto
  de Sopros da Rádio MEC; Mário Tavares, cond
Includes his *Preludio nos. 4 & 5,* and *Etudes* de violão
*See*: W501                                                          D174

## Concerto para violão
MVL 32
III Concurso Internacional de Violão
Paulo Soares, guitar; Orchestra of the Teatro Municipal;
   Henrique Morelenbaum, cond
Includes his *Sexteto místico, Estudos nos. 5 & 10,*
   *Preludio no.2*, and Schottisch-Choro
*See*: W501                                                         D175

## Concerto para violão
PHILIPS 416357-2
Pepe Romero, guitar; Academy of St. Martin in the Fields;
   Neville Marriner, cond
Includes works by Castelnuovo-Tedesco and Rodrigo
*See*: W501                                                         D176

## Concerto para violão
RCA AGL1-4897
Julian Bream, guitar; London Symphony Orchestra; Andre
   Previn, cond
Includes his Schottisch-choro, *Preludes nos.1-5,* and
   *Etude* in c-sharp
*See*: W501                                                         D177

## A condessa
COMPANHIA BRASILEIRA DE PROJETOS E OBRAS  803.401
Miguel Proença, pf
For complete listing of contents see *Bachianas*
   *brasileiras no.5* D046
*See*: W220                                                         D178

## A condessa (Ciranda No.2)
LONDON LLB 1110
Ney Salgado, pf
For complete listing of contents see *Bachianas*
   *brasileiras no.4* D038
*See*: W220                                                         D179

## O cravo brigou com a rosa
COMPANHIA BRASILEIRA DE PROJETOS E OBRAS  803.401
Miguel Proença, pf
For complete listing of contents see *Bachianas*
   *brasileiras no.5* D046
*See*: W220                                                         D180

**Dança do índio branco**
CARAVELLE CAR 43007
O piano de Villa-Lobos
Arnaldo Estrella, pf
For complete listing of contents see *À procura de uma
    agulha* D001
*See*: W374                                                    D181

**Dança do índio branco**
DESTO 6426
Hilda Somer, pf
Includes his *Choros no.5*, and works by Castro, Chávez,
    Ginastera and Revueltas
*See*: W374                                                    D182

**Dança do índio branco**
FUNARET PROMEMUS MMB 82.028
I Concurso Nacional - Jovens Intérpretes da Música
    Brasileira
Nelson José Goes Neves, pf
Includes works by Almeida Prado, Henrique Oswald, Camargo
    Guarnieri, Guilherme Bauer, Joaquim A. da Silva
    Callado, Francisco Mignone, and Bruno Kiefer
*See*: W374                                                    D183

**Danças africanas**
LOUISVILLE ORCHESTRA FIRST EDITION RECORDS LS-695
Louisville Orchestra; Jorge Mester, cond
Includes: John Addison, *Concerto* for Trumpet and
    Strings
*See*: W107                                                    D184

**Danças características africanas**
EMI/LA VOIX DE SON MAITRE 2 C 165-16250/9
L'oeuvre de piano
Anna Stella Schic, pf
For complete listing of contents see *Amazonas* D003
*See*: W085                                                    D185

**Descobrimento do Brasil** (first suite)
EMI 2 C 153-14090/9
Villa-Lobos par lui-même
Orchestre National de la Radiodiffusion Française; Villa-
    Lobos, cond

For complete listing of contents see *Bachianas
brasileiras no.1* D010
*See*: W377                                                    D186

**Descobrimento do Brasil** (second suite)
EMI 2 C 153-14090/9
Villa-Lobos par lui-même
Orchestre National de la Radiodiffusion Française; Villa-
Lobos, cond
For complete listing of contents see *Bachianas
brasileiras no.1* D010
*See*: W378                                                    D187

**Descobrimento do Brasil** (third suite)
EMI 2 C 153-14090/9
Villa-Lobos par lui-même
Orchestre National de la Radiodiffusion Française; Villa-
Lobos, cond
For complete listing of contents see *Bachianas
brasileiras no.1* D010
*See*: W379                                                    D188

**Descobrimento do Brasil** (fourth suite)
EMI 2 C 153-14090/9
Villa-Lobos par lui-même
Orchestre National de la Radiodiffusion Française; Villa-
Lobos, cond
For complete listing of contents see *Bachianas
brasileiras no.1* D010
*See*: W380                                                    D189

**Descobrimento do Brasil** (Oratório) (4th suite)
TAPECAR GRAVAÇÕES MEC/MVL/DAC/PAC/014
Orchestra and chorus of the Teatro Municipal of Rio de
Janeiro; Michel Rochat, cond
Also includes his *Noneto* and *Choros no.10*
*See*: W380                                                    D190

**Desejo**
CLAVES D 8401
Teresa Berganza, mezzo; Juan Antonio Alvarez Parejo, pf
For complete listing of contents see *Adeus Ema* D002
*See*: W216                                                    D191

**Desejo**
EMI 31C 064 422957
Trem Caipira
Egberto Gismonti, performer
For complete listing of contents see *Bachianas
brasileiras no.4* D037
*See*: W216                                                        D192

**Desejo**
PHILIPS 6598 309  Serie de Luxo
Maria Lúcia Godoy,S; Sérgio Abreu, guitar
For complete listing of contents see *Bachianas
brasileiras no.5* D053
*See*: W216                                                        D193

**Deuxième sonate** (Cello and piano)
MEC/MVL/FUNARTE - 017/1976
Concurso Internacional de Violoncelo 1976
Antônio Jerônimo de Menezes Neto, vc; F. Egger, pf
Includes his *Fantasia* para violoncelo e orquestra
*See*: W103                                                        D194

**Duas lendas ameríndias**
ENIR ECL-002
Coral Ars Nova (da Universidade Federal de Minas Gerais);
 Carlos Alberto Pinto da Fonseca, cond
For complete listing of contents see *Ave Maria* D007
*See*: W506                                                        D195

**Duas lendas ameríndias**
TAPECAR GRAVAÇÕES MEC/MVL 024
I Concurso Internacional de Coro Misto
University of Texas Chamber Singers; Morris J. Beachy,
 cond
For complete listing of contents see *Ave Maria* D006
*See*: W506                                                        D196

**Duas paisagens**
SFP 31024/5/6
L'Oeuvre pour Voix et Instruments
Anna-Maria Bondi, S, Françoise Petit, pf; les Solistes
   de Paris; Henri-Claude Fantapie, cond
For complete listing of contents see *Bachianas
   brasileiras no.5*, D055
*See*: W462                                                      D197

**Duo** (Violin and viola)
CRYSTAL RECORDS S 632
Violin & Viola Virtuosic Duos
Charmain Gadd, vn; Yizhak Schotten, va
Includes works by Martinu, Handel/Halvorsen, and Toch
*See*: W463                                                      D198

**The Emperor Jones**
TAPECAR GRAVAÇÕES MEC/MVL/PAC/011
Symphony orchestra of the Teatro Municipal of Rio de
   Janeiro; Laszlo Halasz, cond
Includes his *Suite no.2* for chamber orchestra
*See*: W531                                                      D199

**Erosão**
CSP AML 4615
Louisville Orchestra; Robert Whitney, cond
Includes a work by Norman Dello Joio
*See*: W495                                                      D200

**Erosão** (Lenda ameríndia no.1 - Origem do Rio Amazonas)
MEC/MVL/DAC/PAC - 015/1975
Villa-Lobos Festival 1975
Orquestra Sinfônica Brasileira; Sérgio Magnani, cond
Includes his *Papagaio do moleque* (Episódio Sinfônico)
*See*: W495                                                      D201

**Estrela é lua nova**
TAPECAR GRAVAÇÕES MEC/MVL 024
I Concurso Internacional de Coro Misto
University of Texas Chamber Singers; Morris J. Beachy,
   cond
For complete listing of contents see *Ave Maria* D006
*See*: W158, W159                                                D202

## Étude in C-Sharp Minor

RCA AGL1-4897
Julian Bream, guitar
Includes his *Concerto para violão, Preludes nos.1-5,* and
  Schottisch-choro
*See*: W235                                              D203

## Étude no.1
ANGEL S-36064
Claire de lune
Laurindo Almeida, guitar
Includes his *Prelude no.3,* and works by Falla, Debussy,
  Granados, Albéniz, and Ravel
*See*: W235                                              D204

## Étude no.1
ANGEL S-36020
In the Spanish Style
Christopher Parkening, guitar
Includes his *Prelude no.2,* and works by Albéniz, Tárrega,
  Torroba, Mudarra, Guerau, Sor, Lauro, and Ponce
*See*: W235                                              D205

## Étude no.1
COMPANHIA BRASILEIRA DE PROJETOS E OBRAS  803.401
Turibio Santos, guitar
For complete listing of contents see *Bachianas
  brasileiras no.5* D046
*See*: W235                                              D206

## Étude no. 5
MVL 32
III Concurso Internacional de Violão
Various performers
For a complete listing of contents see *Concerto para
  violão e orquestra* D175
*See*: W235                                              D207

## Étude no.10
MVL 32
III Concurso Internacional de Violão

Various performers
For a complete listing of contents see *Concerto para violão e orquestra* D175
*See*: W235                                                         D208

**Étude no.12**
WERGO WER 60 105
Guitar Music of our Time
Konrad Rgaossnig, guitar
Includes his Mazurka-Choro, *Choro no.1*, and *Prelude no.4*,
and works by Vogel, Zehm, Mittergradnegger, Brindle,
and Dohl
*See*: W235                                                         D209

**Études** (8)
TURNABOUT TV 34676
Manuel Barruenco, guitar
Includes his *Suite populaire brésilienne*, and works by
Guarnieri, and Chávez
*See*: W235                                                         D210

**Études** (12)
BAM 5832
Maria Livia São Marcos, guitar
*See*: W235                                                         D211

**Études** (12)
DEUTSCHE GRAMMOPHON DG 2530140
Narciso Yepes, guitar
Includes his *Preludes* (5)
*See*: W235                                                         D212

**Études** (12)
EMI 1C 067 14-6757-1
Eliot Fisk, guitar
Includes works by Agustin Barrios Mangore, Vincente
Emilio Sojo, and Jorge Morel
*See*: W235                                                         D213

**Études** (12)
KUARUP KLP BV1-4
Villa-Lobos 100 Anos
Turibio Santos, guitar
For complete listing of contents see *Bachianas*

*brasileiras no.2* D023
*See*: W235                                                    D214

**Études** (12)
RCA AGL1-4295
Julian Bream, guitar
Includes his *Suite populaire brésilienne*
*See*: W235                                                    D215

**Études** (Selections)
CAPITOL P8497
Music for the Spanish Guitar
Laurindo Almeida, guitar
Includes *Preludes 1, 3, & 5,* and *Études 1, 7, & 8*
*See*: W235                                                    D216

**Études** (Selections)
MEC/SEAC/FUNARTE/MVL - 025
II Concurso Internacional de Violão
Various guitarists
Includes his *Concerto para violão e orquestra,* and
  *Preludio nos. 4 & 5*
*See*: W235                                                    D217

**Études** (Selections)
PAV ADW 7097
Oscar Cáceres, guitar
Includes his *Études nos. 5 & 10, Choros no.1, Preludes
  nos. 1, 3, & 4, Suite populaire brésilienne,* and a
  work by Marlos Nobre
*See*: W235                                                    D218

**Fantasia para saxofone** (Soprano Saxophone, 3 horns and strings)
Zephyr Z23
François Daneels, sax; l'Orchestre de Chambre de la
  B.R.T, Jan Segers, cond
Includes works by Frank Martin, Paul Harvey, and Victor
  Legley
*See*: W490                                                    D219

**Fantasia concertante**
CID MEC/MVL-007
Concurso Internacional de Conjuntos Instrumentais 1972
Sexteto do Rio

Includes his *Assobio a jato, Choros no.2;* and Guerra-
Peixe, Duo
*See:* W517                                                                D220

**Fantasia concertante** (Piano, clarinet and bassoon)
ENIR ECL-001
Various instrumentalists; Mário Tavares, cond
Includes his *Choros no.7,* and *Fantasia concertante* (pf,
cl, & bn)
*See:* W517                                                                D221

**Fantasia concertante** (Piano, clarinet and bassoon)
GC 4115
Academy Trio
Includes works by Poulenc and Wilder
*See:* W517                                                                D222

**Fantasia concertante** (Para orquestra de violoncelos)
MEC/MVL/FUNARTE - 016/1976
Associação dos Violoncelistas do Brasil
Includes his *Bachianas brasileiras no.1* D013
*See:* W549                                                                D223

**Fantasia concertante for orchestra of cellos**
TAPECAR GRAVAÇÕES MEC/MVL 016
Associação dos Violoncelistas do Brasil
Also includes his *Bachianas brasileiras no.1* D016
*See:* W549                                                                D224

**Fantasia para violoncelo e orquestra**
MEC/MVL/FUNARTE - 017/1976
Concurso Internacional de Violoncelo 1976
Csaba Onczay, vc; F. Egger, pf
Includes his *Deuxième sonate* (Cello and piano)
*See:* W454                                                                D225

**Farrapós**
ANGEL SBR-XLD-12.276
Magda Tagliaferro, pf
For complete listing of contents see *Choros no.5* D138
*See:* W085                                                                D226

**Festa no sertão**
ANGEL S-37110

Cristina Ortiz, pf
For complete listing of contents see *Choros no.5* D137
*See*: W374                                                    D227

**Festa no sertão**
ANGEL SBR-XLD-12.276
Magda Tagliaferro, pf
For complete listing of contents see *Choros no.5* D138
*See*: W374                                                    D228

**Festa no sertão**
COMPANHIA BRASILEIRA DE PROJETOS E OBRAS  803.401
Miguel Proença, pf
For complete listing of contents see *Bachianas
brasileiras no.5* D046
*See*: W374                                                    D229

**A fiandeira**
DEUTSCHE GRAMMOPHON 2530 634
Roberto Szidon, pf; with Richard Metzler, pf
For complete listing of contents see *Carnaval das
crianças* D104
*See*: W176                                                    D230

**A fiandeira**
EMI/LA VOIX DE SON MAITRE 2 C 165-16250/9
L'oeuvre de piano
Anna Stella Schic, pf
For complete listing of contents see *Amazonas* D003
*See*: W176                                                    D231

**Floresta do Amazonas**
UNITED ARTIST RECORDS UAS-5506
Bidu Sayão, S; Symphony of the Air; Villa-Lobos, cond
*See*: W551                                                    D232

**Francette et Pià**
EMI/LA VOIX DE SON MAITRE 2 C 165-16250/9
L'oeuvre de piano
Anna Stella Schic, pf
For complete listing of contents see *Amazonas* D003
*See*: W237                                                    D233

**A freira** (From *Guia prático Album 3*)
CARAVELLE CAR 43007
O piano de Villa-Lobos
Arnaldo Estrella, pf
For complete listing of contents see À *procura de uma agulha* D001
*See*: W279                                            D234

**Fuga**
TAPECAR GRAVAÇÕES MEC/MVL 024
I Concurso Internacional de Coro Misto
University of Texas Chamber Singers; Morris J. Beachy, cond
For complete listing of contents see *Ave Maria* D006
*See*: W445                                            D235

**Fui no Toróró**
CARAVELLE CAR 43007
O piano de Villa-Lobos
Arnaldo Estrella, pf
For complete listing of contents see À *procura de uma agulha* D001
*See*: W220                                            D236

**A gaita de um precoce fantasiado**
ANGEL SBR-XLD-12.276
Magda Tagliaferro, pf
For complete listing of contents see *Choros no.5* D138
*See*: W157                                            D237

**A gaita de um precoce fantasiado**
CARAVELLE CAR 43007
O piano de Villa-Lobos
Arnaldo Estrella, pf
For complete listing of contents see À *procura de uma agulha* D001
*See*: W157                                            D238

**Garibaldi foi à missa** (From *Guia prático Album 3*)
CARAVELLE  CAR 43007
O piano de Villa-Lobos
Arnaldo Estrella, pf
For complete listing of contents see *À procura de uma
agulha* D001
*See*: W45 and W279                                             D239

**O gatinho de papelão** (From *A prole do bebê* no.2)
CARAVELLE  CAR 43007
O piano de Villa-Lobos
Arnaldo Estrella, pf
For complete listing of contents see *À procura de uma
agulha* D001
*See*: W180                                                     D240

**O gato e o rato**
EMI/LA VOIX DE SON MAITRE 2 C 165-16250/9
L'oeuvre de piano
Anna Stella Schic, pf
For complete listing of contents see *Amazonas* D003
*See*: W076                                                     D241

**Gavota-choro**
COMPANHIA BRASILEIRA DE PROJETOS E OBRAS  803.401
Turibio Santos, guitar
For complete listing of contents see *Bachianas
brasileiras no.5* D046
*See*: W20, W395, and W396                                      D242

**Genesis**
MEC/MVL 003/ST  1970
Orchestra of the Teatro Municipal of Rio de Janeiro;
Mário Tavares, cond
Includes his *Mandu-çarará*
*See*: W522                                                     D243

**Guia prático**
EMI/LA VOIX DE SON MAITRE 2 C 165-16250/9
L'oeuvre de piano
Anna Stella Schic, pf
For complete listing of contents see *Amazonas* D003
*See*: W277, W278, W279, W280, W281, W282, W283,
W358, W359, W284, W473                                          D244

**Guriatã do coqueiro**
CARAVELLE MEC-MVL 002
Villa-Lobos, O Intérprete
Beate Roseroiter, S; Villa-Lobos, pf and guitar
For complete listing of contents see *Um canto que saiu
das senzalas*, D102                                           D245

**Histórias da carochinha**
EMI/LA VOIX DE SON MAITRE 2 C 165-16250/9
L'oeuvre de piano
Anna Stella Schic, pf
For complete listing of contents see *Amazonas* D003
*See*: W148                                                   D246

**Homenagem a Chopin**
MEC/MVL/PAC/012
Villa-Lobos Concurso Internacional de Piano 1974
Adam Fellegi, Jorge Fortes, and Yuri Smirnov, pf
Includes his *A prole do bebê* (Selections), and *Prelúdio
no.2*; and Marlos Nobre, *Variações*; Francisco Mignone,
IV *Sonata*; Camargo Guarnieri, *Lundu*
*See*: W474                                                   D247

**Hommage à Chopin**
EMI/LA VOIX DE SON MAITRE 2 C 165-16250/9
L'oeuvre de piano
Anna Stella Schic, pf
For complete listing of contents see *Amazonas* D003
*See*: W474                                                   D248

**Ibericarabé**
EMI/LA VOIX DE SON MAITRE 2 C 165-16250/9
L'oeuvre de piano
Anna Stella Schic, pf
For complete listing of contents see *Amazonas* D003
*See*: W078                                                   D249

**Impressões seresteiras**
ANGEL S-37110
Cristina Ortiz, pf
For complete listing of contents see *Choros no.5* D137
*See*: W374                                                   D250

**Impressões seresteiras**
ANGEL SBR-XLD-12.276
Magda Tagliaferro, pf
For complete listing of contents see *Choros no.5* D138
*See*: W374                                                                  D251

**Impressões seresteiras**
COMPANHIA BRASILEIRA DE PROJETOS E OBRAS 803.401
Miguel Proença, pf
For complete listing of contents see *Bachianas
brasileiras no.5* D046
*See*: W374                                                                  D252

**Improviso** (Violin and piano)
FUNARTE PROMEMUS MMB 79.009
Oscar Borgerth, vn; Ilara Gomes Grosso, pf
Includes his *Sonata fantasia* no.1 (Désespérance), *Sonata
fantasia* No.2, and *Sonata* no.3
*See*: W096                                                                  D253

**Invocação em defesa da pátria**
EMI 2 C 153-14090/9
Villa-Lobos par lui-même
Orchestre National de la Radiodiffusion Française; Villa-
Lobos, cond
For complete listing of contents see *Bachianas
brasileiras* no.1 D010
*See*: W439                                                                  D254

**Jaquibáu**
TAPECAR GRAVAÇÕES MEC/MVL 024
I Concurso Internacional de Coro Misto
University of Texas Chamber Singers; Morris J. Beachy,
cond
For complete listing of contents see *Ave Maria* D006
*See*: Collections, G.P. v.2 #38                                             D255

**Jardim fanado**
EMI ODEON SC-10.114
Cristina Maristany, S; Alceo Bocchino, pf
For complete listing of contents see *Canção de cristal*
D086
*See*: W525                                                                  D256

**Jardim fanado**
SFP 31024/5/6
L'Oeuvre pour Voix et Instruments
Anna-Maria Bondi, S, Françoise Petit, pf; les Solistes
    de Paris; Henri-Claude Fantapie, cond
For complete listing of contents see *Bachianas
    brasileiras no.5,* D055
*See*: W525                                                         D257

**João Cambuête** (From *Guia prático Album 3*)
CARAVELLE  CAR 43007
O piano de Villa-Lobos
Arnaldo Estrella, pf
For complete listing of contents see *À procura de uma
    agulha* D001
*See*: W279                                                         D258

**A lenda do caboclo**
ANGEL SBR-XLD-12.276
Magda Tagliaferro, pf
For complete listing of contents see *Choros no.5* D138
*See*: W156                                                         D259

**A lenda do caboclo**
CARAVELLE MEC-MVL 002
Villa-Lobos, O Interprete
Beate Roseroiter, S; Villa-Lobos, pf and guitar
For complete listing of contents see *Um canto que saiu
    das senzalas,* D102
*See*: W156                                                         D260

**A lenda do caboclo**
DEUTSCHE GRAMMOPHON 2530 634
Roberto Szidon, pf; with Richard Metzler, pf
For complete listing of contents see *Carnaval das
    crianças* D105
*See*: W156                                                         D261

**A lenda do caboclo**
EMI/LA VOIX DE SON MAITRE 2 C 165-16250/9
L'oeuvre de piano
Anna Stella Schic, pf
For complete listing of contents see *Amazonas* D003
*See*: W156                                                         D262

**A lenda do caboclo**
PHILIPS 6747 313  Série de luxo
Vol.9 PERSONALIDADES
Arnaldo Estrella, pf
Includes his *Valsa da dor*, and *Poema singelo*; and works
  by Leopoldo Miguez, Henrique Oswald, Alexandre Levy,
  Alberto Nepomuceno, Barrozo Netto, Fructuoso Viana,
  Radamés Gnattali, Luís Cosme, Souza Lima, Lorenzo
  Fernandez, Camargo Guarnieri, and Francisco Mignone
*See*: W156                                                                D263

**Lundu da Marquêsa de Santos**
PHILIPS 6598 309  Serie de Luxo
Maria Lúcia Godoy,S; Sérgio Abreu, guitar
For complete listing of contents see *Bachianas
  brasileiras no.5* D054
*See*: W365 and W406                                          D264

**Magnificat-Alleluia**
FESTA LDR-5020
Associação de Canto Coral do Rio, Coro Canarinhos de
  Petrópolis; Orquestra Sinfônica Brasileira; Edoardo de
  Guarnieri, cond
Includes his *Bachianas brasileiras no.4* (Prelude), and
  *Quarteto de cordas no.11*
*See*: W553                                                                D265

**Mandu çarará**
MEC/MVL 003/ST  1970
Orquestra Sinfônica Brasileira; Henrique Morelenbaum,
  cond
Includes his *Gênesis*
*See*: W417                                                                D266

**A maré encheu**
ANGEL SBR-XLD-12.276
Magda Tagliaferro, pf
For complete listing of contents see *Choros no.5* D138
*See*: W277                                                                D267

**Mazurka-choro**
COMPANHIA BRASILEIRA DE PROJETOS E OBRAS  803.401
Turíbio Santos, guitar
For complete listing of contents see *Bachianas*

brasileiras no.5 D046
*See*: W020                                                          D268

**Mazurka-choro**
WERGO WER 60 105
Guitar Music of our Time
Konrad Rgaossnig, guitar
Includes his *Choro no.1, Prelude no.4*, and *Étude*
no.12, and works by Vogel, Zehm, Mittergradnegger,
Brindle, and Dohl
*See*: W020                                                          D269

**Missa São Sebastião**
COLUMBIA ML 4516
University of California at Berkley Chorus; Werner
Janssen, cond
*See*: W383                                                          D270

**Missa São Sebastião**
MEC/DAC/MVL 022
Associação de Canto Coral; Cleofe Person de Mattos, cond
Includes his *Bachianas brasileiras no.9* D075
*See*: W383                                                          D271

**Modinha**
PHILIPS 6598 309  Série de Luxo
Maria Lúcia Godoy,S; Sérgio Abreu, guitar
For complete listing of contents see *Bachianas
brasileiras no.5* D053
*See*: W534                                                          D272

**Modinhas e canções**
SFP 31024/5/6
L'Oeuvre pour Voix et Instruments
Anna-Maria Bondi, S, Françoise Petit, pf; les Solistes
de Paris; Henri-Claude Fantapie, cond
For complete listing of contents see *Bachianas
brasileiras no.5,* D055
*See*: W360, W406, W441, W563                                        D273

**Momoprecoce**
ANGEL 35179
Magda Tagliaferro, pf; Orchestre National de la
Radiodiffusion Française; Villa-Lobos, cond

Includes his *Bachianas brasileiras no.8* D069
*See*: W240                                                         D274

**Momoprecoce**
ANGEL 37439
Christina Ortiz, pf; Vladimir Ashkenazy, cond
Includes his *Bachianas brasileiras no.3* D024
*See*: W240                                                         D275

**Momoprecoce**
EMI 2 C 153-14090/9
Villa-Lobos par lui-même
Orchestre National de la Radiodiffusion Française; Villa-
   Lobos, cond
For complete listing of contents see *Bachianas
   brasileiras no.1* D010
*See*: W240                                                         D276

**Momoprecoce**
EMI-Reference-2909621
Magda Tagliaferro, pf; Orchestre National de la
   Radiodiffusion Française; Villa-Lobos, cond
Includes Hahn, Reynaldo - *Concerto pour piano*
*See*: W240                                                         D277

**Na paz do outono**
PHILIPS 6598 309   Serie de Luxo
Maria Lúcia Godoy,S; Sérgio Abreu, guitar
For complete listing of contents see *Bachianas
   brasileiras no.5* D053                                           D278

**New York Skyline**
DEUTSCHE GRAMMOPHON 2530 634
Roberto Szidon, pf; with Richard Metzler, pf
For complete listing of contents see *Carnaval das
   crianças* D104
*See*: W407                                                         D279

**New York Skyline**
EMI/LA VOIX DE SON MAITRE 2 C 165-16250/9
L'oeuvre de piano
Anna Stella Schic, pf
For complete listing of contents see *Amazonas* D003
*See*: W407                                                         D280

## Nhapopê
CARAVELLE MEC-MVL 002
Villa-Lobos, O Intérprete
Beate Roseroiter, S; Villa-Lobos, pf and guitar
For complete listing of contents see *Um canto que saiu das senzalas*, D102
*See*: W406                                                             D281

## Noneto
CAPITOL CLASSICS P8191
Concert Arts Ensemble; Roger Wagner Chorale; Roger Wagner, cond
Includes his *Quatuor* (fl, sax, cel, harp & female voices)
*See*: W191                                                             D282

## Noneto
RCA LCT1143
Brazilian Festival Orchestra; Schola Cantorum of New York; Hugh Ross, cond
Includes his *Bachianas brasileiras no.1, Canção do carreiro*, and various songs performed by Elsie Houston
*See*: W191                                                             D283

## Noneto
TAPECAR GRAVAÇÕES MEC/MVL 014
Orchestra and chorus of the Teatro Municipal of Rio de Janeiro; Roberto Ricardo Duarte, cond
Also includes his *Descobrimento do Brasil* (4th suite) and *Choros no.10*
*See*: W191                                                             D284

## Ondulando
EMI/LA VOIX DE SON MAITRE 2 C 165-16250/9
L'oeuvre de piano
Anna Stella Schic, pf
For complete listing of contents see *Amazonas* D003
*See*: W082                                                             D285

## Padre nosso
ENIR ECL-002
Coral Ars Nova (da Universidade Federal de Minas Gerais); Carlos Alberto Pinto da Fonseca, cond
For complete listing of contents see *Ave Maria* D007
*See*: W026                                                             D286

**Panis angelicus**
ENIR ECL-002
Coral Ars Nova (da Universidade Federal de Minas Gerais);
Carlos Alberto Pinto da Fonseca, cond
For complete listing of contents see *Ave Maria* D007
*See*: W509                                                    D287

**O papagaio do moleque** (Episódio Sinfônico)
MEC/MVL/DAC/PAC - 015/1975
Villa-Lobos Festival 1975
Orquestra Sinfônica Brasileira; Sergio Magnani, cond
Includes his *Erosão* (Lenda ameríndia no.1 - Origem do Rio
Amazonas)
*See*: W302                                                    D288

**Passa, passa, gavião**
COMPANHIA BRASILEIRA DE PROJETOS E OBRAS  803.401
Miguel Proença, pf
For complete listing of contents see *Bachianas
brasileiras no.5* D046
*See*: W220                                                    D289

**O pastorzinho**
CARAVELLE  CAR 43007
O piano de Villa-Lobos
Arnaldo Estrella, pf
For complete listing of contents see *À procura de uma
agulha* D001
*See*: W279                                                    D290

**Pater noster**
ENIR ECL-002
Coral Ars Nova (da Universidade Federal de Minas Gerais);
Carlos Alberto Pinto da Fonseca, cond
For complete listing of contents see *Ave Maria* D007
*See*: Collections, M.S. v1 #12                               D291

**Pequena suíte**
FJA - 112 (MVL 30)
II Concurso Internacional de Violoncelo
Mário Tavares, cond
For complete listing of contents see *Bachianas
brasileiras no.1* D011
*See*: W064                                    ·                D292

**Pequena suíte**
TAPECAR GRAVAÇOES MEC/MVL 019
Victor Addiego and Laurien Laufmann, vc; F. Eger, pf
Includes his *O canto de nossa terra, O trenzinho do caipira, O canto do cisne negro*, and works by Guerra Vicente and Camargo Guarnieri
*See*: W064                                          D293

**Petizada**
EMI/LA VOIX DE SON MAITRE 2 C 165-16250/9
L'oeuvre de piano
Anna Stella Schic, pf
For complete listing of contents see *Amazonas* D003
*See*: W048                                          D294

**O pião**
CARAVELLE  CAR 43007
O piano de Villa-Lobos
Arnaldo Estrella, pf
For complete listing of contents see *À procura de uma agulha* D001
*See*: W279                                          D295

**Pobre cega**
EMI 31C 064 422957
Trem caipira
Egberto Gismonti, performer
For complete listing of contents see *Bachianas brasileiras no.4* D037
*See*: W220                                          D296

**Pobrezinha**
CARAVELLE  CAR 43007
O piano de Villa-Lobos
Arnaldo Estrella, pf
For complete listing of contents see *À procura de uma agulha* D001
*See*: W140                                          D297

**Poema singelo**
EMI/LA VOIX DE SON MAITRE 2 C 165-16250/9
L'oeuvre de piano
Anna Stella Schic, pf
For complete listing of contents see *Amazonas* D003
*See*: W434                                                          D298

**Poema singelo**
PHILIPS 6747 313  Série de luxo
Vol.9 PERSONALIDADES
Arnaldo Estrella, pf
For complete listing of contents see *A lenda do caboclo*
  D263
*See*: W434                                                          D299

**Poema singelo**
SPECTRUM SR-198
Claudio Vasquez, pf
Includes his *A prole do bebê no.2, Chôros no.5, As três
  Marias, Bachianas brasileiras no.4* (Prelude)
*See*: W434                                                          D300

**Poême de l'enfant et de sa mère**
SFP 31024/5/6
L'Oeuvre pour Voix et Instruments
Anna-Maria Bondi, S, Françoise Petit, pf; les Solistes
  de Paris; Henri-Claude Fantapie, cond
For complete listing of contents see *Bachianas
  brasileiras no.5*, D056
*See*: W193                                                          D301

**O polichinelo**
CARAVELLE MEC-MVL 002
Villa-Lobos, O Intérprete
Beate Roseroiter, S; Villa-Lobos, pf and guitar
For complete listing of contents see *Um canto que saiu
  das senzalas*, D102
*See*: W140                                                          D302

**Preludes** (Complete)
ADES 14095-2
Anna Stella Schic, pf
Includes his *Cirandas* and *A prole do bebê no.1*
*See*: W419                                                          D303

**Preludes** (Complete)
ADES 14096-2
Anna-Stella Schic, pf
Includes his *Choros nos. 1 & 5, Ciclo brasileiro, A prole
do bebê no.2*
*See*: W419                                                    D304

**Preludes** (Complete)
DEUTSCHE GRAMMOPHON DG 2530140
Narciso Yepes, guitar
Includes his *Études* (12)
*See*: W419                                                    D305

**Preludes** (Complete)
EMI/LA VOIX DE SON MAITRE 2 C 165-16250/9
L'oeuvre de piano
Anna Stella Schic, pf
For complete listing of contents see *Amazonas* D003
*See*: W419                                                    D306

**Preludes** (Selections)
CAPITOL P8497
Music for the Spanish Guitar
Laurindo Almeida, guitar
Includes *Preludes 1, 3*, and *5*, and *Études 1, 7*, and *8*
*See*: W419                                                    D307

**Preludes** (Selections)
CBS IM-37829
Virtuoso
Liona Boyd, guitar
Includes *Preludes 1, 2*, and *4*
*See*: W419                                                    D308

**Preludes** (Selections)
CBS M-34198
John Williams, guitar
Includes *Sonatas* by Scarlatti
*See*: W419                                                    D309

**Preludes** (Selections)
RCA AGL1-4897
Julian Bream, guitar
Includes his *Concerto para violão, Schottisch-choro*, and

*Etude* in c-sharp minor
See: W419                                                    D310

**Preludes** (Selections)
PAV ADW 7097
Oscar Cáceres, guitar
Includes his *Preludes 1, 3,* and *4, Etudes 5* and *10,*
  *Choros no.1, Suite populaire brésilienne,* and a work by
  Marlos Nobre
See: W419                                                    D311

**Prelúdio no.1**
CARAVELLE MEC-MVL 002
Villa-Lobos, O Intérprete
Beate Roseroiter, S; Villa-Lobos, pf and guitar
For complete listing of contents see *Um canto que saiu
  das senzalas,* D102
See: W419                                                    D312

**Prelúdio no.1**
DA CAMERA SONG  SM 95033
Musique intime pour guitare II
Rudolf Wangler, guitar
Includes his *Prelúdio no.3,* and works by Falla, Tárrega,
  Albéniz, Logy, Sor, and Visée
See: W419                                                    D313

**Prelúdio no.2**
ANGEL S-36020
In the Spanish Style
Christopher Parkening, guitar
Includes his *Étude no.l,* and works by Albéniz, Tárrega,
  Torroba, Mudarra, Guerau, Sor, Lauro, and Ponce
See: W419                                                    D314

**Prelúdio no.2**
COMPANHIA BRASILEIRA DE PROJETOS E OBRAS  803.401
Turíbio Santos, guitar
For complete listing of contents see *Bachianas
  brasileiras no.5* D046
See: W419                                                    D315

**Prelúdio no.2**
MEC/MVL/PAC/012

Villa-Lobos Concurso Internacional de Piano 1974
Adam Fellegi, Jorge Fortes, and Yuri Smirnov, pf
For complete listing of contents see *Homenagem a Chopin*
D247
*See*: W419                                                      D316

**Prelúdio no.2**
MVL 32
III Concurso Internacional de Violão
Various performers
For a complete listing of contents see *Concerto para*
   *violão e orquestra* D175
*See*: W419                                                      D317

**Prelúdio no. 3**
ANGEL S-36064
Clair de lune
Laurindo Almeida, guitar
Includes his *Étude no.1*, and works by Falla, Debussy,
   Granados, Albéniz, and Ravel
*See*: W419                                                      D318

**Prelúdio no.3**
DA CAMERA SONG  SM 95033
Musique intime pour guitare II
Rudolf Wangler, guitar
Includes his *Prelúdio no.1*, and works by Falla, Tárrega,
   Albéniz, Logy, Sor, and Visée
*See*: W419                                                      D319

**Prelúdio no.4**
MEC/SEAC/FUNARTE/MVL - 025
II Concurso Internacional de Violão
Rodolfo M. Lahoz, guitar
Includes his *Concerto para violão e orquestra, Études*
   de violão, and *Preludio no.5*
*See*: W419                                                      D320

**Prelúdio no.4**
WERGO WER 60 105
Guitar Music of our Time
Konrad Rgaossnig, guitar
Includes his *Mazurka-Choro, Choro no.1*, and *Étude*
   *no.12,* and works by Vogel, Zehm, Mittergradnegger,

Brindle, and Dohl
*See*: W419                                                    D321

**Prelúdio no.5**
MEC/SEAC/FUNARTE/MVL - 025
II Concurso Internacional de Violão
Marcelo Jeha Kayath, guitar
Includes his *Concerto para violão e orquestra, Études*
  de violão, and *Prelúdio no.4*
*See*: W419                                                    D322

**Prole do bebê**
DENON OX-7113-ND
Arthur Moreira-Lima, pf
Includes his *Choros no.5, Valsa da dor*, and *Rudepoema*
*See*: W140                                                    D323

**Prole do bebê** (Selections)
MEC/MVL/PAC/012
Villa-Lobos Concurso Internacional de Piano 1974
Adam Fellegi, Jorge Fortes, and Yuri Smirnov, pf
For complete listing of contents see *Homenagem a Chopin*
  D247
*See*: W140                                                    D324

**Prole do bebê no.1**
ADES 14095-2
Anna Stella Schic, pf
Includes his *Cirandas* and *Preludes*
*See*: W140                                                    D325

**Prole do bebê no.1**
ANGEL S-37110
Cristina Ortiz, pf
For complete listing of contents see *Choros no.5* D137
*See*: W140                                                    D326

**Prole do bebê no.1**
DA CAMERA 93106
Iberoamerikanische Klaviermusik im 20. Jahrhundert
Alex Blin, pf
Includes his *Saudade das selvas brasileiras no.2,* and
   works by Ginastera, Tauriello, Castro, Roldan, and
   Revueltas
*See:* W140                                                        D327

**Prole do bebê no.1**
EMS 10
Jacques Abram, pf
Includes his *Rudepoema* and *As três Marias*
*See:* W140                                                        D328

**Prole do bebê no.1**
TELEFUNKEN  SAT 22547  6.41299
Nelson Freire, pf
Includes his *Bachianas brasileiras no.4* (Prelúdio), *As
   três Marias,* and *Rudepoêma*
*See:* W141                                                        D329

**Prole do bebê no.1**
WESTMINSTER WN 18065
Jose Echaniz, pf
Includes his *Prole do bebê no.2*
*See:* W141                                                        D330

**Prole do bebê no.2**
ADES 14096-2
Anna Stella Schic, pf
Includes his *Choros nos.1,2,* and  *5,* and *Ciclo
   brasileiro*
*See:* W180                                                        D331

**A prole do bebê no.2**
SPECTRUM SR-198
Claudio Vasquez, pf
Includes his *Chôros no.5, Poema singelo, As três Marias,
   Bachianas brasileiras no.4* (Prelude)
*See:* W180                                                        D332

**Prole do bebê no.2**
WESTMINSTER WN 18065

Jose Echaniz, pf
Includes his *Prole do bebê no.1*
*See*: W180                                          D333

**A prole do bebê nos.1 and 2**
EMI/LA VOIX DE SON MAITRE 2 C 165-16250/9
L'oeuvre de piano
Anna Stella Schic, pf
For complete listing of contents see *Amazonas* D003
*See*: W140 and W180                                 D334

**A prole do bebê nos.1 and 2**
EMI 2 C 153-14090/9
Villa-Lobos par lui-même
Orchestre National de la Radiodiffusion Française; Villa-
  Lobos, cond
For complete listing of contents see *Bachianas
  brasileiras no.1* D010
*See*: W140 and W180                                 D335

**A prole do bebê nos.1 and 2** (Selections)
EDUCO 3091
Huybregts, pf
Includes works by Chopin, Liszt, Satie, and Scriabin
*See*: W140 and W180                                 D336

**A prole do bebê nos.1 and 2**
RCA 5670-1-RC
Artur Rubinstein, pf
Includes works by Albéniz, Debussy, Prokofiev, Schumann,
  and Szymanowski
*See*: W140 and W180                                 D337

**Quarteto**
RAVENNA RAVE 702
Soni Ventorum Wind Quintet
Includes his *Bachianas brasileiras no.6, Choros no.2* and
  *Trio*
*See*: W230                                          D338

**Quarteto de cordas no.1**
RBM Records RMB 3034
University of Brasilia String Quartet
Includes works by Mário Ficarelli and Lindembergue

Cardoso
*See*: W099                                                    D339

**Quarteto de cordas no.5**
VICTOR 11 212
Quarteto Carioca
*See*: W263                                                    D340

**Quarteto de cordas no.6**
COLUMBIA FCX 467
Le Quatuor Hongrois
*See*: W399                                                    D341

**Quarteto de cordas no.11**
FESTA LDR-5020
Quarteto da Rádio Ministério de Educação e Cultura
Includes his *Bachianas brasileiras no.4* (Prelude), and
   *Magnificat-alleluia*
*See*: W481                                                    D342

**Quarteto de cordas no.11**
MEC/DAC/MVL 013
Concurso Internacional de Quarteto de Cordas 1966
Quarteto de cordas Mário de Andrade
Includes his *Quarteto de cordas no.16*
*See*: W481                                                    D343

**Quarteto de cordas no.15**
CARAVELLE MEC/MVL 004
Quarteto Santiago; various soloists
Includes his *Choros nos.2* and *4*, and *Quatuor* (fl, ob, cl
   and bn)
*See*: W523                                                    D344

**Quarteto de cordas no.16**
CBS 160174
Quarteto U.F.R.J
Includes Henrique Oswald, *Quarteto brasileiro*
*See*: W526                                                    D345

**Quarteto de cordas no.16**
MEC/DAC/CFC/MVL 020/1977
Concurso Internacional de Quartetos de Cordas
Quarteto de Cordas de la Universidad Nacional de la Plata

Includes his *Quarteto de cordas no.17*
*See*: W526                                             D346

**Quarteto de cordas no.16**
MEC/DAC/MVL 013
Concurso Internacional de Quarteto de Cordas 1966
Quarteto Rio de Janeiro
Includes his *Quarteto de cordas no.11*
*See*: W526                                             D347

**Quarteto de cordas no.17**
MEC/DAC/CFC/MVL 020/1977
Concurso Internacional de Quartetos de Cordas
Audubon Quartet
Includes his *Quarteto de cordas no.16*
*See*: W537                                             D348

**Quarteto de cordas no.17**
ODYSSEY 32 16 0176
Brazilian String Quartet
Includes Alberto Nepomuceno: *Quartet no.3* in d,
   "Brasileiro"
*See*: W537                                             D349

**Quatuor** (Flute, oboe, clarinet and bassoon)
CALIG CAL 30840
Blaserwerke fur Trio, Quartett und Quintett
Residenz-Quintett Munchen
Includes his *Quintette en forme de choros,* and *Trio* (ob,
   cl, & bn)
*See*: W230                                             D350

**Quatuor** (Flute, oboe, clarinet and bassoon)
CARAVELLE MEC/MVL 004
Quarteto Santiago; various soloists
Includes his *Choros nos.2* and *4,* and *Quarteto de cordas
   no.15*
*See*: W230                                             D351

**Quatuor** (Flute, oboe, clarinet and bassoon)
WESTMINSTER WL 5360
New Art Wind Quintet
Includes his *Quinteto em forma de choros*, and *Trio*
  (Oboe, clarinet and bassoon)
*See*: W230                                                        D352

**Quatuor** (Flute, saxophone, celeste, harp and female voices)
CAPITOL CLASSICS P8191
Concert Arts Ensemble; Roger Wagner Chorale; Roger
  Wagner, cond
Includes his *Noneto*
*See*: W181                                                        D353

**Quintet** (with harp)
ADDA 581035
Group Instrumental de Paris
Includes his *Quintette en forme de choros* and *Trio*
  (strings)
*See*: W538                                                        D354

**Quintette en forme de choros**
ADDA 581035
Group Instrumental de Paris
Includes his *Quintet* (with harp) and *Trio* (strings)
*See*: W231                                                        D355

**Quintette en forme de choros**
CALIG CAL 30840
Blaserwerke fur Trio, Quartett und Quintett
Residenz-Quintett Munchen
Includes his *Quatuor* (fl, ob, cl & bn) and *Trio* (ob,
  cl, & bn)
*See*: W231                                                        D356

**Quintette en forme de choros**
CBS MK-39558
Ensemble Wien-Berlin
Includes works by Bozza, Danzi, Haydn and Ibert
*See*: W231                                                        D357

**Quintette en forme de choros**
CDM  78836
Les choros de chambre

For complete listing of performers and contents see
  *Choros bis* D107
  *See*: W231                                        D358

**Quinteto em forma de choros**
  KUARUP KLP BV1-4
  Villa-Lobos 100 Anos
  Quinteto Villa-Lobos
  For complete listing of contents see *Bachianas*
    *brasileiras no.2* D023
  *See*: W231                                        D359

**Quintette en forme de choros**
  LYRICHORD LLST 7168
  Soni Ventorum Wind Quintet
  Includes works by Mozart
  *See*: W231                                        D360

**Quintette en forme de choros**
  NONESUCH 71030E
  New York Woodwind Quintet
  Includes his *Bachianas brasileiras no.6*, and works by
    Glazunov and Ibert
  *See*: W231                                        D361

**Quintette en forme de choros**
  PAN VERLAG VLEUGELS OV-75004
  Aulos Wind Quintet of Stuttgart
  Includes works by Hindemith and Ravel
  *See*: W231                                        D362

**Quintette en forme de choros**
  WESTMINSTER WL 5360
  New Art Wind Quintet
  Includes his *Quatuor*, and *Trio* (Oboe, clarinet and
    bassoon)
  *See*: W231                                        D363

**Remeiro do São Francisco**
  PHILIPS 6598 309 Série de Luxo
  Maria Lúcia Godoy,S; Sergio Abréu, guitar
  For complete listing of contents see *Bachianas*
    *brasileiras no.5* D053
  *See*: W365                                        D364

**Rosa amarela**
ANGEL SBR-XLD-12.276
Magda Tagliaferro, pf
For complete listing of contents see *Choros no.5* D138
*See*: W280                                                    D365

**Rudá**
MEC/MVL 005-1972
Orchestra of the Teatro Municipal of Rio de Janeiro;
  Mário Tavares, cond
*See*: W504                                                    D366

**Rudepoema**
DENON OX-7113-ND
Arthur Moreira-Lima, pf
Includes his *Prole do bebê no.1, Valsa da dor*, and
  *Choros no.5*
*See*: W184                                                    D367

**Rudepoema**
DEUTSCHE GRAMMOPHON 2530 634
Roberto Szidon, pf; with Richard Metzler, pf
For complete listing of contents see *Carnaval das
  crianças* D104
*See*: W184                                                    D368

**Rudepoema**
EMI/LA VOIX DE SON MAITRE 2 C 165-16250/9
L'oeuvre de piano
Anna Stella Schic, pf
For complete listing of contents see *Amazonas* D003
*See*: W184                                                    D369

**Rudepoema**
EMS 10
Jacques Abram, pf
Includes his *Prole do bebê* and *As três Marias*
*See*: W184                                                    D370

**Rudepoema**
TELEFUNKEN SAT 22547 6.41299
Nelson Freire, pf
Includes his *Bachianas brasileiras no.4* (Prelúdio), *Prole do bebê no.1*, and *As três Marias*
*See*: W184                                                      D371

**Rudepoema**
WERGO WER 60110
Volker Banfield, pf
Includes Muller-Siemens, Detlev - *Under Neonlight* II
*See*: W184                                                      D372

**Samba clássico**
CLAVES D 8401
Teresa Berganza, mezzo; Juan Antonio Alvarez Parejo, pf
For complete listing of contents see *Adeus Ema* D002
*See*: W497                                                      D373

**Saudades das selvas brasileiras**
DA CAMERA 93106
Iberoamerikanische Klaviermusik im 20. Jahrhundert
Alex Blin, pf
Includes his *A prole do bebê no.1*, and works by
Ginastera, Tauriello, Castro, Roldan, and Revueltas
*See*: W226                                                      D374

**Saudades das selvas brasileiras**
DEUTSCHE GRAMMOPHON 2530 634
Roberto Szidon, pf; with Richard Metzler, pf
For complete listing of contents see *Carnaval das crianças* D104
*See*: W226                                                      D375

**Saudades das selvas brasileiras**
EMI/LA VOIX DE SON MAITRE 2 C 165-16250/9
L'oeuvre de piano
Anna Stella Schic, pf
For complete listing of contents see *Amazonas* D003
*See*: W226                                                      D376

**Schottish-choro**
MVL 32
III Concurso Internacional de Violão

Various performers
For a complete listing of contents see *Concerto para
violão e orquestra* D175
*See*: W020                                                    D377

**Schottish-choro**
RCA AGL1-4897
Julian Bream, guitar
Includes his *Preludes nos.1-5, Étude in C-sharp minor*,
and *Concerto for guitar*
*See*: W020                                                    D378

**Senhora dona sancha**
CARAVELLE  CAR 43007
O piano de Villa-Lobos
Arnaldo Estrella, pf
For complete listing of contents see *À procura de uma
agulha* D001
*See*: W220                                                    D379

**Serestas** (14)
PHILIPS 4122111
Maria Lúcia Godoy, S.; Miguel Proença, pf
*See*: W216                                                    D380

**Serestas**
SFP 31024/5/6
L'Oeuvre pour Voix et Instruments
Anna-Maria Bondi, S, Françoise Petit, pf; les Solistes
de Paris; Henri-Claude Fantapie, cond
For complete listing of contents see *Bachianas
brasileiras no.5*, D055
*See*: W215                                                    D381

**Serestas**
SFP 31024/5/6
L'Oeuvre pour Voix et Instruments
Anna-Maria Bondi, S, Françoise Petit, pf; les Solistes
de Paris; Henri-Claude Fantapie, cond
For complete listing of contents see *Bachianas
brasileiras no.5*, D055
*See*: W215                                                    D382

**Sexteto místico**
MVL 32
III Concurso Internacional de Violão
Various performers
For a complete listing of contents see *Concerto para violão e orquestra* D175
*See*: W131                                                    D383

**Simples coletânea**
EMI/LA VOIX DE SON MAITRE 2 C 165-16250/9
L'oeuvre de piano
Anna Stella Schic, pf
For complete listing of contents see *Amazonas* D003
*See*: W134                                                    D384

**Sonata fantasia no.1** (Désespérance) (Violin and piano)
FUNARTE PROMEMUS MMB 79.009
Oscar Borgerth, vn; Ilara Gomes Grosso, pf
Includes his *Sonata fantasia no.2, Sonata no.3*, and *Improviso no.7*
*See*: W051                                                    D385

**Sonata fantasia no.1** (Désespérance) (Violin and piano)
MVL-31
I Concurso Internacional de Violino
Leonid Levin, vn; Luiz Henrique Senise, pf
Includes his *Sonata fantasia no.2,* and *Sonata no.3*
*See*: W051                                                    D386

**Sonata fantasia no.2** (Violin and piano)
FUNARTE PROMEMUS MMB 79.009
Oscar Borgerth, vn; Ilara Gomes Grosso, pf
Includes his *Sonata fantasia no.1* (Désespérance), *Sonata no.3*, and *Improviso no.7*
*See*: W083                                                    D387

**Sonata fantasia no.2** (Violin and piano)
MVL-31
I Concurso Internacional de Violino
Jean Paul Jourdan, vn; Sonia Goulart, pf
Includes his *Sonata fantasia no.1* (Désespérance), and *Sonata no.3*
*See*: W083                                                    D388

**Sonata no.2** (Cello and piano)
FESTA IG 79.013
Radamés Gnattali, pf; Iberê Gomes Grosso, vc
Includes Radamés Gnattali - *Sonata* para violoncelo e
piano, *Modinha e baião*, and *Flor da noite*
*See*: W103                                                     D389

**Sonata no.3** (Violin and piano)
FUNARTE PROMEMUS MMB 79.009
Oscar Borgerth, vn; Ilara Gomes Grosso, pf
Includes his *Sonata fantasia no.1* (Désespérance) *Sonata
fantasia no.2*, and *Improviso no.7*
*See*: W171                                                     D390

**Sonata no.3** (Violin and piano)
MVL-31
I Concurso Internacional de Violino
Anibal Castanho de Lima, vn; Luiz Medalha, pf
Includes his *Sonata fantasia no.1* (Désespérance) and
*Sonata fantasia no.2*
*See*: W171                                                     D391

**Suíte floral**
COPACABANA CLP 11.641
Panorama da música brasileira para piano
Belkiss Carneiro de Mendonça
Includes works by Henrique Oswald, Lorenzo Fernandez,
  Fructuoso Vianna, Francisco Mignone, Osvaldo Lacerda,
  Marlos Nobre, Claudio Santoro, and Camargo Guarnieri
*See*: W117                                                     D392

**Suíte floral**
DEUTSCHE GRAMMOPHON 2530 634
Roberto Szidon, pf; with Richard Metzler, pf
For complete listing of contents see *Carnaval das
crianças* D104
*See*: W117                                                     D393

**Suíte floral**
EMI/LA VOIX DE SON MAITRE 2 C 165-16250/9
L'oeuvre de piano
Anna Stella Schic, pf
For complete listing of contents see *Amazonas* D003
*See*: W117                                                     D394

**II (Second) suite for chamber orchestra**
TAPECAR GRAVAÇÕES MEC/MVL/PAC/011
Symphony orchestra of the Teatro Municipal of Rio de
 Janeiro; Laszlo Halasz, cond
Includes his *The Emperor Jones*
*See*: W567                                                                      D395

**Suíte infantil (1 & 2)**
EMI/LA VOIX DE SON MAITRE 2 C 165-16250/9
L'oeuvre de piano
Anna Stella Schic, pf
For complete listing of contents see *Amazonas* D003
*See*: W053 abd W067                                                   D396

**Suíte para canto e violino**
PHILIPS 6598 309  Série de Luxo
Maria Lúcia Godoy,S; Sérgio Abreu, guitar
For complete listing of contents see *Bachianas
 brasileiras no.5* D053
*See*: W195                                                                     D397

**Suíte para canto e violino**
SFP 31024/5/6
L'Oeuvre pour Voix et Instruments
Anna-Maria Bondi, S, Françoise Petit, pf; les Solistes
 de Paris; Henri-Claude Fantapie, cond
For complete listing of contents see *Bachianas
 brasileiras no.5*, D055
*See*: W195                                                                     D398

**Suite populaire brésilienne**
BIS  LP-233
Favourite Guitar Music
Diego Blanco, guitar
Includes his *Choros no.1*, and works by Tárrega, Myers,
 Yocoh, and Albéniz
*See*: W020                                                                     D399

**Suite populaire brésilienne**
DA CAMERA MAGNA  SM 93609
Sonja Prunnbauer, guitar
Includes works by Turina, Tárrega, Sor, and Ponce
*See*: W020                                                                     D400

**Suite populaire brésilienne**
PAV ADW 7097
Oscar Caceres, guitar
Includes his *Études nos. 5* & *10, Choros no.1, Preludes nos. 1, 3,* & *4,* and a work by Marlos Nobre
*See*: W020                                                                                      D401

**Suíte populaire brésilienne**
TURNABOUT TV 34676
Manuel Barruenco, guitar
Includes his *Études*, and works by Guarnieri, and Chavez
*See*: W020                                                                                      D402

**Sul América**
EMI/LA VOIX DE SON MAITRE 2 C 165-16250/9
L'oeuvre de piano
Anna Stella Schic, pf
For complete listing of contents see *Amazonas* D003
*See*: W217                                                                                      D403

**Symphony no.4** (A Vitória)
EMI 2 C 153-14090/9
Villa-Lobos par lui-même
Orchestre National de la Radiodiffusion Française; Villa-Lobos, cond
For complete listing of contents see *Bachianas brasileiras no.1* D010
*See*: W153                                                                                      D404

**Teresinha de Jesus**
CARAVELLE CAR 43007
O piano de Villa-Lobos
Arnaldo Estrella, pf
For complete listing of contents see *À procura de uma agulha* D001
*See*: W220                                                                                      D405

**Teresinha de Jesus**
DA CAMERA MAGNA SM 93602
Ilse and Nicolaus Alfonso, guitars
Includes works by Vivaldi, Rosenmuller, J.S. Bach, Carulli, Falla, Cervantes, Absil, and Alfonso
*See*: W220                                                                                      D406

**O trenzinho do caipira**
EMI 31C 064 422957
Trem Caipira
Egberto Gismonti, performer
For complete listing of contents see *Bachianas brasileiras no.4* D037
*See*: W247 and W254

D407

**O trenzinho do caipira**
FJA - 112 (MVL 30)
II Concurso Internacional de Violoncelo
Mário Tavares, cond
For complete listing of contents see *Bachianas brasileiras no.1* D011
*See*: W247 and W254

D408

**O trenzinho do caipira**
TAPECAR GRAVAÇÕES MEC/MVL 019
Victor Addiego and Laurien Laufmann, vc; F. Eger, pf
Includes his *Pequena suíte, O canto da nossa terra, O canto do cisne negro*, and works by Guerra Vicente and Camargo Guarnieri
*See*: W247 and W254

D409

**As três Marias**
EMI/LA VOIX DE SON MAITRE 2 C 165-16250/9
L'oeuvre de piano
Anna Stella Schic, pf
For complete listing of contents see *Amazonas* D003
*See*: W411

D410

**As três Marias**
EMS 10
Jacques Abram, pf
Includes his *A prole do bebê* and *Rudepoema*
*See*: W411

D411

**As três Marias**
SPECTRUM SR-198
Claudio Vasquez, pf
Includes his *A prole do bebê no.2, Choros no.5, Poema singelo, Bachianas brasileiras no.4* (Prelude)
*See*: W411

D412

**As três Marias**
   TELEFUNKEN  SAT 22547  6.41299
   Nelson Freire, pf
   Includes his *Bachianas brasileiras no.4* (Prelúdio), *A prole do bebê no.1*, and *Rudepoema*
   *See*: W411                                                          D413

**Trio** (Oboe, clarinet and bassoon)
   CALIG CAL 30840
   Blaserwerke fur Trio, Quartett und Quintett
   Residenz-Quintett Munchen
   Includes his *Quatuor* (fl, ob, cl & bn) and *Quintette en forme de choros*
   *See*: W182                                                          D414

**Trio** (Oboe, clarinet,and bassoon)
   PHILOTSOM MVL-001
   Paolo Nardi, ob; José Botelho, cl; Noël Devos, bn
   Includes his *Trio no.2* (pf, vn, & vc)
   *See*: W182                                                          D415

**Trio** (Oboe, clarinet, and bassoon)
   RAVENNA RAVE 702
   Soni Ventorum Wind Quintet
   Includes his *Bachianas brasileiras no.6, Choros no.2* and *Quarteto* (Fl, ob, cl, and bn)
   *See*: W182                                                          D416

**Trio** (Oboe, clarinet and bassoon)
   WESTMINSTER WL 5360
   New Art Wind Quintet
   Includes his *Quatuor*, and *Quinteto em forma de choros*
   *See*: W182                                                          D417

**Trio** (No.1 for piano and strings)
   GOLDEN CREST GC 4213
   Macalester Trio
   Includes a work by Turina
   *See*: W042                                                          D418

**Trio** (Strings)
   ADDA 581035
   Group Instrumental de Paris
   Includes his *Quintet* (with harp) and *Quintette en forme*

*de choros*
See: W460

D419

**Trio** (Strings)
CARAVELLE MEC/MVL 007
Quarteto Guanabara
Includes his *Choros bis*
See: W460

D420

**Trio no.2** (Piano, violin, and cello)
PHILOTSOM MVL-001
Trio Novo Pro Arte
Includes his *Trio* (ob, cl, bn)
See: W105

D421

**Trio no.2** (Piano, violin, and cello)
CENTAUR 1004
Philadelphia Trio
Includes a work by Kirchner
See: W105

D422

**Tristorosa**
CARAVELLE CAR 43007
O piano de Villa-Lobos
Arnaldo Estrella, pf
For complete listing of contents see *À procura de uma
  agulha* D001
See: W034

D423

**Tristorosa**
EMI/LA VOIX DE SON MAITRE 2 C 165-16250/9
L'oeuvre de piano
Anna Stella Schic, pf
For complete listing of contents see *Amazonas* D003
See: W034

D424

**Uirapuru**
EVEREST SDBR 3016
Stadium Symphony Orchestra of New York; Leopold
  Stokowski, cond
Also includes his *Bachianas brasileiras no.1* (Modinha);
  Prokofiev - *Cinderella* (Ballet suite)
See: W133

D425

**Valsa-choro**
COMPANHIA BRASILEIRA DE PROJETOS E OBRAS  803.401
Turíbio Santos, guitar
For complete listing of contents see *Bachianas
brasileiras no.5* D046
*See*: W020                                                                D426

**Valsa-choro**
MVL 32
III Concurso Internacional de Violão
Various performers
For a complete listing of contents see *Concerto para
violão e orquestra* D175
*See*: W020                                                                D427

**Valsa da dor**
CARAVELLE  CAR 43007
O piano de Villa-Lobos
Arnaldo Estrella, pf
For complete listing of contents see *À procura de uma
agulha* D001
*See*: W316                                                                D428

**Valsa da dor**
COMPANHIA BRASILEIRA DE PROJETOS E OBRAS  803.401
Miguel Proença, pf
For complete listing of contents see *Bachianas
brasileiras no.5* D046
*See*: W316                                                                D429

**Valsa da dor**
DENON OX-7113-ND
Arthur Moreira-Lima, pf
Includes his *A prole do bebê no.1, Choros no.5,* and
*Rudepoema*
*See*: W316                                                                D430

**Valsa da dor**
PHILIPS 6747 313  Série de luxo
Vol.9 PERSONALIDADES
Arnaldo Estrella, pf
For complete listing of contents see *A lenda do caboclo*
D263
*See*: W316                                                                D431

**Valse-scherzo**
EMI/LA VOIX DE SON MAITRE 2 C 165-16250/9
L'oeuvre de piano
Anna Stella Schic, pf
For complete listing of contents see *Amazonas* D003
*See*: W070                                                    D432

**Vamos atrás da serra, oh! calunga**
ANGEL SBR-XLD-12.276
Magda Tagliaferro, pf
For complete listing of contents see *Choros no.5* D138
*See*: W282                                                    D433

**Vamos atrás da serra, oh! calunga**
CARAVELLE CAR 43007
O piano de Villa-Lobos
Arnaldo Estrella, pf
For complete listing of contents see *À procura de uma
   agulha* D001
*See*: W282                                                    D434

**Viola quebrada**
CLAVES D 8401
Teresa Berganza, mezzo; Juan Antonio Alvarez Parejo, pf
For complete listing of contents see *Adeus Ema* D002
*See*: W159                                                    D435

**Vira português**
EMI ODEON SC-10.114
Cristina Maristany, S; Alceu Bocchino, pf
For complete listing of contents see *Canção de cristal*
D085
*See*. W225                                                    D436

**Vôo (Seresta No.14)**
SFP 31024/5/6
L'Oeuvre pour Voix et Instruments
Anna-Maria Bondi, S, Françoise Petit, pf; les Solistes
de Paris; Henri-Claude Fantapie, cond
For complete listing of contents see *Bachianas
   brasileiras no.5*, D055
*See*: W216                                                    D437

## Xangô
CARAVELLE MEC-MVL 002
Villa-Lobos, O Intérprete
Beate Roseroiter, S; Villa-Lobos, pf and guitar
For complete listing of contents see *Um canto que saiu
das senzalas*, D102
*See*: W158 and W159                                    D438

## Xangô
CLAVES D 8401
Teresa Berganza, mezzo; Juan Antonio Alvarez Parejo, pf
For complete listing of contents see *Adeus Ema* D002
*See*: W158 and W159                                    D439

## Xô xô, passarinho
LONDON LLB 1110
Ney Salgado, pf
For complete listing of contents see *Bachianas
brasileiras no.4* D038
*See*: W220                                             D440

# Bibliography

## Books

The bibliography of books and articles about and by Villa-Lobos is a representative selection of books and articles. The enormous body of Portuguese language and European newspaper articles required that a careful selection to be made. The Villa-Lobos Museum in Rio de Janeiro contains eleven volumes of catalogued news clippings, many without date or complete information concerning the newspaper in which articles were published. The Museum also contains a large collection of uncatalogued letters, news items and memorablia. The bibliography in this book includes a number of important items from this collection.

Appleby, David P. *The Music of Brazil*. Austin, TX:
    University of Texas Press, 1983.

> Villa-Lobos' contribution to the awakening of
> musical Nationalism in Brazil is included as well
> as a brief discussion of his life and works.          B001

Appleby, David P. *La Musica de Brasil*. Mexico, D.F.:
    Fondo de Cultura Economica, 1985.

> A Spanish translation of *The Music of Brazil*.        B002

Barros, C. Paula. *O romance de Villa-Lobos*. Rio de
    Janeiro: Editôra A Noite, n.d.

A highly romanticized biography of Villa-Lobos, authored by a Brazilian poet and admirer of the composer.                    B003

Batista, Marta Rossetti; Lopez, Tele Porto Ancona; and Lima, Yone Soares de. *Brasil: Primeiro tempo modernista- 1917/1929 Documentação.* São Paulo: Instituto de estudos brasileiros, 1972.

Pages 303-392 present articles about and by Villa-Lobos, reviews of concerts in Brazil and in France.    B004

Beaufils, Marcel. *Villa-Lobos Musicien et Poète du Brésil.* 2d ed. Rio de Janeiro: Museu Villa-Lobos - Fundação Nacional proMEMORIA, 1982.

A brief biography by a professor of the Paris Conservatory. Villa-Lobos made his international reputation in Paris.                    B005

Béhague, Gerard. *Music in Latin America*, an Introduction. Englewood Cliffs, N.J.: Prentice Hall, 1979.

A comprehensive, scholarly account of the history of the music of Latin America, places the contribution of Villa-Lobos in historical perspective.                    B006

Belo, José de Andrade. *Villa-Lobos.* Rio de Janeiro: Grafica editora, Arte Moderna, 1979.

A short biography for the Brazilian public.    B007

Boff, Ruy Celso. "Les Choros de Heitor Villa-Lobos- La Transfiguration de l'élément populaire." Thesis, Catholic University of Louvain, Institut Superieur d'Archéologie et l'Histoire de l'Art, Louvain, France, n.d.

A thesis by a Brazilian university student provides
insight into the popular elements in the choros of
Villa-Lobos.                                                    B008


Brandão, José Vieira. "O nacionalismo na música
  brasileira para piano." Master's thesis, University of
  Brazil, 1949.

         José Vieira Brandão was assistant to Villa-Lobos
         during the period when he reorganized music education
         in Brazil. An informative discussion of national
         elements in Villa-Lobos' piano music.                B009


Brazilian American Cultural Institute. Commentary on the
  Tenth Anniversary of the Death of Heitor Villa-Lobos
  (1887-1959). Washington, D.C. 1969

         Information concerning recordings, publishers, and
         performance times of individual works. Information is
         dated but useful.                                     B010


Brazilian Embassy in Paris. *Heitor Villa-Lobos: compositeur*
  *1877-1959.* (Biographical sketch illustrated
  by excerpts from the book by Marcel Beaufils: *Villa-*
  *Lobos-Musicien et poète du Brésil*) Paris: Brazilian
  Embassy, 1979.

         A biographical sketch of Villa-Lobos, mainly based on
         the Beaufils book.                                    B011


Caldi, Catalina Estela. "A execução da ritmica brasileira
  no Rudepoema para piano de Heitor Villa-Lobos."
  Master's thesis, Universidade Federal do Rio de
  Janeiro, 1985.

         Identification and discussion of typically Brazilian
         rhythm patters from popular music present in
         *Rudepoema*, Villa-Lobos' most extended piano work.   B012

Clément, Jeanne Venzo. "Villa-Lobos, Éducateur." Doctoral
    dissertation, Université de Paris-Sorbonne, 1978-
    1980.

> A comprehensive dissertation contains documentation
> and information concerning Villa-Lobos'
> reorganization of music education in Brazil during
> the period of the 1930's and 1940's.                    B013


Coelho, Aurea Regina de Oliveira. Villa-Lobos, sua
    *repercussão no exterior*. Rio de Janeiro: Museu Villa-
    Lobos, 1977.

> A short book on the international influence of
> Villa-Lobos.                                            B014


*l'Éducation musicale, trait d'union entre les peuples*;
    Rapports et discours sur l'éducation musicale dans les
    divers pays. Prague, Societé d'Éducation Musicale.
    1937.

> Papers of an international conference on music
> education held in Prague in 1936.                       B015


Elkins, Laurine Annette. "An Examination of Compositional
    Technique in Selected Piano Works of Heitor Villa-
    Lobos." Master of Music Thesis, University of Texas at
    Austin, August, 1971.

> A study of compositional techniques in piano works
> by Villa-Lobos.                                         B016


Enyart, John William. "The Symphonies of Heitor Villa-
    Lobos." Ph.D. diss., University of Cininnati, 1984.

> The symphonies of Villa-Lobos are among his least
> known works. This dissertation provides both
> background information and analyses.                    B017

Estrella, Arnaldo. *Os quartetos de cordas de Villa-Lobos.*
Rio de Janeiro: Ministério da Educação e Cultura -
Museu Villa-Lobos, 1970.

> For several years the Museu Villa-Lobos sponsored
> competitions for critical essays on various bodies
> of Villa-Lobos works. The essay on the string
> quartets is by a pianist intimately acquainted with
> his music.                                             B018


Farmer, Virginia. "An Analytical Study of the Seventeen
String Quartets of Heitor Villa-Lobos." Thesis,
University of Illinois-Urbana, 1973.

> The string quartets are important expressions of
> Villa-Lobos stylistic evolution and development as
> composer. Farmer is a student and performer of the
> Villa-Lobos quartet literature.                        B019


França, Eurico Nogueira. *A evolução de Villa-Lobos na
música de câmera.* Rio de Janeiro: Ministério da
Educação e Cultura-Departamento de Assuntos Culturais -
Museu Villa-Lobos, 1976.

> Eurico Nogueira França knew Villa-Lobos personally
> and has worked for many years in the Museu Villa-
> Lobos. The essay on Villa-Lobos' stylistic evolution
> in his music chamber music writing is informative
> and useful.                                            B020


França, Eurico Nogueira. *Villa-Lobos síntese crítica e
biografica.* 3d ed. Rio de Janeiro: Ministério da
Educação e Cultura-Departamento de Assuntos Culturais -
Museu Villa-Lobos, 1978.

> An essay in Portuguese with Spanish translation
> provides various items of information and a
> bibliography of writings about Villa-Lobos. Although
> much of the information is incomplete, it provides
> information not available elsewhere.                   B021

Giacomo, Arnaldo Magalhães de. *Villa-Lobos, alma sonora do Brasil.* (Biography for children and youth) São Paulo: Edições Melhoramentos, 1972.    B022


Guimarães, Luiz, Oldemar Guimarães, Dinorah Guimarães Campos, and Alvaro de Oliveira Guimarães. *Villa-Lobos visto da platéia e na intimidade* (1912/1935). Rio de Janeiro: Grafica Editôra Arte Moderna Ltda., 1972.

A biography compiled by the Guimarães family provides information and anecdotes concerning the early years of Villa-Lobos' marriage and his early struggles to establish himself as a composer. Reviews of his first public concerts and program information are essential to a student of Villa-Lobos' early years.    B023


Horta, Luis Paulo. *Heitor Villa-Lobos.* Rio de Janeiro: Edições Alumbramento: Livroarte Editora, 1986.

A biography and list of works prepared for the celebrations of the Villa-Lobos' centennial, amply illustrated with photographs.    B024


Julianelli, José Salvador, ed. *Homenagem a Villa-Lobos.* Rio de Janeiro: Ministério da Educação e Cultura, 1960

Short stories and reminiscences by friends and collaborators.    B025


Kiefer, Bruno. *Villa-Lobos e o modernismo na música brasileira.* Porto Alegre: Movimento, 1981.

An assesment of the influence of Villa-Lobos on the "Modernist" movement in Brazil.    B026


Lima, Souza. *Comentários sobre a obra pianística de Villa-Lobos.* 2d ed. Rio de Janeiro: Ministério da Educação e Cultura-Departamento de Assuntos Culturais - Museu Villa-Lobos, 1976.

Commentaries on various piano works by a pianist
intimately acquainted with Villa-Lobos as a person,
and with performing experience of his piano music.     B027


Mariz, Vasco. *A canção brasileira*. Rio de Janeiro:
   Civilização brasileira, 1977.

A chapter on the songs of the first generation of
Nationalist composers includes a discussion of the
songs of Villa-Lobos. A valuable source of
information from a biographer and performer of song
literature.     B028


Mariz, Vasco. *Historia da música no Brasil*. Rio de
   Janeiro; Civilização brasileira, 1981.

Chapter Eight is devoted to the contribution of
Villa-Lobos to the Nationalist Movement.     B029


Mariz, Vasco. *Hector Villa-Lobos, l'Homme et son Oeuvre*.
   Catalogue des Oeuvres, Discographie, Illustration.
   Paris: Seghers, 1967.

Based on the Portuguese language biography.     B030


Mariz, Vasco. *Heitor Villa-Lobos compositor brasileiro*.
   Rio de Janeiro: Zahar Editores S.A., 1983.

Vasco Mariz is the foremost Brazilian biographer of
Villa-Lobos. The first edition of his biography was
published in 1947. Several editions of his biography
have appeared prior to the 1983 edition.     B031


Mariz, Vasco. *Heitor Villa-Lobos*: Life and Work of the
   Brazilian Composer. 2d rev.ed. Washington, D.C.:
   Brazilian American Cultural Institute, Inc., 1970

A translation of the Portuguese biography of Villa-
Lobos.     B032

Maul, Carlos. *A glória escandalosa de Heitor Vila Lôbos.*
Rio de Janeiro: Livraria Imperio Editora, 1960.

> An attack on what the author perceives to be the
> undeserved glory of Villa-Lobos.                                    B033

Muricy, José Candido de Andrade, *Villa-Lobos*, uma
interpretação. Rio: Ministério da Educação e Cultura,
Serviço de Documentação, 1961.

> An assessment of the significance of the work of
> Villa-Lobos and one of the most comprehensive early
> attempts to provide a complete chronological list of
> his works.                                                         B034

Museu Villa-Lobos. *Presença de Villa-Lobos.* Vol. 1. Rio
de Janeiro: MVL, 1965.

> The "Presença" books published by the Museu
> Villa-Lobos are a multi-volume series of short
> testimonials and stories by twentieth century musicians
> regarding their personal experiences with the man and
> his works. Although many of the essays are romanticized
> story-telling, they provide a unique source of
> information for the student of the life and works of
> the composer.                                                      B035

Museu Villa-Lobos. *Presença de Villa-Lobos.* Vol. 1. 2d
ed. Rio de Janeiro: MVL, 1977.                                       B036

Museu Villa-Lobos. *Presença de Villa-Lobos.* Vol. 2. Rio
de Janeiro: MVL, 1966.                                               B037

Museu Villa-Lobos. *Presença de Villa-Lobos.* Vol. 2. 2d
ed. Rio de Janeiro: MVL, 1982.                                       B038

Museu Villa-Lobos. *Presença de Villa-Lobos.* Vol. 3. Rio
de Janeiro: MVL, 1969.                                               B039

Museu Villa-Lobos. *Presença de Villa-Lobos*. Vol. 4. Rio
de Janeiro: MVL, 1969.                                       B040

Museu Villa-Lobos. *Presença de Villa-Lobos*. Vol. 5. Rio
de Janeiro: MVL, 1970.                                       B041

Museu Villa-Lobos. *Presença de Villa-Lobos*. Vol. 6. Rio
de Janeiro: MVL, 1971.                                       B042

Museu Villa-Lobos. *Presença de Villa-Lobos*. Vol. 7. Rio
de Janeiro: MVL, 1972.                                       B043

Museu Villa-Lobos. *Presença de Villa-Lobos*. Vol. 8. Rio
de Janeiro: MVL, 1973.                                       B044

Museu Villa-Lobos. *Presença de Villa-Lobos*. Vol. 9. Rio
de Janeiro: MVL, 1974.                                       B045

Museu Villa-Lobos. *Presença de Villa-Lobos*. Vol. 10. Rio
de Janeiro: MVL, 1977.                                       B046

Museu Villa-Lobos. *Presença de Villa-Lobos*. Vol. 11. Rio
de Janeiro: MVL, 1980.                                       B047

Museu Villa-Lobos. *Presença de Villa-Lobos*. Vol. 12. Rio
de Janeiro: MVL, 1981.                                       B048

Museu Villa-Lobos. *Villa-Lobos, sua obra.* 2d ed. Rio de
    Janeiro: Ministério da Educação e Cultura-Departamento
    de Assuntos Culturais - MVL, 1972.

        A uniquely useful book for the Villa-Lobos scholar.
        Although the second edition, which is currently
        being revised, contains considerable information
        which is incorrect, it provides a list of works,

publishers, decdications, performance times and
comments by Villa-Lobos and associates regarding
his most important works.                          B049


Neves, José Maria. *Villa-Lobos, O Choro e os Choros.*
   Milan: G. Ricordi, 1977.

      A valuable study of the *Choros*, Villa-Lobos' most
      uniquely national and original genre.           B050


Neves, José Maria. *Música contemporânea brasileira.* São
   Paulo: Ricordi Brasileira, 1981.

      A thesis on Brazilian contemporary music. Villa-Lobos
      and Mario de Andrade are the beginning point for a
      discussion of contemporary Brazilian music.       B051


Nóbrega, Adhemar. *As Bachianas brasileiras de Villa-
   Lobos.* Rio de Janeiro: Museu Villa-Lobos - Ministério
   da Educação e Cultura-Departamento de Assuntos
   Culturais, 1971.

      A study and analysis of the Bachianas brasileiras
      by a collaborator and personal secretary of Villa-
      Lobos.                                           B052


Nóbrega, Adhemar. *Os Choros de Villa-Lobos.* Rio de
   Janeiro: Museu Villa-Lobos - Ministério da Educação e
   Cultura-Departamento de Assuntos Culturais, 1975.

      The study of the choros of Villa-Lobos by Nobrega
      has special interest because of his comments
      regarding Choros No. 13 and 14. The manuscripts for
      these works were lost, but Nobrega found sketches of
      the works and includes a few comments regarding the
      lost works.                                       B053


Palma, Enos da Costa, and Edgard de Brito Chaves, Jr. *As
   Bachianas brasileiras de Villa-Lobos.* Rio de Janeiro:

Companhia Editora Americana, 1971.

>Comments on the *Bachianas brasileiras* and a brief
>discography. B054

Peppercorn, Lisa M. *Heitor Villa-Lobos*. Zurich: Atlantis
Musikbuch-Verlag, 1972.

>The German language biography of Villa-Lobos is based
>on personal   interviews with Villa-Lobos during the
>1940's. It contains much information not found in
>any other source, a discussion of the artistic
>evolution of Villa-Lobos as a composer, and analyses
>of various works in the last portion of the book. The
>Peppercorn biography provides interesting contrast
>with other sources since her opinions frequently
>are at variance with opinions of Portuguese language
>biographies. B055

Riedel, W. Rudolph Emmen. *Trois grades ad Parnassum les
derniers quatuors à cordes* (Nos. 15,16 & 17) *de Heitor
Villa-Lobos* (1887-1959). The Hague: Albersen & Co.,
1977.

>Comments on the last three Villa-Lobos string
>quartets. B056

Rodrigues, Lindalva. *Concurso escolar de monografia*,
organizado pelo Museu Villa-Lobos: estudantes do
primeiro e segundo grau, 1974-1976. Award-winning
drawings. Museu Villa-Lobos. Rio de Janeiro: Museu
Villa-Lobos, 1976.

>A book of award-winning drawings by Brazilian
>schoolchildren on subjects related to the music of
>Villa-Lobos. B057

Santos, Turíbio. *Heitor Villa-Lobos e o violão*. Rio de
Janeiro: Museu Villa-Lobos - Ministerio da Educação e
Cultura-Departamento de Assuntos Culturais, 1975.

Villa-Lobos performed most frequently on the guitar
and cello. A discussion of his works for guitar
by the Director of the Villa-Lobos Museum, a
guitarrist who has recorded the complete Villa-
Lobos works for guitar.                              B058

Silva, Francisco Pereira da, and Americo Jacobina
Lacombe, ed. *Villa Lobos.* A vida dos grandes
brasileiros. São Paulo: Editora Três, 1974.

A biography combining fact and legend.        B059

Villa-Lobos, Heitor. *Canto orfeônico.* Vol. 1. São Paulo:
Irmãos Vitale S/A., 1937.

A collection of melodies for use in choral groups in
Brazilian schools. (*See*: Collections)        B060

Villa-Lobos, Heitor. *Canto orfeônico.* Vol. 2. São Paulo:
Irmãos Vitale S/A., 1951.                        B061

Villa-Lobos, Heitor. *Coleção escolar de músicas de
vários autores estrangeiros e nacionais,* arranjados e
adotados por H. Villa-Lobos. Rio: Departamento de
Educação do Distrito Federal, Superintendência de
Educação Musical e Artística, n.d.

A collection of melodies collected and arranged by
Villa-Lobos.                                     B062

Villa-Lobos, Heitor. *O ensino popular da música no
Brasil.* Rio: Oficina Gráfica da Secretaria Geral de
Educação e Cultura, 1937.

A description of the organization of music curricula
during the period when Villa-Lobos was director of
music education in Brazil.                       B063

Villa-Lobos, Heitor. *Guia prático*. Vol. 1. São Paulo:
Irmãos Vitale S/A., 1941.

    A practical guide to musical and artistic education.
For a description of contents, see Collections.     B064

Villa-Lobos, Heitor. *Programa de música*: Escola
Elementar e Secundária Técnica: Curso
de Especialização e Cursos de Orientação,
Aperfeiçoamento do Canto Orfeônico. Rio: Oficina
Gráfica do Departamento de Educação, 1934.

    A description of requirements for various levels of
instruction in orpheonic singing.     B065

Villa-Lobos, Heitor. *Programa do ensino da música*: Jardim
da Infância; Escola Elementar Experimental e Técnica
Secundária; Curso de Especialização e Cursos de
Orientação e Aperfeiçoamento do Ensino de Música e
Canto Orfeônico. Rio: Oficina Gráfica da Secretaria
Geral de Educação e Cultura, 1937.

    The organization of curricula of music education at
various levels.     B066

Villa-Lobos, Heitor. *Solfejos*. Vol. 1. São Paulo: Irmãos
Vitale, S/A., 1940.

    For a description of contents of the solfeggio
volumes one and two, see Collections.     B067

Villa-Lobos, Heitor. *Solfejos*. Vol. 2. São Paulo: Irmãos
Vitale S/A., 1951.     B068

Wisnik, José Miguel. O coro dos contrários: a música em
torno da Semana de 22. São Paulo: Duas Cidades, Secretaria da Cultura, Ciência e Tecnologia, 1977.

A master's thesis describing the events and the
signficance of the "Week of Modern Art" in
February 1922, and Villa-Lobos' participation.          B069

Wright, Simon. "Villa-Lobos and His Position in Brazilian
    Brazilian Music after 1930." Cardiff, Wales: University
    College, thesis, 1976.

A study of the influence of Villa-Lobos after 1930          B070

## Articles

Andrade, Mário de. "Mundo Musical" *Folha da Manhã*
(Rio) October 9, 1945: 47a.                                        B071

Andrade, Mário de. "Villa-Lobos" *Revista do Brasil* (Rio)
May 23, 1923: 50-53.                                              B072

Appleby, David P. "A Lenda do Caboclo." *Clavier* 26:3
(March 1987): 19-26.                                              B073

Appleby, David P. "A Visit to the Villa-Lobos Museum."
*The American Music Teacher* (June/July 1976): 24.               B074

Appleby, David P. "Villa-Lobos."*Ícaro* (Varig Inflight
Magazine  Ano IV, No. 32, 1987: 12-20.                           B075

Azevedo, Luiz Heitor Correa de. "Brazilian Orchestral
Music of Villa-Lobos, Lorenzo Fernandez, and
Francisco Mignone" (Rio) Ministry of Foreign
Affairs of Brazil, Cultural Division, 1947.                       B076

Azevedo, Luiz Heitor Correa de. "Villa-Lobos" Volume 19,
pp. 763-767, *The New Grove Dictionary of Music and
Musicians,* ed. by Stanley Sadie, MacMillan Publishers
Ltd, 1980.                                                        B077

Barros, Jayme de. "Villa-Lobos e Portinari" *O Globo*
(Rio) Oct. 1, 1973.                                              B078

Barros, João de. "Obras de Villa-Lobos" *Seis anos de divulgação musical* 2 (1939): pp. 441-459 Conference and Concert in the Club brasileiro, Rio de Janeiro, March 15, 1933.                                               B079

Bellez, Jorge Cesar. "Villa-Lobos, o popular erudíto" *O Globo* (Rio) Dec. 4, 1969: p. 51-56.                         B080

Bettencourt, Gastão de. "O sentido da terra brasileira na obra de Villa-Lobos" *Jornal de Música* V, May 1952, p.3    B081

Bret, Gustave. "Musique" *l'Intransigeant*, (Paris) February 17, 1929.                                              B082

Cabral, Mário. "Três fases na vida de Heitor Villa-Lobos" (Rio) *Boletin Social da U.B.C.* No. 57 Oct./Dec. 1959: p. 15-16.                                            B083

Carvalho, Herminio Bello de. "O som livre de Villa" (Rio) *Arte e a educação,* May 1971.                            B084

Carvalho, Ilmar. "O popular no universo de Villa-Lobos" *O Correio da Manhã*, (Rio) Nos. 23 and 24, November 1969: p. 25.                                             B085

Castro, Enio de Freitas. "Villa-Lobos fez a síntese da música brasileira com a europeia" *Jornal do Brasil* (Rio) November 4, 1971.                                      B086

"O centenário de Villa-Lobos" *O Globo* (Rio) Feb. 9, 1986: p. 8.                                                               B087

Chimanovitch, Mario. "Villa-Lobos, o gênio e o homem, sempre presentes" *Correio da manhã* (Rio) Nov. 16 and 17, 1969.                                                   B088

Coelho, João Marcos. "Um concerto de Villa-Lobos, na regencia do padrão-Globo-de-qualidade" *Folha de São Paulo*, (São Paulo) July 25, 1977.                     B089

Coelho, João Marcos. "Villa-Lobos, além dos folclorismos" *Folha de São Paulo*, (São Paulo) Nov. 18, 1984, p. 61.                                              B090

Coelho, João Marcos. "Villa-Lobos, os noventa anos de
um folclórico maestro" Ultima Hora (Rio) May 2, 1977.          B091

Coelho, Lauro Machado. "Villa-Lobos; a genialidade de
um compositor lírico e selvagem" Jornal da Tarde
(São Paulo) Nov. 17, 1984: p.5.                                B092

Composers of the Americas, Volume III,"Heitor Villa
Lobos", Washington, D.C.: Pan American Union, 1957:
1-59.                                                          B093

Decaudin, Jacques. "Symphonie de M. Villa-Lobos"
Le Courier Musicale (January 1, 1930)                          B094

"Da mulher, a mais grata lembrança" O Estado de São
Paulo (São Paulo) Nov. 17, 1981: p. 14.                        B095

Demarquez, Suzanne. "Villa-Lobos" La Revue Musicale 10:4
(November 1, 1929): 1-22.                                      B096

Dezarnaux, Robert. "l'Esthetique de Momoprecoce"
La Liberté, Febrruary 25, 1930.                                B097

"E.U.A. fazem homenagem a Villa-Lobos" Jornal do Brasil.
(Rio) July 19, 1977.                                           B098

Efegê, Jota. "Villa-Lobos também queria of Brasil p'rá
frente" Jornal do Brasil (Rio) Jan. 21,1971.                   B099

"Enterrada ontem no Rio a viúva de Villa-Lobos" Folha
de São Paulo (São Paulo) Aug. 7, 1985: p. 3f.                  B100

Estolano, Helio. "Mestre das bachianas cresce cada vez
mais" Ultima Hora (Rio) Nov. 17, 1975.                         B101

Estrela, Arnaldo. "Música de câmara no Brasil." Boletin
latino-americano de musica VI (April 1946): 255-281.           B102

Fernandez, Oscar Lorenzo. "A contribuição harmônica de
Villa-Lobos para a música brasileira" Boletin latino-
americano de musica VI (April 1946): 283-300.                  B103

França, Eurico Nogueira. "O compositor Villa-Lobos"
Provincia de São Pedro, X (1947) p. 72-74.                     B104

França, Eurico Nogueira. "Villa-Lobos" *Revista brasileira de música* I, 3 (Oct./Dec. 1962): p. 11-12.  B105

França, Eurico Nogueira. "Villa-Lobos permanece" *Correio da manhã* (Rio) June 26, 1980.  B106

Freitag, Lea Vinocur. "Música que exprime um Brasil exuberante" *Estado de São Paulo* (São Paulo) Nov. 17, 1984: p. 14.  B107

Freitag, Lea Vinocur. "O que os franceses dizem da obra de Villa-Lobos" *O Estado de São Paulo* (São Paulo) Nov. 14, 1979: p. 7.  B108

Galm, John K. "The Use of Brazilian Percussion Instruments in the Music of Villa-Lobos" *Musicology at the University of Colorado*, Williams Kearns, ed., a collection of essays by the faculty and graduates, Dec. 1977: 182-197.  B109

Gresh, Ruth. "Bruno Kiefer, Villa-Lobos e o modernismo na música brasileira" *Latin American Music Review* 4:2 (Fall-Winter 1983): 273-276.  B110

Gropillo, Cilea. "Villa-Lobos- 25 anos depois, lembranças de um gênio brasileiro" *Jornal do Brasil* (Rio) July 16, 1984: p. B1.  B111

Guaspari, Silvia. "Considerações em torno da obra pianística de Heitor Villa-Lobos." *Música Viva* 1 (January/February 1941).  B112

Heller, Alfred. "A Conductor's Guide to Villa-Lobos' Bachianas Brasileiras Nos. 2, 3, and 8" Indiana University, Bloomington, Indiana, 1974.  B113

Hernandez, Antonio. "Glórias póstumas. E um tesouro ainda não revelado." *O Globo*. (Rio) Nov. 17, 1979.  B114

Hernandez, Antonio. "Villa-Lobos e o novo som da O.S.B." *O Globo* (Rio) July 22, 1977.  B115

"A homenagem da escola a Villa-Lobos" *Jornal do Brasil*. (Rio) March 5, 1985, p. 20.  B116

"A homenagem dos E.U.A. nos 90 de Villa-Lobos" *Ultima Hora* (Rio) May 6, 1977.                    B117

Horta, Luiz Paulo. "Adeus à Mindinha" *Jornal do Brasil* (Rio) Aug. 9, 1985, p. 2.                   B118

Horta, Luiz Paulo. "Em memória de Villa-Lobos" *Jornal do Brasil* (Rio) Jan. 24, 1979.               B119

Kater, Carlos. "Villa-Lobos e a 'Melodia das Montanhas'." *Latin American Music Review* 5:1 (Spring/Summer 1984): 102-105.                    B120

Krieger, Edino. "Florestas e montanhas no som de Villa-Lobos" *Jornal do Brasil* (Rio) Nov. 23, 1976.       B121

Lange, Francisco Curt. "Villa-Lobos, um pedagogo creador" *Boletin latino-americano de musica* VI (April 1946): 189-196.                    B122

Leite, Rogério C. Cerqueira. "O tardio resgate da obra para piano de Villa-Lobos" *Folha de São Paulo* (São Paulo) Feb. 2, 1985: p. 89.                B123

Lima, João de Souza. "Impressões sobre a música pianística de Villa-Lobos" *Boletin latino-americano de musica* VI (April 1946): 149-155.           B124

Mariz, Vasco. "Música de Villa-Lobos (Sétimo quarteto de cordas)" Ministério das Relações Exteriores (Rio) Divisão Cultural, 1947.                B125

Massarani, Renzo. "A semana Villa-Lobos" *Jornal do Brasil* (Rio) Nov. 26, 1973.                 B126

Massarani, Renzo. "Villa-Lobos em ampla visão" *Jornal do Brasil* (Rio) April 6, 1972.             B127

Medaglia, Júlio. Villa-Lobos e o índio de casaca" *Folha de São Paulo* (São Paulo) Jan. 13, 1986.       B128

"Memória preservada" *Veja*, (Rio de Janeiro), Nov. 21, 1973.                    B129

Mendes, Gilberto. "O tropicalista dos anos 30" *Folha de São Paulo,* (São Paulo), Nov. 18, 1984, p. 61.                    B130

Menegale, Heli. "Villa-Lobos e a educação"  Escola Técnica Federal (Rio de Janeiro), 1969.                    B131

Milhaud, Darius. "Brésil" *La Revue Musicale* 1:1 (November 1, 1920): 60-61.                    B132

Note: The highly important article by Milhaud is probably the first reference to Villa-Lobos in the European press.

"Mindinha Villa-Lobos, a companheira perfeita" *Jornal do Brasil* (Rio) Nov. 21, 1969.                    B133

Miranda, Ronaldo. "Villa-Lobos e a música coral" *Jornal do Brasil* (Rio) Nov. 19, 1974.                    B134

"Morreu Villa-Lobos" *Música Sacra* No. 6, (Nov./Dec. 1959): p. 89-92.                    B135

"Morte chega sem dor para Dona Mindinha Villa-Lobos" *O Globo* (Rio) August 6, 1985, p. 3.                    B136

"A morte de Arminda Villa-Lobos, aos 73 anos" *O Estado de São Paulo*" (São Paulo) August 6, 1985: p. 21.                    B137

Note: According to members of her family, Arminda Villa-Lobos was 78 years of age at the time of her death. The press  graciously accepted her own statement regarding her age.

Muricy, Andrade. "Villa-Lobos" *Bulletin of the Pan American Union* 79:1  (January 1945): 1-10.                    B138

"Museu lança livros sobre Villa-Lobos" *Jornal do Brasil* (Rio) April 27, 1976.                    B139

Museu Villa-Lobos. "Villa-Lobos em discografia" (Rio) Escola de Artes Graficas do S.E.N.A.I. 1965.                    B140

*Música Viva,* January-February 1941 (A special Villa-Lobos
issue containing articles by various author
Rio, 1941.                                                    B141

"O músico Heitor Villa-Lobos." *Folha de São Paulo* (São
Paulo) Nov. 14, 1969.                                         B142

"Musicólogo analisa obra e mostra como Villa-Lobos
interpretava sua obra" *Jornal do Brasil* (Rio) Nov. 6,
1971.                                                         B143

Obussier, Robert. "Momoprecoce, de Villa-Lobos. *La Revue
Musicale* 11:103 (April 1, 1930): 356-357.                    B144

"87, ano de Villa-Lobos." *Folha de São Paulo,* (São
Paulo) Feb. 24, 1986: p. 21.                                  B145

Oliveira, Jamary. "Black Key vs. White Key: a Villa-Lobos
Device" *Latin American Music Review* 5:1 (Spring/Summer
1984): 33-47.                                                 B146

Oliveira, José da Veiga. "Aspetos de Villa-Lobos" *O
Estado de São Paulo* (São Paulo) April 15, 1973, p. 7.        B147

Orrego-Salas, Juan A. "Heitor Villa-Lobos 'Man, Work,
Style'" *Inter-American Music Bulletin* 52 (March 1966):
1-36.                                                         B148

Orrego-Salas, Juan A. "Heitor Villa-Lobos, Figura, Obra y
Estilo" *Revista Musical Chilena* 19:93 (July-September
1965): 25-62.                                                 B149

"Peças de Villa-Lobos, na Austria, recebem elogíos"
*O Estado de São Paulo* (São Paulo) Feb. 23, 1985,
p.15.                                                         B150

Pedrosa, Mário. "Villa-Lobos et son Peuple - le point de
vue Bresilien" *La Revue Musicale* 10:4 (November 1,
1929): 23-28.                                                 B151

Peppercorn, Lisa M. "Correspondence between Heitor Villa-
Lobos and His Wife Lucilia" *Music and Letters* 61:
3 & 4 (July-October 1980): 284-291.                           B152

Peppercorn, Lisa M. "The Fifteen-Year Periods in Villa-Lobos's Life" *Ibero-Amerikanisches Archiv* N.F., Jg.5, Heft 2, (1979): 179-197.                                        B153

Peppercorn, Lisa M. "Foreign Influences in Villa-Lobos's Music" *Ibero-Amerikanisches Archiv* N.F., Jg.3, Heft 1, (1977): 37-51.                                              B154

Peppercorn, Lisa M. "Heitor Villa-Lobos in Paris" *Latin American Music Review* 6:2 (Fall/Winter 1985): 235-248.     B155

Peppercorn, Lisa M. "Heitor Villa-Lobos: Profilo del Compositore Brasiliano" *Nuova Rivista Musicale Italiana* 19, no.2 (April/June 1985): 254-267.                    B156

Peppercorn, Lisa M. "The History of Villa-Lobos Birth Date" London: *Monthly Musical Record* 78: 898 (July/August 1948: 153-155.                                              B157

Peppercorn, Lisa M. "Le Influenze del Folklore Brasiliano nella Musica di Villa-Lobos" *Nuova Rivista Musicale Italiana*. X:2, (April-June 1976): 179-184.                   B158

Peppercorn, Lisa M. "A Letter of Villa-Lobos to Arnaldo Guinle" *Studi Musicali* X:1, 1981: 172-179.                 B159

Peppercorn, Lisa M. "Menschen, Masken, Mythen: Heitor Villa-Lobos und die Brasilianische Musik" *Neue Zeitschrift fur Musik* (September 1984): 8-11.                      B160

Peppercorn, Lisa M. "Musical Education in Brazil." *Bulletin of the Pan American Union* 74, no.10 (October 1940): 689-693.                                              B161

Peppercorn, Lisa M. "New Villa-Lobos Works" *New York Times* (October 11, 1942): VIII, 5.                            B162

Peppercorn, Lisa M. "The Paris Bibliothèque National's Autograph Letter of Villa-Lobos to His Sponsor" *Journal of Musicological Research* 3:3/4 (1981): 423-433.                                                   B163

Peppercorn, Lisa M. "Some Aspects of Villa-Lobos
Principles of Composition." *The Music Review* 4:3
(Feb. 1943): 28-34.                                                           B164

Peppercorn, Lisa M. "A Villa-Lobos Autograph Letter at
the Bibliothèque Nationale (Paris)." *Latin American
Music Review* 1:2 (Fall/Winter 1980): 253-264.                    B165

Peppercorn, Lisa M. "Villa-Lobos: Father and Son"
*Americas* 24, no.4 (April 1972): 19-23.                              B166

Peppercorn, Lisa M. "The Villa-Lobos Museum" *Americas*
25, nos. 11/12 (November/December 1973): 18-23.              B167

Peppercorn, Lisa M. "A Villa-Lobos Opera" *The New York
Times* (April 28, 1940): IX, 8.                                            B168

Peppercorn, Lisa M. "Villa-Lobos's Brazilian Excursions"
*The Musical Times* 113, no.1549 (March 1972): 263-265.     B169

Peppercorn, Lisa M. "Villa-Lobos's Commissioned
Compositions" *Tempo*, no.151 (December 1984): 28-31.      B170

Peppercorn, Lisa M. "Villa-Lobos's Last Years" *The Music
Review* 40, no.4 (November 1979): 285-299.                       B171

Peppercorn, Lisa M. "Violin Concerto by Villa-Lobos" *New
York Times* (June 8, 1941): IX, 5.                                       B172

Pereira, Carmen. "O autor das 'Bachianas' morreu há 17
anos" *Ultima Hora*. Rio: Nov. 17, 1976.                             B173

Picchia, Menotti del. "In Memorian: Villa-Lobos" Rio:
*Revista de música*, Nos. 6 and 7 (Dec./Jan. 1960: p. 18-
21).                                                                                   B174

"Prêmio Villa-Lobos será disputado por conjuntos"
*Correio da manhã*. Rio: Oct. 19, 1972.                              B175

Prunières, Henry. "Oeuvres de Villa-Lobos" *La Revue
Musicale* 9:3 (January 1, 1928): 258-259.                          B176

Reys, Luis da Câmara. "Obras de Villa-Lobos (Segunda
Série) conferência e concerto realizado no Club

brasileiro em 29 de novembro de 1934" *Seis anos de divulgação musical*, v.3 (1936): p. 165-183.    B177

"O retorno de Villa-Lobos" *Jornal do Brasil* (Rio) June 1, 1965: p. B2.    B178

Schiller, Beatriz. "Noventa anos de Villa-Lobos; no Kennedy Center, a homenagem dos americanos ao gênio brasileira" *Jornal do Brasil* (Rio) May 14, 1977.    B179

Schmitt, Florent. "Les Arts et la Vie" *La Revue de France* 8:1 (January 1, 1928): 137-142.    B180

Schmitt, Florent. "Sur H. Villa-Lobos" *Revue de France* (October 1, 1927): p. 522-523.    B181

Scholoezer, Boris de. "Les Miniaturas de Villa-Lobos" *La Revue Musicale* 2:9 (July 1, 1921): 65-66.    B182

Scholoezer, Boris de. "Oeuvres de Villa-Lobos" *La Revue Musicale* 5:9 (July 1, 1924): p. 69-70.    B183

Schwerke, Irving. "Villa-Lobos: Rabelais da música moderna" *Musica viva* 1 (January-February 1941)    B184

"Semana mostrará que Villa-Lobos tambêm era muito bom de chorinho" *O Globo* (Rio) Aug. 21, 1984, p. 7.    B185

Smith, Carleton Sprague. "Heitor Villa-Lobos (1889-1959)" *Inter-American Music Bulletin* 15 (January 1960): 1-8.    B186

Smith, Carleton Sprague. "Lisa M. Peppercorn: Heitor Villa-Lobos: Leben und Werk des brasilianischen Komponisten" *Inter-American Music Bulletin* 8 (1972): 174-176.    B187

"A sobrevida de Villa-Lobos" *Correio da manhã*, (Rio) Jan. 28, 1972.    B188

Squeff, Enio. "Sinfônica resgata a obra de Villa-Lobos" *Folha de São Paulo*. (São Paulo) Dec. 22, 1982, p. 27.    B189

Squeff, Enio. "Villa-Lobos, as grandes contradições de
um gênio" *O Estado de São Paulo* (São Paulo) May 22,
1977.                                                                    B190

Squeff, Enio. "Villa-Lobos quase desconhecido" *O Estado
de São Paulo* (São Paulo) Nov. 17, 1974, p. 38-39.                       B191

Torres, Geraldo. "Heitor Villa-Lobos" *Boletim de
Brasilia*, June 1961, p. 40-43.                                          B192

"Um som internacional com Villa-Lobos" *Jornal do
Brasil.* Rio: June 1, 1973.                                              B193

Utzeri, Fritz. "França comemora 100 anos de Villa-Lobos"
*Jornal do Brasil.* Rio: May 1, 1986, p. 9.                              B194

Utzeri, Fritz. "A França o festeja no centenário" *Jornal
do Brasil.* Rio: Oct. 14, 1985, p. B1.                                   B195

Vassburg, David E. "Villa-Lobos: Music as a Tool for
Nationalism" *Luso-Brazilian Review* VI: 2, Dec. 1969                    B196

Vergueiro, Carlos. "Villa-Lobos para voz feminina" *O
Estado de São Paulo* (São Paulo) Jan 15, 1978.                           B197

"Vida de Villa-Lobos na TV Russa" *O Estado de São Paulo,*
(São Paulo) Feb. 28, 1974.                                               B198

"Villa-Lobos. As primeiras respostas da posteridade"
*O Globo* (Rio) Nov. 19, 1972.                                           B199

"Villa-Lobos, esse desconhecido" *Jornal do Brasil*
(Rio) March 8, 1969.                                                     B200

"Villa-Lobos em discografia" Escola de artes gráficas
(Rio de Janeiro), S.E.N.A.I. 1965.                                       B201

"Villa-Lobos: gênio, ufanista, irreverente, o próprio
folclore, e seguramente imortal" *Jornal da Tarde,*
(São Paulo) March 24, 1979.                                              B202

"Villa-Lobos- Há 20 anos morreu o criador do canto
orfeônico" *Jornal do Brasil.* (Rio) January 15, 1979.                   B203

"Villa-Lobos- Homenagem sem precedentes em Paris."
Jornal do Brasil (Rio) Nov. 4, 1979.                    B204

"Villa-Lobos, moderno antes da semana de 22" O Estado
de São Paulo (São Paulo) May 8, 1972              B205

"Villa-Lobos morreu há dez anos e a mulher zela por sua
obra em sala do M.E.C." Jornal do Brasil (Rio)
March 5, 1969.                                         B206

"Villa-Lobos: na morte, exemplo da vida" Ultima Hora
(Rio) Feb. 24, 1973.                                   B207

"Villa-Lobos-um revolucionário" Jornal do Brasil (Rio)
Nov. 22, 1969: p. B4.                                 B208

"Villa-Lobos via suas obras como cartas à posteridade sem
esperança de resposta" Jornal do Brasil (Rio) Nov. 17,
1964.                                                  B209

Villa-Lobos, Arminda. "Um brasileiro autêntico" Jornal
do Brasil. Rio: November 16, 1971.                    B210

Villa-Lobos, Heitor. "Las actividades de la S.E.M.A. de
1932 a 1936" Boletin latino-americano de musica III
(1937) p. 369-405.                                    B211

Villa-Lobos, Heitor. "Catalogo cronologico de las obras
del compositor brasileño" Compositores de America
No. 3 (1957), p. 1-59.                                B212

Villa-Lobos, Heitor. "Educação Musical" Boletin latino-
americano de musica VI (April 1946): 495-588.        B213

Villa-Lobos, Heitor. "Minha filosofia" Jornal do Brasil
(Rio) Oct. 16, 1971.                                  B214

Villa-Lobos, Heitor. "Oscar Lorenzo Fernândez" Boletin
latino-americano de musica VI (April 1946): 589-593.  B215

"Viúva de Villa quer museu em sede própria" Folha de
São Paulo (São Paulo) Jan. 26, 1983. s               B216

# Appendix I
# Alphabetical Listing
# of Compositions

The numbers following each title, e.g. W17, refer to the Works and Performances section of this book.

À praia W352
A abelhinha, W342
Abertura, W366
Acalentando, W318
Aglaia, W021
Alvorada na floresta tropical, W513
Amazonas (Ballet and symphonic poem) (Orchestra), W118
Amazonas (Bailado indígena brasileiro) (Piano), W119
Amor y perfidia, W135
Argentina, W353
Assobio a jato, W493
Ave Maria (Moteto) (Four part mixed a cappella chorus), W319
Ave Maria (Voice, cello and organ), W022
Ave Maria (Voice and organ), W044
Ave Maria (Voice and strings), W058
Ave Maria no.6 (Voice and piano), W072
Ave Maria no. 18 (Voice, piano or harmonium) W121
Ave Maria no. 18 (Four part mixed a cappella chorus) W120
Ay-ay-ay, W354

Bachianas brasileiras no.1, W246
Bachianas brasileiras no.2 (Orchestra), W247
Bachianas brasileiras no.2 (Cello and piano), W568
Bachianas brasileiras no.2 (Piano),W569

Bachianas brasileiras no.3, W388
Bachianas brasileiras no.4 (Orchestra), W424
Bachianas brasileiras no.4 (Piano), W264
Bachianas brasileiras no.5 (Voice and guitar), W391
Bachianas brasileiras no.5 (Voice and orchestra of cellos), W389
Bachianas brasileiras no.5 (Voice and piano), W390
Bachianas brasileiras no.6 , W392
Bachianas brasileiras no.7, W432
Bachianas brasileiras no.8, W444
Bachianas brasileiras no.9, W449
Bailado infantil, W035
Bailado infernal, W160
Um beijo, W025
Bendita sabedoria, W543
Berceuse (Violin and piano), W089
Berceuse (Cello and piano), W088
Big Ben (Voice and orchestra), W485
Big Ben (Voice and piano), W484
Boris Godunov, W320
Il bove, W090
Brasil (Dobrado), W010
Brasil novo (Chorus and orchestra), W185
Brasil novo (Band), W186
O brasileiro (Gritos da rua), W255
Brincadeira de pegar, W343
Brinquedo de roda, W045

Cabocla (also Caboca) do Caxangá, W570
Cair da tarde (Voice and orchestra), W545
Cair da tarde (Voice and piano), W544
Caixinha de boas festas, W265
Caixinha de música quebrada, W256
Canarinho, W355
Canção a José de Alencar, W321
Canção árabe, W073
Canção brasileira, W027
Canção da folha morta, W571
Canção da imprensa (Band), W412
Canção da imprensa (Chorus and orchestra), W413
Canção da saudade, W322
Canção da terra (Female chorus and orchestra), W2010
Canção da terra (Voice and piano), W202
Canção das águas claras (Voice and orchestra), W529
Canção das águas claras (Voice and piano), W530

Canção de cristal, W494
Canção do amor, W546
A canção do barqueiro do Volga (Six part mixed a
  cappella chorus), W356
Canção do barqueiro do Volga (Voice and orchestra), W323
Canção do operário brasileiro, W405
Canção do parachoque, W203
Canção do poeta do século XVIII (Voice and guitar), W514
Canção do poeta do século XVIII (Voice and orchestra), W564
Canção do poeta do século XVIII (Voice and piano), W486
Canção dos caçadores de esmeraldas (Two part chorus), W414
Canção dos caçadores de esmeraldas (Voice and piano), W572
Canção ibérica, W074
Canções de cordialidade (Orchestra), W450
Canções de cordialidade (Voice and orchestra), W451
Canções de cordialidade (Voice and piano), W452
Canções indígenas (Voice and orchestra), W248
Canções indígenas (Voice and piano), W249
Canções típicas brasileiras (Chansons typiques brésiliennes)
  (Voice and orchestra), W158
Canções típicas brasileiras (Chansons typiques brésiliennes)
  (Voice and piano), W159
Cânones perpétuos, W357
A canoa virou, W266
Canta, canta, passarinho, W415
Cântico do Colégio Santo André, W547
Cântico do Pará, W425
Cânticos sertanejos (Fantasia característica) (Chamber
  orchestra), W014
Cânticos sertanejos (Fantasia característica) (String
  quintet and piano), W013
Cantiga boêmia, W172, W573
Cantiga de roda (Female chorus and orchestra), W205
Cantiga de roda (Female chorus and piano), W204
Cantilena da paz, W520
O canto da nossa terra, W250
O canto do capadócio, W251
O canto do cisne negro (Cello and
  piano), W122
O canto do cisne negro (Violin and piano), W123
Canto do pajé, W324
Canto orfeônico (Volume I), W416
Canto orfeônico (Volume II), W500
Canto oriental (Violin and piano), W124

Canto oriental (Voice and piano), W036
Capriccio (Cello and piano), W091
Capriccio (Violin and piano, W092
Carnaval das crianças, W157
Cascavel, W125
A cegonha, W093
Celestial, W005
Centauro de ouro, W106
Chansons typiques brésiliennes (*See*: Canções típicas
    brasileiras W158 and W159)
Chile-Brasil (Canção sertaneja), W393
Choros bis, W227
Choros no.1, W161
Choros no.2 (Flute and clarinet), W197
Choros no.2 (Piano), W198
Choros no.3, W206
Choros no.4, W218
Choros no.5, W207
Choros no.6, W219
Choros no.7, W199
Choros no.8, W208
Choros no.9, W232
Choros no.10, W209
Choros no.11, W228
Choros no.12, W233
Choros no.13, W234
Choros no.14, W229
Ciclo brasileiro, W374
Ciranda das sete notas (Bassoon and string orchestra), W325
Ciranda das sete notas (Bassoon and piano), W548
Ciranda das sete notas (Voice and piano), W574
O' ciranda, ó cirandinha, W301
Cirandas, W220
Cirandinhas, W210
Coleção brasileira (Voice and orchestra), W190
Coleção brasileira (Voice and piano), W211
Comédia lírica em 3 atos, W037
Concerto brasileiro, W326
Concerto grosso, W565
Concerto no.1 (Piano and orchestra), W453
Concerto no.2 (Piano and orchestra), W487
Concerto no.3 (Piano and orchestra), W512
Concerto no.4 (Piano and orchestra), W505
Concerto no.5 (Piano and orchestra), W521

Concerto para harmônica e orquestra, W524
Concerto para harpa e orquestra, W515
Concerto para violão (Guitar and orchestra), W501
Concerto para violão (Guitar and piano), W502
Concerto para violoncelo e orquestra no.2, W516
Confidência (canção), W017
Conselhos, W488
Consolação, W267
Constância, W268
O contra-baixo, W327
Coração inquieto, W489
Corrupio, W328
Cortejo nupcial, W491
As costureiras, W329
As crianças, W018
Currupira, W376

Dança da terra, W437
Dança de roda, W344
Dança diabólica, W162
Dança dos mosquitos, W187
Dança frenética, W144
Dança infernal, W163
Danças aéreas, W075
Danças africanas (Octet), W087
Danças características africanas (Piano), W085
Danses africaines (Danses des indiens métis du Brésil)
  (Orchestra), W107
Descobrimento do Brasil (1st suite), W377
Descobrimento do Brasil (2nd suite), W378
Descobrimento do Brasil (3rd suite), W379
Descobrimento do Brasil (4th suite), W380
Desfile aos heróis do Brasil, W367
Dime perché, W003
Dinga-donga, W492
Distribuição de flores (Flute and guitar), W381
Distribuição de flores (Female chorus) W575
Divagação, W461
Dobrado pitoresco, W028
Dobrados, W026
Duas lendas ameríndias, W506
Duas paisagens, W462
Duo (Violin and viola), W463
Duo (Oboe and bassoon), W535

Élégie (Cello and piano), W108
Élégie (Mixed a cappella chorus, tenor and soprano
  soloists), W269
Élégie (Orchestra), W094
Élégie (Violin and piano), W109
Elisa, W029
The Emerald Song, W471
The Emperor Jones, W531
Ena-Môkôcê, W330
Entrei na roda, W270
Epigramas irônicos e sentimentais (Voice and orchestra),
  W173
Epigramas irônicos e sentimentais (Voice and piano), W183
Erosão, W495
Estrela é lua nova, W331
12 Études (12 Estudos) (Guitar), W235
Eu te amo (Voice and orchestra), W532
Eu te amo (Voice and piano), W533
Evolução dos aeroplanos, W271

Fábulas características, W076
Fado, W236
Fantasia (Guitar), W023
Fantasia (Cello and orchestra), W454
Fantasia concertante (Piano, clarinet and bassoon), W517
Fantasia concertante (Orchestra of cellos), W549
Fantasia de movimentos mistos (Violin and orchestra), W174
Fantasia de movimentos mistos (Violin and piano), W175
Fantasia e fuga no.6, W394
Fantasia em três movimentos, W550
Fantasia para saxofone, W490
Felix anima, W332
Festim pagão, W145
A fiandeira (La fileuse), W176
Filhas de Maria, W221
Fleur fanée, W059
Floresta do Amazonas, W551
Folia de um bloco infantil, W146
Food for Thought, W472
Francette e Piá (Orchestra), W552
Francette et Pià (Piano), W237
Fuga (Cello and piano), W030
Fuga (Four part a cappella chorus), W445
Fuga no.1 (Four voice mixed a cappella chorus), W272

Fuga no.5 (Four voice mixed a cappella chorus), W273
Fuga no.8 (Four voice mixed a cappella chorus), W274
Fuga no.10 (Cello and piano), W257
Fuga no.21 (Four voice mixed a cappella chorus), W275
Fugas nos.1, 8, & 21, W426
Funil, W238

A gaita de fole, W375
Gavião de penacho, W345
Gênesis, W522
Gondoleiro, W427
Grande concerto para violoncelo e orquestra, W095
Guia prático (Various choral ensembles [Collections]), W276
Guia prático (Album 1), W277
Guia prático (Album 2), W278
Guia prático (Album 3), W279
Guia prático (Album 4), W280
Guia prático (Album 5), W281
Guia prático (Album 6), W282
Guia prático (Album 7), W283
Guia prático (Album 8), W358
Guia prático (Album 9), W359
Guia prático (Album 10), W284
Guia prático (Album 11), W473

Hino à vitória (Chorus and band), W428
Hino à vitória (Chorus and orchestra), W429
Hino a vitória (Voice and piano), W430
Hino acadêmico, W368
Hino às arvores, W285
Hino da independencia do Brasil, W286
Hino da juventude brasileira, W438
Hino dos artistas, W147
Hino escolar (Two part a cappella chorus), W360
Hino escolar (Two part a cappella chorus) (Cultura e afeto
  às nações), W369
Hino nacional brasileiro, W287
História de Pierrot, W006
Histórias da carochinha, W148
Historiettes (Historietas) (Voice and orchestra), W164
Historiettes (Historietas) (Voice and piano), W165
Hommage à Chopin, W474
Iara (Symphonic poem), W126
Ibericarabé (Piano), W078

Ibericarabé (Orchestra), W077
Il pleut, il pleut, bergère, W475
Imploro, W011
Improviso no.7 (Melodia), W096
A infância, W346
Introdução aos choros, W239
Invocação à cruz, W332
Invocação em defesa da pátria (Soloist, chorus, and
  orchestra), W439
Iphigénie en Aulide, W288
Izaht (Opera), W055
Izaht (Oratorio), W577
Izi, W536

Japonesa, W015
Jardim fanado, W525
Jesus, W136
José, W455
Juventude, W289

Kyrie, W347

Lá na ponte da vinhaça , W290
Lamento, W291
Lembrança do sertão, W252
A lenda do caboclo (Piano), W166
A lenda do caboclo (Orchestra), W188
El libro brasileño, W464
Lobisomem (Werewolf), W127
Louco (Voice and orchestra), W079
Louco (Voice and piano), W060
Luar do sertão, W382

Madona, W456
Magdalena (First Suite), W477
Magdalena (Second Suite), W478
Magdalena (Soloists, chorus and orchestra), W476
Magdalena (Voice and piano), W479
Magnificat aleluia (Soloist, mixed choir and orchestra),
  W553
Magnificat aleluia (Soloist, mixed choir and organ), W554
Mal secreto, W046
Malazarte, W177
Mandu çarará (Orchestra, mixed chorus and children's choir),

W417
Mandu çarará (Piano, mixed chorus and children's choir), W418
Marcha religiosa, W137
Marcha religiosa no.1, W097
Marcha religiosa no.3, W138
Marcha religiosa no.6, W579
Marcha religiosa no.7, W139
Marcha solene no.3, W061
Marcha solene no.6, W167
Marcha solene no.8, W212
Marcha triunfal, W168
Maria, W333
Marquesa de Santos (Orchestra), W395
Marquesa de Santos (Piano), W396
A marselhesa, W292
Martírio dos insetos (Violin and orchestra), W213
Martírio dos insetos (Violin and piano), W214
Mazurka em ré maior, W004
Mazurlesca, W038
Melodia sentimental (Voice and orchestra), W555
Melodia sentimental (Voice and piano), W556
Memorare (Two part chorus and orchestra), W128
Memorare (Two part chorus and organ), W024
A menina nas nuvens, W540
Les mères, W080
Meu benzinho, W293
Meu jardim (Chorus and band), W466
Meu jardim (Four part a cappella chorus), W465
Meu país (Chorus and orchestra), W149
Meu país (Chorus and band), W258
Minha mãe, W294
Minha terra, W440
Miniaturas (Voice and orchestra), W057
Miniaturas (Voice and piano), W056
Missa São Sebastião, W383
Modinha, W534
Modinhas e canções (Album 1) (Voice and orchestra), W406
Modinhas e canções (Album 1) (Voice and piano), W365
Modinhas e canções (Album 2) (Voice and orchestra), W563
Modinhas e canções (Album 2) (Voice and piano), W441
Os moinhos, W295
Momoprecoce (piano and band), W259
Momoprecoce (piano and orchestra), W240
Moteto, W296

Motivos gregos, W580
Música sacra  Volume 1, W507
My Bus and I, W480
Myremis (Symphonic poem), W110

Na Bahia tem (Band), W297
Na Bahia tem (Chorus and band), W582
Na Bahia tem (Four part male chorus), W581
Na risonha madrugada, W298
Na roça, W299
Naufrágio de Kleônicos (Symphonic poem and ballet), W111
Nésta rua, W300
New York Skyline Melody (Orchestra), W408
New York Skyline Melody (Piano), W407
Noite de insônia, W334
Noite de luar, W047
Il nome di Maria, W098
Noneto, W191
Nossa América, W433
Noturno Op.9, No.2 (Cello and piano), W260
Num berço de fadas, W039
Nuvens, W007

O' ciranda, ó cirandinha, W301
O' salutaris, W012
Octeto, W081
Odisséia de uma raça, W518
L'oiseau blessé d'une flèche, W062
Ondulando, W082
Oração ao diabo, W583
Ouverture de l'homme tel, W508

Pai do mato, W253
Panis angelicus (Four part mixed a cappella chorus), W509
Panqueca, W002
O papagaio do moleque, W302
Papai curumiassú, W336
Paraguai, W008
Pátria (Two part male chorus and military drums), W303
Pátria (Mixed chorus and orchestra), W348
Pedra bonita, W338
Pequena sonata, W063
Pequena suíte, W064
Petizada, W048

Pião, W361
Pierrot, W178, W584
Poema de Itabira (Voice and Orchestra), W442
Poema de Itabira (Voice and Piano), W443
Poema de l'enfant et de sa mère (Voice, flute, clarinet and cello), W192
Poema de l'enfant et de sa mère (Voice and piano), W193
Poema de palavras (Voice and piano), W541
Poema de palavras (Voice and orchestra), W542
Poema do menestrel, W169
Poema singelo, W434
Poema úmido, W179
Possessão, W241
Prelúdio (Six part mixed a cappella chorus), W349
Prelúdio e fuga no.4, W397
Prelúdio e fuga no.6, W398
Prelúdio em fá sustenido menor, W031
Prelúdio em ré maior (Six part mixed a cappella chorus),W467
Prelúdio no.2, W065
Prelúdio no.4, W350
Prelúdio no.8 (Cello and piano), W261
Prelúdio no.8 (Six part mixed a cappella chorus), W304
Prelúdio no.14 (Cello and piano), W262
Prelúdio no.14 (Four part mixed a cappella chorus), W305
Prelúdio no.22, W306
Prelúdios (Guitar), W419
Prelúdios nos.8, 14, and 22, W431
Primeira missa no Brasil, W384
Procissão da cruz, W385
A prole do bebê no.1 (A Familia do Bebê), W140
A prole do bebê no.2 (Os bichinhos), W180
A prole do bebê no.3 (Esportes) , W222
Prólogo do Mefistofle, W337
Pro-pax, W049

Quadrilha, W032
Quadrilha de roça, W585
Quadrilha brasileira, W370
Quarteto de cordas no.1, W099
Quarteto de cordas no.2, W100
Quarteto de cordas no.3, W112
Quarteto de cordas no.4, W129
Quarteto de cordas no.5, W263
Quarteto de cordas no.6, W399

Quarteto de cordas no.7, W435
Quarteto de cordas no.8, W446
Quarteto de cordas no.9, W457
Quarteto de cordas no.10, W468
Quarteto de cordas no.11, W481
Quarteto de cordas no.12, W496
Quarteto de cordas no.13, W503
Quarteto de cordas no.14, W519
Quarteto de cordas no.15, W523
Quarteto de cordas no.16, W526
Quarteto de cordas no.17, W537
Quatuor (Flute, E-flat alto saxophone, harp, celeste and
    female voices), W181
Quatuor (Quarteto para instrumentos de sopro) (Flute, oboe,
    clarinet, and bassoon), W230
Quero amar-te, W469
Quinteto, W113
Quinteto duplo de cordas, W050
Quinteto em forma de choros, W231
Quinteto instrumental, W538

Ratoeira, W470
Recouli, W019
Redemoinho, W371
Redenoilha, W386
Redondilhas de Anchieta, W586
Regozijo de uma raça, W387
Rêverie, W307
O Rio, W308
A roseira (Wind quintet), W362
A roseira (Saxophone quintet), W309
Rudá, W504
Rudepoema (Orchestra), W310
Rudepoema (Piano), W184
Rumo à escola, W372

Saci pererê, W130
Salutaris hostia (motet), W101
Samba clássico (Voice and orchestra), W497
Samba clássico (Voice and piano), W498
Saudação a Getúlio Vargas, W400
Saudade da juventude (Suite no. 1), W420
Saudades das selvas brasileiras, W226
Scène de Paris, W482

Os sedutores, W001
A sementinha, W311
Serenata, W339
Serestas (Voice and orchestra), W215
Serestas (Voice and piano), W216
Sertanejo do Brasil, W401
Sertão no estio (Voice and orchestra), W151
Sertão no estio (Voice and piano), W150
Sete vezes (Voice and orchestra), W557
Sete vezes (Voice and piano), W558
Sexteto místico (Sextuor Mystique), W131
Simples, W040
Simples coletânea, W134
Sinfonia ameríndia no.10, W511
Sinfonia no.1, W114
Sinfonia no.2 (Ascenção), W132
Sinfonia no.3 (A Guerra), W152
Sinfonia no.4 (A Vitória), W153
Sinfonia no.5 (A Paz), W170
Sinfonia no.6, W447
Sinfonia no.7, W458
Sinfonia no.8, W499
Sinfonia no.9, W510
Sinfonia no.11, W527
Sinfonia no.12, W539
Sinfonieta no.1, W115
Sinfonieta no.2, W483
Sinos, W402
Sonata fantasia no.1 (Première Sonate Fantaisie-
  Désespérance) (Violin and Piano), W051
Sonata fantasia no.2 (Deuxième Sonate-Fantaisie) (Violin and
  piano), W083
Sonata no.1 (Cello and piano), W102
Sonata no.2 (Cello and piano), W103
Sonata no.3 (Violin and piano), W171
Sonata no.4 (Violin and piano), W194
Sonhar (Cello and piano), W086
Sonhar (Violin and piano), W084
Suíte brasileira, W052
Suíte da terra, W066
Suíte floral, W117
I Suite for Chamber Orchestra, W566
II Suite for Chamber Orchestra, W567
Suíte infantil no.1, W053

Suíte infantil no.2, W067
Suíte oriental, W587
Suíte para canto e violino (Voice and violin), W195
Suíte para canto e violino (Voice, violins and violas), W196
Suíte para piano e orquestra, W068
Suíte para quinteto duplo de cordas, W054
Suíte pitoresca, W588
Suíte populaire brésilienne, W020
Suíte sugestiva (Chamber orchestra, soprano and baritone),W242
Suíte sugestiva (Voice and piano), W243
Sul América, W217

O tamborzinho, W312
Tantum ergo (Chorus and orchestra), W104
Tantum ergo (Four part mixed a cappella chorus), W141
Tão doce luz, W363
Tarantela (Guitar), W033
Tarantela (Piano), W041
Tédio de alvorada, W116
Terezinha de Jesus (Band), W314
Terezinha de Jesus (Guitar), W559
Terra natal, W313
Tico-tico, W351
Tiradentes (Voice, mixed chorus and harpsichord), W410
Tiradentes (Voice and piano), W409
Tiradentes (Chorus and orchestra), W403
Tocata e fuga no.3, W404
Trenzinho, W340
Trenzinho do caipira, W254
Três Marias (As), W411
Três poemas indígenas (Voice and piano), W223
Três poemas indígenas (Voice, mixed chorus and orchestra),W224
Trio (Flute, cello and piano), W069
Trio (Oboe, clarinet and bassoon),W182
Trio (Violin, viola and cello), W460
Trio no.1, W042
Trio no.2, W105
Trio no.3, W142
Tristorosa, W034
Trovas, W589

Uirapuru (Mixed a cappella chorus), W448
Uirapuru (Orchestra), W133
Uruguai-Brasil, W422

Valsa (Six part mixed a cappella chorus), W315
Valsa brasileira, W143
Valsa brilhante, W009
Valsa da dor, W316
Valsa lenta, W043
Valsa romântica, W016
Valsa-scherzo, W070
Valsa sentimental, W373
Veleiros (Voice and orchestra), W561
Veleiros (Voice and piano), W560
Veleiros (Voice and two guitars), W562
Veículo, W244
Vem cá, siriri, W317
Verde velhice, W184
Vidapura (Orchestra, mixed chorus and soloists), W155
Vidapura (Organ, mixed chorus,and soloists), W154
Vira, W225
A virgem, W071
A virgem dos santos, W341
Viva a nossa América, W590
Vocalises-estudos, W245
Vocalismo (Four part chorus), W423
Vocalismo no.11, W364
Voz do povo, W436

Xango, W591

Yerma (Voice chorus and orchestra), W528
Yerma (Voice chorus and piano reduction), W592

Zoé (Bailado Infernal), W156

# Appendix II
# Classified Listing
# of Compositions

DRAMATIC

Aglaia (Opera), W021
Amazonas (Ballet and Symphonic Poem) W118
Caixinha de boas festas (Symphonic Poem and Children's
  Ballet) W265
Comédia lírica em 3 atos (Opera), W037
Dança da terra (Ballet), W437
Descobrimento do Brasil (Four suites, music based on a
  a film version) W377, W378, W379, and W380
Elisa (Opera), W029
Floresta do Amazonas (Music used in film: Green Mansions) W551
Funil (ballet), W238
A gaita de fole (Music for the film version of Descobrimento
  do Brasil) W375
Izaht (Opera), W055
Izaht (Oratorio), W577
Jesus (Opera), W136
Jurapary (Ballet version of Choros No. 10, *See*: W209)
Magdalena (Musical Adventure in Two Acts), W476
Malazarte (Opera), W177
Marquesa de Santos, music for a play by Viriato Correa, W395
A menina das nuvens, W540
Naufragio de Kleônicos, (Symphonic Poem and Ballet), W111
Pedra bonita (Ballet), W338
Possessão (Ballet), W241
Rudá (Dio d'Amore) (Ballet), W504

Suíte sugestiva (Cinema) W242, W243
Veículo (Ballet) W244
Yerma (Opera) (Voice, chorus and orchestra), W528
Yerma (Opera) (Voice, chorus and piano reduction), W592
Zoé (Bailado Infernal) (Opera), W156

## CHORAL

A abelhinha (Three part chorus), W342
À praia (Two part chorus), W352
Acalentando (Three part a cappella chorus), W318
Argentina (Three part chorus), W353
Ave Maria (Moteto) (Four part mixed a cappella chorus), W319
Ay-ay-ay (Six part a cappella chorus), W354
Bachianas brasileiras no. 9 (String orchestra or voices) W449
Bendita sabedoria (Six part a cappella chorus), W543
Brasil novo (Chorus and orchestra), W185
Brincadeira de pegar (Two part a cappella chorus), W343
Cabocla do Caxangá (Soloist and four part chorus), W570
Canarinho (Two part chorus), W355
Canção a José de Alencar (Two part chorus), W321
Canção da folha morta (Chorus and orchestra), W571
Canção da imprensa (Chorus and orchestra), W413
Canção da saudade (Four part a cappella chorus), W322
Canção da terra (Female voices and piano), W201
A canção do barqueiro do Volga (Six part mixed a cappella
    chorus), W356
Canção do operário brasileiro (Chorus and band), W405
Canção do parachoque (Three part a cappella chorus), W203
Canção dos caçadores de esmeraldas (Two part chorus), W414
Cânones perpétuos (Four part a cappella chorus), W357
Canta, canta, pasarinho (Two part chorus), W415
Cantico do Pará (Three part a cappella chorus), W425
Cantiga de roda (Female chorus and orchestra), W205
Cantiga de roda (Female chorus and piano), W204
Cantilena da paz (Six part a cappella chorus), W520
Chile-Brasil (Canção sertaneja) (Three part a cappella
    chorus), W393
Choros no.10 (Orchestra and mixed chorus), W209
Choros no.14 (Orchestra, band and choirs), W229
Concerto brasileiro (Two pianos and mixed chorus), W326
Consolação (Four part mixed a cappella chorus), W267
O contra-baixo (Three part a cappella childrens chorus), W327

As costureiras (Five part female a cappella chorus), W329
As crianças (Four part a cappella chorus), W018
Dança da terra (Mixed chorus and percussion), W437
Dança de roda (Two part chorus, string quintet & bassoon), W344
Distribuição de flores (Female chorus), W575
Duas lendas ameríndias (Four part mixed a cappella chorus), W506
Élégie (Mixed a cappella chorus, tenor and soprano
   soloists), W269
Elisa (Opera), W029
Fuga (Four part a cappella chorus), W445
Fuga no.1 (Four voice mixed a cappella chorus), W272
Fuga no.5 (Four voice mixed a cappella chorus), W273
Fuga no.8 (Four voice mixed a cappella chorus), W274
Fuga no.21 (Four voice mixed a cappella chorus), W275
Gavião de penacho (Mixed a cappella chorus), W345
Gondoleiro (Two part chorus and band), W427
Guia prático (Various choral ensembles, See: Collections, W276
Hino à vitória (Chorus and band), W428
Hino à vitória (Chorus and orchestra), W429
Hino acadêmico (Two part chorus and band), W368
Hino às árvores (Two part a cappella chorus), W285
Hino da independencia do Brasil (Three part a cappella
   chorus), W286
Hino da juventude brasileira (Four part mixed a cappella
   chorus), W438
Hino escolar (Two part a cappella chorus), W360
Hino escolar (Two part a cappella chorus) (Cultura e afeto
   às nações), W369
Hino nacional brasileiro (Two part a cappella chorus), W287
Il pleut, il pleut, bergère (Three part a cappella chorus), W475
A infância (Two part a cappella chorus), W346
Invocação à cruz (Four part mixed a cappella chorus), W332
Invocação em defesa da pátria (Soloist, chorus, and
   orchestra), W439
Iphigénie en aulide (Four part mixed a cappella chorus),
   W288
Izaht (Opera), W055
Izaht (Oratorio version), W577
Jesus (Opera), W136
José (Four part male a cappella chorus), W455
Juventude (Three part a cappella chorus), W289
Kyrie (Mixed chorus), W347
Lamento (Six part mixed a cappella chorus), W291
El libro brasileño (Two part chorus), W464

Luar do sertão (Four part mixed a cappella chorus), W382
Magdalena (Soloists, chorus and orchestra), W476
Magnificat aleluia (Soloist, mixed choir and orchestra), W553
Magnificat aleluia (Soloist, mixed choir and organ), W554
Malazarte (Opera), W177
Mandu çarará (Orchestra, mixed chorus and children's choir), W417
Mandu çarará (Piano, mixed chorus and children's choir), W418
A marselhesa (Two part a cappella chorus), W292
Memorare (Two part chorus and orchestra), W128
Memorare (Two part chorus and organ), W024
Meu jardim (Chorus and Band), W466
Meu jardim (Four part a cappella chorus), W465
Meu país (Chorus and orchestra), W149
Meu país (Chorus and band), W258
Minha mãe (Four part mixed a cappella chorus), W294
Minha terra (Three part a cappella chorus), W440
Missa São Sebastião (Three part a cappella chorus), W383
Os moinhos (Four part mixed a cappella chorus), W295
Moteto (Three part mixed a cappella chorus), W296
Música sacra (Various choral ensembles), W507
Na Bahia tem (Four part male chorus), W581
Na Bahia tem (Chorus and band), W582
Na risonha madrugada (Four part female a cappella chorus), W298
Na roça (Two part a cappella chorus), W299
Nossa América (Two part chorus), W433
O' felix anima (four part chorus), W335
O' salutaris (Chorus and piano or harmonium), W012
Panis angelicus (Four part mixed a cappella chorus), W509
Papai curumiassú (Soloist and mixed a cappella chorus), W336
Pátria (Two part male chorus and military drums), W303
Pátria (Mixed chorus and orchestra), W348
Prelúdio (Six part mixed a cappella chorus), W349
Prelúdio em ré maior (Six part mixed a cappella chorus), W467
Prelúdio no.4 (Four part mixed a cappella chorus), W350
Prelúdio no.8 (Six part mixed a cappella chorus), W298
Prelúdio no.14 (Four part mixed a cappella chorus), W304
Prelúdio no.22 (Six part mixed a cappella chorus), W306
Primeira missa no Brasil (Mixed chorus, children's chorus
   and instrumental ensemble), W384
Procissão da cruz (Four part chorus), W385
Prólogo do Mefistofle (Mixed a cappella chorus), W337
Quadrilha brasileira (Three part a cappella childrens
   chorus), W370
Quero amar-te (Three part a cappella chorus), W469

Ratoeira (Three part a cappella chorus), W470
Redondilhas de Anchieta (Three part chorus), W586
Regozijo de uma raça (Tenor soloist, mixed chorus and
  percussion), W387
Rêverie (Six part mixed a cappella chorus), W307
O Rio (Four part mixed a cappella chorus), W308
Rumo à escola (Two part chorus), W372
Salutaris hostia (motet) (Four part mixed a cappella
  chorus), W101
Saudação a Getúlio Vargas (Chorus and orchestra), W400
A sementinha (Two part a cappella chorus), W311
Serenata (Six part mixed a cappella chorus), W339
Sertanejo do Brasil (Chorus and band), W401
Sinos (Three part a cappella chorus), W402
O tamborzinho (Four part female a cappella chorus), W312
Tantum ergo (Chorus and orchestra), W104
Tão doce luz (Three part a cappella childrens chorus), W363
Terra natal (Four part female a cappella chorus), W313
Tico-tico (Two part a cappella chorus), W351
Tiradentes (Voice, mixed chorus and harpsichord), W410
Tiradentes (Chorus and orchestra), W403
Trenzinho (Three part a cappella chorus), W340
Três poemas indígenas (Voice, mixed chorus and orchestra), W224
Uirapuru (Mixed a cappella chorus), W448
Uruguai-Brasil (Mixed chorus), W422
Valsa (Six part mixed a cappella chorus), W315
Vidapura (Orchestra, mixed chorus and soloists), W155
Vidapura (Organ, mixed chorus,and soloists), W154
Viva a nossa América (Two part chorus), W590
A Virgem dos santos (Two part female a cappella chorus), W341
Vocalismo (Four part chorus), W423
Vocalismo no.11 (Four part chorus), W364
Yerma (Opera) (Voice, chorus and orchestra), W528
Yerma (Opera) (Voice, chorus and piano reduction), W592
Zoé (Bailado infernal) (Opera), W156


ORCHESTRAL

Abertura (Orchestra), W366
Aglaia (Opera), W021
Alvorada na floresta tropical (Orchestra), W513
Amazonas (Ballet and symphonic poem) (Orchestra), W118
Bachianas brasileiras no.1 (Orchestra of celli), W246

Bachianas brasileiras no.2 (Orchestra), W247
Bachianas brasileiras no.3 (Piano and orchestra), W388
Bachianas brasileiras no.4 (Orchestra), W424
Bachianas brasileiras no.7 (Orchestra), W432
Bachianas brasileiras no.8 (Orchestra), W444
Bachianas brasileiras no.9 (String orchestra or voices), W449
Caixinha de boas festas (Orchestra), W265
Canções de cordialidade (Orchestra), W450
Cantiga boêmia, W573
Centauro de ouro (Orchestra), W106
Choros no.6 (Orchestra), W219
Choros no.8 (Two pianos and orchestra), W208
Choros no.9 (Orchestra), W232
Choros no.11 (Piano and orchestra), W228
Choros no.12 (Orchestra), W233
Choros no.13 (Two orchestras and band), W234
Ciranda das sete notas (Bassoon and string orchestra), W325
Comédia lírica em 3 atos (Opera), W037
Concerto grosso (Woodwind ensemble), W565
Concerto no.1 (Piano and orchestra), W453
Concerto no.2 (Piano and Orchestra), W487
Concerto no.3 (Piano and orchestra), W512
Concerto no.4 (Piano and orchestra), W505
Concerto no.5 (Piano and Orchestra), W521
Concerto para harmônica e orquestra, W524
Concerto para harpa e orquestra, W515
Concerto para violão (Guitar and orchestra), W501
Concerto para violoncelo e orquestra no.2, W516
Cortejo nupcial (Orchestra and organ), W491
Currupira (Orchestra), W376
Dança diabólica (Orchestra), W162
Dança dos mosquitos (Orchestra), W187
Dança frenética (Orchestra), W144
Danses africaines (Danses des indiens métis du Brésil)
    (Orchestra), W107
Descobrimento do Brasil (1st suite) (Orchestra), W377
Descobrimento do Brasil (2nd suite) (Orchestra), W378
Descobrimento do Brasil (3rd suite) (Orchestra), W379
Descobrimento do Brasil (4th suite) (Orchestra), W380
Élégie (Orchestra), W094
The Emperor Jones (Orchestra with alto and baritone
    solos), W531
Erosão (Orchestra), W495
Evolução dos aeroplanos (Orchestra), W271

Fantasia (Cello and orchestra), W454
Fantasia concertante (Orchestra of cellos), W549
Fantasia de movimentos mistos (Violin and orchestra), W174
Fantasia e fuga no.6 (Orchestra), W394
Fantasia em três movimentos (Orchestra), W550
Floresta do Amazonas (Orchestra, soloist, and male chorus), W551
Folia de um bloco infantil (Piano and orchestra), W146
Francette e Piá (Orchestra), W552
Funil (Orchestra), W238
Gênesis (Orchestra), W522
Grande concerto para violoncelo e orquestra, W095
Iara (symphonic poem), W126
Ibericarabé (Orchestra), W077
Introdução aos choros (Orchestra and guitar), W239
Izi (Orchestra), W536
A lenda do caboclo (Orchestra), W188
Lobisomem (Orchestra), W127
Madona (Orchestra), W456
Magdalena (First Suite) (Orchestra, soloists and mixed
    chorus), W477
Magdalena (Second Suite) (Orchestra, soloists and mixed
    chorus), W478
Marcha religiosa (Orchestra), W137
Marcha religiosa no.1 (Orchestra), W097
Marcha religiosa no.3 (Orchestra), W138
Marcha religiosa no.6 (Orchestra), W579
Marcha religiosa no.7 (Orchestra), W139
Marcha solene no.3 (Orchestra), W061
Marcha solene no.6 (Orchestra), W167
Marcha solene no.8 (Orchestra), W212
Marcha triunfal (Orchestra), W168
Marquesa de Santos (Orchestra), W395
Martírio dos insetos (Violin and orchestra), W213
A menina nas nuvens (Soloists, chorus and orchestra), W540
Momoprecoce (Piano and orchestra), W240
Myremis (Orchestra), W110
Naufragio de Kleônicos (Symphonic poem and ballet)
    (Orchestra), W111
New York Skyline Melody (Orchestra), W408
Noneto (Orchestra), W191
Odisséia de uma raça (Orchestra), W518
Oração ao diabo, W583
Ouverture de l'homme tel (Orchestra), W508
O papagaio do moleque (Orchestra), W302

Pedra bonita (Orchestra), W338
Pierrot (Orchestra) , W584
Possessão (Orchestra), W241
Prelúdio e fuga no.4 (Orchestra), W397
Prelúdio e fuga n.6 (Orchestra), W398
Recouli (Orchestra), W019
Rudá (Orchestra), W504
Rudepoema (Orchestra), W310
Saci pererê (Orchestra), W130
Saudade da juventude (Suíte no. 1) (Orchestra), W420
Sinfonia ameríndia no.10 (Orchestra, mixed chorus, tenor,
    baritone and bass soloists), W511
Sinfonia no.1 (Orchestra), W114
Sinfonia no.2 (Ascenção) (Orchestra), W132
Sinfonia no.3 (A Guerra) (Orchestra), W152
Sinfonia no.4 (A Vitória) (Orchestra), W153
Sinfonia no.5 (A Paz) (Orchestra), W170
Sinfonia no.6 (Orchestra), W447
Sinfonia no.7 (Orchestra), W458
Sinfonia no.8 (Orchestra), W499
Sinfonia no.9 (Orchestra), W510
Sinfonia no.11 (Orchestra), W527
Sinfonia no.12 (Orchestra), W539
Sinfonieta no.1 (Orchestra), W115
Sinfonieta no.2 (Orchestra), W483
Suíte da terra, W066
Suíte brasileira (Orchestra), W052
Suíte para piano e orquestra, W068
Suíte pitoresca (Piano and orchestra), W588
Tédio de alvorada (Orchestra), W116
Tocata e fuga no.3 (Orchestra), W404
Trovas, W589
Uirapuru (Orchestra), W133
Veículo (Orchestra), W244
Verde velhice (Orchestra), W189


CHAMBER MUSIC

Assobio a jato (Flute and cello), W493
Bachianas brasileiras no. 2 (Cello and piano), W568
Bachianas brasileiras no.6 (Flute and bassoon), W392
Berceuse (Violin and piano), W089
Berceuse (Cello and piano), W088

Cânticos sertanejos (Fantasia característica) (Chamber orchestra), W014
Cânticos sertanejos (Fantasia característica) (String quintet and piano), W013
O canto da nossa terra (Cello and piano), W250
Canto do capadócio (Cello and piano), W251
O canto do cisne negro (Cello and piano), W122
O canto do cisne negro (Violin and piano), W123
Canto oriental (Violin and piano), W124
Capriccio (Cello and piano), W091
Capriccio (Violin and piano), W092
Choros bis (Violin and cello), W227
Choros no.2 (Flute and clarinet), W197
Choros no.3 (Clarinet, alto sax, bassoon, 3 horns, trombone, and male chorus), W206
Choros no.4 (Three horns and trombone), W218
Choros no.7 (Flute, oboe, B-flat clarinet, E-flat alto sax, bassoon, violin, cello and tam-tam), W199
Ciranda das sete notas (Bassoon and piano), W548
Concerto para violão (Guitar and piano), W502
Corrupio (Bassoon and string quintet), W328
Danças aéreas (Chamber orchestra), W075
Danças africanas (Octet), W087
Distribução de flores (Flute and guitar), W381
Divagação (Cello, piano and drum), W461
Duo (Violin and viola), W463
Duo (Oboe and bassoon), W535
Élégie (Cello and piano), W108
Élégie (Violin and piano), W109
Ena-Môkôcê (Soloist, five part mixed chorus and percussion), W330
Fantasia concertante (Piano, clarinet and bassoon), W517
Fantasia de movimentos mistos (Violin and piano), W175
Fantasia para saxofone (Soprano or tenor saxophone, 2 horns and strings), W490
Fuga (Cello and piano), W030
Fuga no.10 (Cello and piano), W257
Fugas nos.1, 8, & 21 (Orchestra of cellos), W426
A gaita de fole (English horn and harmonium), W375
Improviso no.7 (Melodia) (Violin and piano), W096
Martírio dos insetos (Violin and piano), W214
Meu benzinho (Vocal sextet), W293
Motivos gregos (flute, guitar and female chorus), W580
Música sacra  Volume 1 (Various choral ensembles), W507
Noturno op.9, no.2 (Cello and piano), W260

Octeto (Flute, clarinet, bassoon, 2 violins, cello and
 piano), W081
Pequena sonata (Cello and piano), W063
Pequena suíte (Cello and piano), W064
Poème de l'enfant et de sa mère (Voice, flute, clarinet and
 cello), W192
Prelúdio em fá sustenido menor (Cello and piano), W031
Prelúdio no.2 (Cello and piano), W065
Prelúdio no. 8 (Cello and piano), W261
Prelúdio no. 14 (Cello and piano), W262
Prelúdios nos.8, 14, & 22 (Orchestra of cellos), W431
Quarteto de cordas no.1 (String quartet), W99
Quarteto de cordas no.2 (String quartet), W100
Quarteto de cordas no.3 (String quartet), W112
Quarteto de cordas no.4 (String quartet), W124
Quarteto de cordas no.5 (String quartet), W263
Quarteto de cordas no.6 (String quartet), W399
Quarteto de cordas no.7 (String quartet), W435
Quarteto de cordas no.8 (String quartet), W446
Quarteto de cordas no.9 (String quartet), W457
Quarteto de cordas no.10 (String quartet), W468
Quarteto de cordas no.11 (String quartet), W481
Quarteto de cordas no.12 (String quartet), W496
Quarteto de cordas no.13 (String quartet), W503
Quarteto de cordas no.14 (String quartet), W519
Quarteto de cordas no.15 (String quartet), W523
Quarteto de cordas no.16 (String quartet), W526
Quarteto de cordas no.17 (String quartet), W537
Quatuor (Flute, E-flat alto saxophone, harp, celeste and
 female voices), W181
Quatuor (Quarteto para instrumentos de sopro) (Flute, oboe,
 clarinet, and bassoon), W230
Quinteto (Two violins, viola, cello, and piano), W113
Quinteto duplo de cordas (Double string quintet), W050
Quinteto em forma de choros (Flute, oboe, clarinet, English
 or French horn, and bassoon), W231
Quinteto instrumental (Flute, violin, viola, cello and
 harp), W538
A roseira (Wind quintet), W362
A roseira (Saxophone quintet), W309
Sexteto místico (Sextuor Mystique), W131
Sonata fantasia no.1 (Première Sonate Fantaisie-
 Désespérance) (Violin and Piano), W051
Sonata fantasia no.2 (Deuxième Sonate-Fantaisie) (Violin and

piano), W083
Sonata no.1 (Cello and piano), W102
Sonata no.2 (Cello and piano), W103
Sonata no.3 (Violin and piano), W171
Sonata no.4 (Violin and piano), W194
Sonhar (Cello and piano), W086
Sonhar (Violin and piano), W084
I Suite for chamber orchestra, W566
II Suite for chamber orchestra, W567
Suíte para quinteto duplo de cordas, W054
Suíte sugestiva (Chamber orchestra, soprano and baritone), W242
O trenzinho do caipira (Cello and piano), W254
Trio (Flute, cello and piano), W069
Trio (Oboe, clarinet and bassoon),W182
Trio (Violin, viola and cello), W460
Trio no.1 (Piano, violin, and cello), W042
Trio no.2 (Piano, violin, and cello), W105
Trio no.3 (Piano, violin, and cello), W142
Xangô (Voice and chamber ensemble), W582


## SOLO VOCAL

Amor y perfidia (Voice and piano), W135
Ave Maria (Voice, cello and organ), W022
Ave Maria (Voice and organ), W044
Ave Maria (Voice and strings), W058
Ave Maria no.6 (Voice and piano), W072
Bachianas brasileiras no.5 (Voice and guitar), W391
Bachianas brasileiras no.5 (Voice and orchestra of cellos), W389
Bachianas brasileiras no.5 (Voice and piano), W390
Big Ben (Voice and orchestra), W485
Big Ben (Voice and piano), W484
Boris Godunov (Voice and orchestra), W320
Il bove (Voice and piano, cello ad libitum), W090
O brasileiro (Gritos da rua) (Voice), W255
Cair da tarde (Voice and orchestra), W545
Cair da tarde (Voice and piano), W544
Canção árabe (Voice and piano), W073
Canção da terra (Voice and piano), W202
Canção das águas claras (Voice and orchestra), W529
Canção das águas claras (Voice and piano), W530
Canção de cristal (Voice and piano), W494
Canção do amor (Voice and orchestra), W546

Canção do barqueiro do Volga (Voice and orchestra), W323
Canção do poeta do século XVIII (Voice and guitar), W514
Canção do poeta do século XVIII (Voice and orchestra), W564
Canção do poeta do século XVIII (Voice and piano), W486
Canção dos caçadores de esmeraldas (Two part chorus) , W414
Canção dos caçadores de esmeraldas (Voice and piano), W572
Canções de cordialidade (Voice and orchestra), W451
Canções de cordialidade (Voice and piano), W452
Canções indígenas (Voice and orchestra), W248
Canções indígenas (Voice and piano), W249
Canções típicas brasileiras (Chansons typiques brésiliennes)
    (Voice and orchestra), W158
Canções típicas brasileiras (Chansons typiques brésiliennes)
    (Voice and piano), W159
Cântico do Colégio Santo André (Voice and piano), W547
Cantiga boêmia (Voice and orchestra), W172
Canto oriental (Voice and piano), W036
Cascavel (Voice and piano), W125
A cegonha (Voice and piano), W093
Ciranda das sete notas (Voice and piano), W574
Coleção brasileira (Voice and orchestra), W190
Coleção brasileira (Voice and piano), W211
Confidência (canção) (Voice and piano), W017
Conselhos (Voice and piano), W488
Coração inquieto (Voice and piano), W489
Dime perché (Voice and piano), W003
Dinga-donga (Voice and piano), W492
Duas paisagens (Voice and piano), W462
The Emerald Song (Voice and piano), W471
Epigramas irônicos e sentimentais (Voice and orchestra), W173
Epigramas irônicos e sentimentais (Voice and piano), W183
Eu te amo (Voice and orchestra), W532
Eu te amo (Voice and piano), W533
Fado (Voice and piano), W236
Festim pagão (Voice and piano), W145
Filhas de Maria (Voice and piano), W221
Fleur fanée (Voice and piano), W059
Food for Thought (Voice and violin), W472
Hino à vitória (Voice and piano), W430
Hino dos artistas (Voice and piano), W147
Historiettes (Historietas) (Voice and orchestra), W164
Historiettes (Historietas) (Voice and piano), W165
Japonesa (Voice and piano), W015
Jardim fanado (Voice and piano), W525

Louco (Voice and orchestra), W079
Louco (Voice and piano), W060
Magdalena (Voice and piano), W479
Mal secreto (Voice and piano), W046
Maria (Voice and orchestra), W333
Melodia sentimental (Voice and orchestra), W555
Melodia sentimental (Voice and piano), W556
Les mères (Voice and piano), W080
Miniaturas (Voice and orchestra), W057
Miniaturas (Voice and piano), W056
Modinha (Seresta no.5) (Voice and guitar) W534
Modinhas e canções (Album 1) (Voice and orchestra), W406
Modinhas e canções (Album 1) (Voice and piano), W365
Modinhas e canções (Album 2) (Voice and orchestra), W563
Modinhas e canções (Album 2) (Voice and piano), W441
My Bus and I (Voice and piano), W480
Noite de insônia (Voice and orchestra), W334
Noite de luar (Voice and piano), W047
Il nome di Maria (Voice and piano), W098
L'oiseau blessé d'une flèche (Voice and piano), W062
Pai do mato (Voice and piano), W253
Pierrot (Voice and orchestra), W178, W584
Poema de Itabira (Voice and Orchestra), W442
Poema de Itabira (Voice and Piano), W443
Poème de l'enfant et de sa mère (Voice and piano), W193
Poema de palavras (Voice and piano), W541
Poema de palavras (Voice and orchestra), W542
Samba clássico (Voice and orchestra), W497
Samba clássico (Voice and piano), W498
Scène de Paris (Voice and piano), W482
Os sedutores (Voice and piano), W001
Serestas (Voice and orchestra), W215
Serestas (Voice and piano), W216
Sertão no estio (Voice and orchestra), W151
Sertão no estio (Voice and piano), W150
Sete vezes (Voice and orchestra), W557
Sete vezes (Voice and piano), W558
Suíte para canto e violino (Voice and violin), W195
Suíte para canto e violino (Voice, violins and violas), W196
Suíte sugestiva (Voice and piano), W243
Três poemas indígenas (Voice and piano), W223
Veleiros (Voice and orchestra), W561
Veleiros (Voice and piano), W560
Veleiros (Voice and two guitars), W562

Vira (Voice and piano), W225
A Virgem (Voice and piano), W071
Vocalises-estudos (Voice and piano), W245
Voz do povo (Voice and piano), W436
Xangô (Voice and chamber ensemble), W591

## PIANO

Amazonas (Bailado indígena brasileiro), W119
Bachianas brasileiras no. 2 (Dança), W569
Bachianas brasileiras no.4, W264
Bailado infantil, W035
Bailado infernal, W160
Um beijo, W025
Brinquedo de roda, W045
Caixinha de música quebrada, W256
Canção ibérica, W074
Carnaval das crianças, W157
Celestial, W005
Choros no. 2, W198
Choros no.5 (Alma brasileira), W207
Ciclo brasileiro, W374
Cirandas, W220
Cirandinhas, W210
Choros no.2, W198
Dança infernal, W163
Danças características africanas, W085
Fábulas características, W076
A fiandeira (La Fileuse), W176
Francette et Pià, W237
Gavota-choro, See: W396
Guia prático (Album 1), W277
Guia prático (Album 2), W278
Guia prático (Album 3), W279
Guia prático (Album 4), W280
Guia prático (Album 5), W281
Guia prático (Album 6), W282
Guia prático (Album 7), W283
Guia prático (Album 8), W358
Guia prático (Album 9), W359
Guia prático (Album 10), W284
Guia prático (Album 11), W473
Histórias da carochinha, W148

História de Pierrot, W006
Hommage à Chopin, W474
Ibericarabé, W078
Imploro, W011
Lembrança do sertão, W252
A lenda do caboclo, W166
Marquesa de Santos, W396
Mazurlesca, W038
New York Skyline Melody, W407
Num berço de fadas, W039
Nuvens, W007
Ondulando, W082
Petizada, W048
Poema do menestrel, W169
Poema singelo, W434
Poema úmido, W179
A prole do bebê no.1 (A família do bebê), W140
A prole do bebê no.2 (Os bichinhos), W180
A prole do bebê no.3 (Esportes), W222
Quadrilha de roça, W585
Rudepoema, W184
Saudades das selvas brasileiras, W226
Simples coletânea, W134
Suíte floral, W117
Suíte infantil No.1, W053
Suíte infantil No.2, W067
Sul América, W217
Tarantela, W041
As três Marias, W411
Tristorosa, W034
Valsa da dor, W316
Valsa lenta, W043
Valsa romântica, W016
Valsa-scherzo, W070


BAND

Brasil, W010
Brasil novo, W186
Canção da imprensa, W412
A canoa virou, W266
Canto do pajé, W324
Constância, W268

Desfile aos heróis do Brasil, W367
Entrei na roda, W270
Lá na ponte da vinhaça, W290
Na Bahia tem, W297
Nésta rua, W300
O' ciranda, ó cirandinha, W301
Paraguai, W008
O pião, W361
Pro-pax, W049
Terezinha de Jesus, W314
Valsa brasileira, W143
Vem cá, siriri, W317


GUITAR

Choros no.1, W161
Canção brasileira, W027
Dobrados, W026
Dobrado pitoresco, W028
12 Études (12 Estudos), W235
Fantasia, W023
Mazurka em ré maior, W004
Panqueca, W002
Prelúdios, W419
Quadrilha, W032
Simples, W040
Suite populaire brésilienne, W020
Tarantela, W033
Terezinha de Jesus, W559
Valsa brilhante, W009
Valsa sentimental, W373

# Index

The following abbreviations will be used in the index:

W- Works and Performances
D- Discography
B- Bibliography
CO-Collections, *Canto orfeônico* (See Collections)
GP- Collections, *Guia prático* (See Collections)
MS- Collections, *Música sacra* (See Collections)

Guimarães, Antenor (instrumentalist), W362
Guimarães, J. F., see Pernambuco, José
Guimarães, Lelia (soprano), D049
Guimarães, Luiz, B023
Guimarães, Oldemar, B023
Guimarães, Ruy Pinheiro, (poet), W106
Guimarães Filho, Luiz, W015, W056, W057
Guinle, Arnaldo (dedicatee), W199, W207
Guinle, Carlos (dedicatee), W218
Guizos do dominozinho, (Os), W157
Guriatã do coqueiro, D245


Haas, Hugh, W476
Hahn, Reynaldo (composer), D277
Haifa (Israel), W518
Halasz, Laszlo (conductor), D199, D395
Hamelin (instrumentalist), W182
Harmonias soltas, W064
Haroldo, F. (poet), W294, W298
Harrell, Lynn (cellist), D050
Harvey, Paul (composer), D219
Haydn, Joseph, W298, D357
Haydn Quartet, W399, W496
*Hei de namorar,* GP 62
Heller, Alfred, B113
Hendl, Walter, W516
Hendricks, Barbara (soprano), D044
Henrique, M., W540
Henrique, Waldemar (composer), D056, D057
Henze, Hans Werner, D077
*Heranças de nossa raça,* CO v1 #23
Hermione et les bergers, W164, W165
Hernandez, Antonio, B114, B115
Hettich, A. L. (editor), W245
*Higiene,* GP 64
Hilt, F., W476
Hindemith, Paul, D362
*Hino à Santo Agostinho,* MS v1 #20
*Hino à vitoria* (Chorus and band), W428
*Hino à vitoria* (Chorus and orchestra), W429
*Hino à vitória* (Four part a cappella chorus), CO v2 #36
*Hino à vitória* (Voice and piano), W430
*Hino acadêmico,* W368

## About the Author

DAVID P. APPLEBY is Professor of Music at Eastern Illinois University. His previous books include *The Music of Brazil* and *La musica de Brasil*, a Spanish translation.

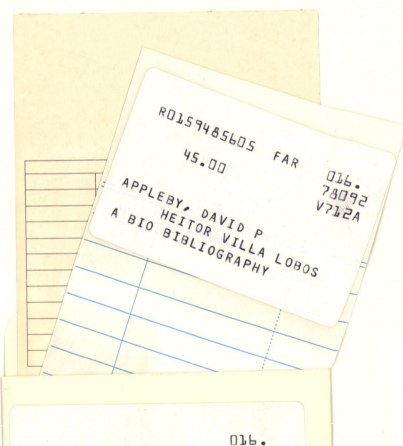